FRANKLIN DELANO ROOSEVELT

The Tribute of the Synagogue

Franklin Delano Roosevelt

FDR Coll.

Franklin Delano ROOSEVELT

THE TRIBUTE OF THE SYNAGOGUE

COMPILED AND EDITED BY

MAX KLEIMAN, Rabbi

FIRST HEBREW CONGREGATION OF PEEKSKILL, N. Y.

WITH A FOREWORD BY THE

Rev. Dr. STEPHEN S. WISE

NEW YORK

BLOCH PUBLISHING COMPANY

1946

"No greater thing could come to our land today than a revival of the spirit of religion—a revival that would stir the hearts of men and women of all faiths to a reassertion of their belief in God. I doubt if there is a problem that would not melt away before the fire of such a spiritual awakening."

—FRANKLIN DELANO ROOSEVELT

PRINTED IN THE UNITED STATES OF AMERICA
AMERICAN BOOK–STRATFORD PRESS, INC., NEW YORK

To My Wife

with deepest affection

FOREWORD

THE following pages constitute an almost wholly unpremeditated tribute to Franklin Delano Roosevelt. I say unpremeditated, for these tributes are for the most part the instinctive outpourings of a deep grief and of a great affection. The writer can think of no tribute comparable save for a parallel tribute of the Synagogue to the memory of Abraham Lincoln, compiled by the late Dr. Emanuel Hertz.

The tributes that will be found in the following pages are not for the most part considered appraisals. They are, I repeat, the first outpourings of a great sorrow over a very great loss. They are of different kinds and types, for they deal with many sides and aspects of a multi-faceted personality.

I have only to add,—and I believe that I made it clear in my own tribute spoken on the day that Roosevelt was laid to rest,—that the American Jewish community did not think of Roosevelt as one to whom, for any special reason, it was indebted. The reverent admiration and love that inform these pages, derive not from any feeling that Roosevelt was friendly to Jews or partial to Jews or helpful to Jews. They derive from something deeper and truer; namely, the sense of all men, who cherish freedom, that Roosevelt was the greatest servant of democracy of this century; that he stood above every thought of racial and religious difference, insofar as he was a friend of man.

Some of the following pages deserve to live; and they will live. And if they live, it will be because they are bound up with a majestic and enduring fame. They catch and reflect gleams of radiant personality which Roosevelt was. In the midst of a great epoch he stood as its greatest figure. He lived in a world which resisted tyranny and fought for freedom and democracy. In that mighty struggle he was leader, exemplar, inspirer. And so he will be remembered not only by his own country and his own countrymen, but through all ages and in all lands which cherish the man who gave himself for the highest irrespective of victory or defeat, who lived and fought immortally for the immortal causes of human freedom, human justice and world peace.

STEPHEN S. WISE

PREFACE

ON APRIL 12, 1945 when the world found itself shocked by the sudden death of Franklin Delano Roosevelt, I felt that the feeling of spontaneous grief that flowed from the hearts and souls of Jews everywhere, and expressed in words uttered by their leaders in America, deserved permanent preservation. It will serve as a glorious memorial and tribute to a man who kept the spirit of mankind high and who always fought for the rights of the under-privileged.

This volume is divided into four sections. They include: a) eulogies and tributes that have been offered by outstanding lay leaders and eminent rabbis in the various groups comprising American Jewry, b) editorials from representative American periodicals, c) memorial prayers, and d) a section of Rooseveltiana in which many of the utterances of the President on Jewish occasions are again made available.

The compiler ventures to hope that in the present volume he was able to bring together a representative collection of sermons, tributes and related material, through which the Jewish people of America have given expression to the grief that was theirs in the demise of a man, who, on more than one occasion, demonstrated his concern with their welfare. May his memory be an enduring blessing.

My thanks are due to the many Orthodox, Conservative, and Reform rabbis who have willingly contributed to this collection and who have spoken so highly of this project as to motivate me to bring it to fruition.

I am especially thankful to Mr. Irving Hinerfeld, Dr. Harry

Seldin, Mrs. Irving Grossman and to my many friends in Peekskill, N. Y. who have encouraged me in this undertaking. I am grateful to the distinguished Rev. Dr. Stephen S. Wise for his charmingly written Foreword, and to Dr. Joshua Block of the New York Public Library for his invaluable aid and assistance.

MAX KLEIMAN

Peekskill, New York
Shevat 5706
January 1946

CONTENTS

TRIBUTES AND EULOGIES

CONTENTS

CONTENTS

CONTENTS

CONTENTS

CONTENTS

TRIBUTES
and
EULOGIES

F. D. R. Enshrined in Jewish Hearts *

DAVID ABARBANEL

FRANKLIN DELANO ROOSEVELT, world leader, whose untimely passing is lamented by peoples of divergent faiths, had one thing especially in common with the Jews: to him, as to us, religion signified the universality of divine guidance which permeates the Old Testament. He lost no opportunity to emphasize this belief throughout his distinguished career as state, national and international figure.

Equally firm was his belief that in the United States "spiritual values count in the long run more than material values." In messages and pronouncements he excoriated those forces that sought to undermine devotion to religious principles, the violators of divine commandments. He affirmed that "God-fearing democracies of the world . . . cannot safely be indifferent to international lawlessness everywhere." In ringing accents he declared: "Whoever seeks to set one religion against another seeks to destroy all religion."

Ironically, the American delegation to the San Francisco Conference voted in favor of admitting that Argentine (under Peron) which less than two years ago provoked from F. D. R. the following condemnation: ". . . I cannot forbear to give expression to my own feeling of apprehension at the taking in this hemisphere of action obviously anti-Semitic in nature and so closely identified with the most repugnant features of Nazi doctrine."

The outpouring of grief among Jews everywhere indicates how deeply Franklin Roosevelt cut across all party and group lines in Israel. To comprehend the well-springs of this wide-spread affection, one needs but examine the highlights of the Roosevelt record,

* Reprinted from *Liberal Judaism.*

which we reproduce below by courtesy of The Universal Jewish Encyclopedia, recently completed.

In 1933, Roosevelt's orders to William E. Dodd, Ambassador to Germany, were that whatever could be done to moderate the general persecution by unofficial and personal influence ought to be done. But not until 1938 was Hugh R. Wilson, who had succeeded Dodd, recalled from his post, in protest against the pogroms that occurred in November of that year. Earlier in 1938 (June), Roosevelt had called a twenty-eight-Power refugee parley at Evian-les-Bains, France, to discuss possible resettlement opportunities for refugees of all kinds.

Anti-immigrant and anti-refugee sentiment was not entirely absent in the United States, even apart from its utilization by pro-Nazi elements. Roosevelt was outspoken in his condemnation of such attitudes, as for instance in his speech to the Daughters of the American Revolution (1938): "All of us, and you and I especially, are descended from immigrants and revolutionaries."

With the progressive continuation of persecution in Germany, Roosevelt suggested to the State Department that the many refugees who were in the United States on six-month visitors' visas be granted an indefinite number of extensions of these visas.

Another anti-Democratic undertone, affecting the Jews as well as other minority groups, which Roosevelt combated was discrimination in industrial employment. In June, 1941, when the country—not yet at war—was under emergency routine, he sent a memorandum to William S. Knudsen and Sidney Hillman, co-administrators of emergency production, stating:

> No nation combating the increasing threat of totalitarianism can afford arbitrarily to exclude large segments of its population from its defense industries. American workers, both organized and unorganized, must be prepared to welcome the general and much-needed employment of fellow workers of all racial and nationality origins in defense industries.

In January, 1942, several weeks after the United States entered the war, Roosevelt, in an official statement, deplored the dismissal of aliens from industry, and his message to the 77th Congress warned against racial discrimination and its use as a technique to create division.

Toward interfaith endeavor as well as to Jewish activities, Roosevelt frequently voiced support that showed familiarity with biblical precepts of religious living. In 1939, he was awarded the American Hebrew medal for outstanding service in promoting better understanding between Christians and Jews. Acknowledging the award, Roosevelt said:

> After all, the majority of Americans, whether they adhere to the ancient teaching of Israel or accept the tenets of the Christian religion, have a common source and inspiration in the Old Testament. In a spirit of brotherhood we should, therefore, seek to emphasize all the many essential things in which we find unity in our common biblical heritage.

Roosevelt repeatedly expressed his interest in the establishment of a Jewish national home in Palestine and reiterated that the United States had an interest in the handling of the British Mandate over Palestine. In 1940 he was represented with a replica of the Jewish National Fund Golden Book, inscribed in tribute to Roosevelt by nearly 1,000 Jewish organizations in the United States. On more recent occasions he boldly committed himself to the aspiration of creating a Jewish Commonwealth in Palestine.

Roosevelt's prolonged term of office, covering a span between national crisis and international struggle, required the introduction of political and intellectual leaders of all kinds into official circles. Roosevelt's approach—stubborn, fearless and democratic to the roots—disregarded any considerations except those of effectiveness. Consequently, the names of Jews figure among his associates, not out of proportion to the contribution they were able to make, but somewhat more plainly than during other periods.

Among these was Herbert H. Lehman, who, at Roosevelt's urging, had first accepted the lieutenant-governor-ship of New York state and who, near the end of his ten years in office as governor (1942), was appointed by Roosevelt director of Relief and Rehabilitation. Another old friend and neighbor was Henry Morgenthau, Jr., who served as Secretary of the Treasury from almost the beginning of Roosevelt's incumbency. Bernard M. Baruch, a lifelong Democrat, first called into war service by Woodrow Wilson, was summoned again by Roosevelt to aid in the coordination and concentration of effort during the Second World War. Samuel Irving Rosenman, as associate of Roosevelt from his days as governor, remained a trusted adviser while Roosevelt was in the White House. Felix Frankfurter, whom Roosevelt had appointed to the Supreme Court in 1933, was likewise a confidant throughout. Isador Lubin was a valued White House aide.

The opportunities which were found by Jews in the Federal government, during the stress of the post-depression and later of the international emergency, were naturally misinterpreted as favoritism, and roused a barrage from Nazi sources. Nazi propaganda also alleged that Roosevelt was of Jewish ancestry.

Philip Slomovitz, editor of the Detroit Jewish Chronicle, wrote Roosevelt in 1935, asking for an authentic reply to the rumor of his Jewish ancestry. Roosevelt, in his answer, said that in the almost three hundred years of their American residence, there had been no intermarriage with Jews:

> In the dim distant past they may have been Jews or Catholics or Protestants. What I am more interested in is whether they were good citizens and believers in God. I hope they were both.

With the precedent-breaking election, to a third term, of Roosevelt in 1940, the struggle that was begun in 1933, when he and Adolf Hitler assumed power on almost the same day, was already in manifest and bloody progress. It did not reach the United States officially for about another year. By that time the attitudes that had motivated Roosevelt's demeanor towards matters in which Jews were concerned—that Jews were human beings, but peculiarly designated as the first victims by elements whose aim was tyranny and destruction for all mankind—these attitudes became recognized as the basis of the contest between freedom and slavery. It was in accord with his frequently enunciated principles that one of the first consequences of the American occupation of Northern Africa, late in 1942, was Roosevelt's demand for the abolition of anti-Semitic laws imposed by the Vichy government.

On December 3, 1942, President Roosevelt received a delegation of representatives of the six leading Jewish organizations (religious and lay) in the United States. The American people more than ever will feel, he told them, the conscience of the United Nations and of free men everywhere was revolted by those deeds of savagery and attempted extermination. Roosevelt reminded the delegation that when the American Jewish organizations which they represented met in Madison Square Garden (July, 1942), to protest against the savagery of the Nazis against their victims, he had said: "The American people not only sympathize with all victims of Nazi crime but will hold the perpetrators of these crimes to strict accountability in a day of reckoning which will surely come." Nor did he doubt that the United Nations will be prepared, as the American government would be, to take every step which will end these crimes.

In his message to Congress (June, 1944), condemning the systematic persecution of helpless minority groups by the Nazis, Roosevelt declared: "To us, the unprovoked murder of innocent people, simply because of race, religion or political creed, is the blackest of all possible crimes."

He had been fully aware of the blood-thirsty ruthlessness of the Nazis long before the ghastly revelations of Buchenwald and other horror spots discovered by Allied armies. He paid no heed to those who mischievously sought to discredit similar reports made much earlier by liberating Russian armies.

Our Pain Is Great

RABBI JACOB BOSNIAK

FRANKLIN D. ROOSEVELT also died in action. Disregarding the state of his health, he performed his duties as the Commander-in-Chief of the armed forces and as the leader of the United Nations, a task that was assigned to him by God and humanity. It is well known that he returned from the Crimea a sick man. The strain of the trip and the conferences was too much for his weakened and tortured body, and he fell under the terrific burden.

Our pain is great. Words cannot express the sentiments of our hearts. Our feelings of disappointment, our fears for the future of the world, for the future of the nations and the future of Israel, cannot be expressed in words.

Like Moses of old, President Roosevelt must have prayed to God in the last days of his life, "Let me cross and see the Promised Land" of tomorrow. The parallel is evident to all. Now that victory is assured on all fronts, now that it is only a question of days or weeks when General Eisenhower will command: "Ye shall proclaim liberty to all inhabitants" of Europe, Franklin D. Roosevelt, the Commander-in-Chief of all armed forces, the saviour of the nations with his lend-lease policy, he who was a true and loyal friend of Israel—he will not be here to rejoice with us, to offer thanks to God with us, and to enjoy the fruit of his labors. You recall the answer of God that came to Moses: It was not granted that he should enter the Promised Land, but another privilege was given unto him. "Walk up to the top of the mountain . . . turn in all directions, East and West, North and South, and feast your eyes on the Land of Promise."

We are thankful to God for this privilege which was also granted to Franklin D. Roosevelt. Until the very last moment of his life, he stood at the head of the world and feasted his vision upon the world of tomorrow. He surveyed the world and made a blueprint of a world based upon the Four Freedoms: Freedom of Government, Freedom of conscience, Freedom from want and Freedom from fear.

If you permit me to continue the parallel. We are told in the Bible: "And Moses died on the mountain . . . by the mouth of God." The Rabbis of old remark "bineshikah meth Mosheh." Moses expired by a kiss received from God. Surely these words were not meant to be taken literally. There are two interpretations of these words and both are beautifully and truthfully applicable to Franklin D. Roosevelt.

One interpretation is that they meant to tell us that Moses died without experiencing the excruciating pains of death. F. D. R. too, passed away without the usual ills and pains which accompany the end of human life. He sat before the fireplace reading official reports, while some artist made drawings of his countenance. He suddenly remarked that he felt terrific pain in the back of his head and immediately fainted and remained unconscious. His lips were sealed by the kiss of God.

The second interpretation is as follows: The kiss is the symbol of love, and our sages express in poetic words that Moses retained the love of God and of Israel until the last moment of his life.

Who can deny that this was also the portion of F. D. R. He died enjoying the love and the gratitude of the entire world and the whole nation. Democrats and Republicans, employers and employees, conservatives and liberals, Jews and Gentiles—all were united in their love, veneration and admiration for his princely magnetic personality, for his humor, sagacity and wisdom, for his courage, honesty and kindness, for his great human heart which bled for the poor, for the "forgotten man," and for Israel, despised, degraded and slaughtered in Germany.

May his immortal soul be bound in the eternal bond of life.

A Symbol of Unity

MAX BRESSLER

IT IS very difficult for me to measure the depth of the tragedy that has befallen not only the American people, but also the freedom-loving nations of this earth upon the death of President Franklin Delano Roosevelt. His Divine Soul rests at peace. At this very moment as I speak to you, the spirit of our great Leader has merged with eternity. The whole world stands bowed in grief and in reverence.

But no matter how great the tragedy for the rest of mankind, the pain of Israel is infinitely greater. In this most tragic period of the history of our martyrdom, saturated as it is with the blood of our heroes, suffering and twitching from torture and pain, the Angel of Death drew the dark clouds over the ray of hope and confidence symbolized by the President—beloved fighter for the rights of the forgotten man—the comman man.

He was one of the very few dynamic personalities who at every moment was ready to do good for all who needed him. As big as was his heart and as open as was his mind, so at all times were his arms open to receive our representatives and to heed our tortured cries for help. At all times was he ready to help alleviate our miseries.

Franklin Delano Roosevelt, of sacred memory, was the one who requested the State Department together with the Treasury Department to assist in sending monies into the land of our enemies (though illegal) in order to free thousands of our brothers and sisters who otherwise would be among the victims of Hitler's wholesale slaughterhouse.

He was the one who urged the nations of the world to consider the problems of the refugee. He was the one who requested Pope Pius XI, through his personal emissary, Myron Taylor, to intercede with the Nazis. Myron Taylor was the one who brought back to America the first peace of soap manufactured from the bodies of the Jewish victims of the Nazi murderers.

Hearing the horrible news of the frightful fate that has befallen our people in the Hitler-occupied territories, Roosevelt created the War Refugee Board. When the time will come, which I hope, will be soon, the world will learn how many thousands of Jewish souls were thus rescued by him.

When the Government of Turkey was ordered by Hitler to tax their Jewish inhabitants without mercy and many of them were thrown into prison cells, it was the Divine Voice of President Roosevelt, through the interocean telephone to the President of Turkey, that stopped the persecution of our brethren.

Surely it will be recorded on the pages of history how President Roosevelt's letter to Dr. Wise, expressing his indignation to Hitler's poisonous anti-Semitism, said, "Those who spread the philosophy of anti-Semitism here in our land shall be considered enemies of our free America."

History will also record the untiring efforts of the best friend of our people, the true lover of humanity, in our behalf.

Like a Prophet, he foretold the great catastrophe that has befallen the freedom-loving peoples of the earth, including our own. He pleaded with the world to arrest the aggressor nations, to quarantine the governments that aspired to conquer, and to frustrate their attempts to enslave the world. He was the first to warn Hitler and his bestial followers that they will be held to strict account for the spilling of Jewish blood.

In contrast to the debauched leadership of the Nazis, we in America and all of the freedom-loving people have had the brightest and the finest of men in the person of the one whom we have now laid to eternal rest.

In the most critical moment in our history when we were so brutally attacked by our enemy, and the very life of the American people was in danger, this Titan of our day not only united the people of America but also the peoples of all the world.

We were not prepared for the conflict. However, the strength of this spiritual giant pierced through our complacency like lightning and wove together a strong resistance to the dark forces of aggression. As a result of this unity created by him, we have thus overcome the greatest of world catastrophes.

Like a father, devoted to his children, he taught the American people to forget their political quarrels, their social and economic differences. Every minute, every hour, every day he reminded us of the true danger and pleaded with us to overcome our differences. By arousing the American people and instilling confidence in the United Nations, he guided us to the shores of Victory. Like Moses and other great leaders of the past, he was not privileged to enter the Promised Land of enduring peace to which he devoted and sacrificed his life.

The Conferences he held with the leaders of the great nations at Casablanca, Quebec, Moscow, Teheran, and Yalta together with his plans of military strategy planted the seeds for the world of tomorrow.

Stalin sensed in Roosevelt a friend of the Soviet people. Chiang Kai-Shek sensed his fatherly feeling to the Chinese people. In every corner of the world, the common people loved him.

It is because of this that the American people expressed their confidence in him, by re-electing him for four consecutive terms. His warm words, "My friends," with which he traditionally began his fireside chats, will forever ring in our ears and remain a testimony to his greatness and warmth.

His attitude to the problem of Jewish homelessness, and his promises to Dr. Stephen S. Wise and other Zionist leaders to help build a home for our dispersed people will remain forever one of the brightest chapters in Jewish history. He understood the importance—the historic importance—and the elementary justice of giving us an opportunity to build a Jewish democratic Commonwealth in Palestine.

The cup of Jewish tragedy and Jewish bitterness runneth over. Let us hope that in the passing of our leader we find the true meaning of the expression "There can be no dawn before complete darkness." Let us hope that hereafter we begin to see and to sense the rays of a brighter day.

We can honor his memory best by following his teachings for unity, to forget our differences, to gather as one, combat our enemies so that together with the help of all nations, we may open the doors of freedom of our People. Not as a people of the Galut, but as a free nation fulfilling the 2,000 year-old dream—a Jewish home for the Jewish People. With it we shall bring to realization his hopes of building a better world.

Even though the passing of our dear President inscribes another black chapter in the already Black Book of Jewish pain and suffering, and even though his death shook our great hopes, we shall not lose our confidence. His ideals will come to pass, and with it, a new, better and brighter world.

The memory of Franklin Delano Roosevelt will serve as the beacon of light that will lead our people to their redemption. Let us hope that the new President, Harry S. Truman, will follow in the footsteps of the most noble citizen of this world. Let us hope that together with the united effort of the people he will labor incessantly to complete the task that was so brutally interrupted by President Roosevelt's death.

As we stand with bowed heads before the fresh grave of our beloved President, let us extend to him his well-deserved honors. Let us vow to carry on his work to build a better world for "the common man" he loved so much.

Peace to his remains—Honor to his memory.

"Captain, My Captain"

RABBI BARNETT R. BRICKNER

I AM still too stunned by the tragic news of the President's death to be able to put into words or to evaluate the effect that his passing is likely to have upon the course of the war, and what is even more important upon the shape of the peace to follow. I wish merely at this time to record a few personal reminiscences and impressions of the man, Roosevelt.

It was a little over a year ago that I saw him at the White House. I had come at his invitation prior to my departure on an overseas mission as the representative of the National Jewish Welfare Board to the men on the fighting fronts, for which he had designated me. As I entered his office, he greeted me with his hand extended—even before I had a chance to grasp his. His hand shake was firm and sincere. The President had a great faculty for putting those who called on him immediately at their ease, and one soon chatted with him as one would with an old friend. I told him how happy I was to see him looking so well and so refreshed. "Mr. President," I said, "you look so different from your picture in the movies," where he appeared so haggard with face drawn and heavy lines under his eyes. "Well," he said to me, "I've had a few days of rest over the weekend, and besides Rabbi, I sleep well, I don't take my troubles to bed with me." It was this remarkable faculty to throw off things which made it possible for him to bear the heaviest load any living man had to carry, and this despite a body that had been impaired by infantile paralysis. I said to him further, "Mr. President, people say you should delegate to others more of the things that come over your desk," and he replied, "I try to do just that, but there are many things that one can't delegate to others," by which he indicated that in this crisis he had a great sense of personal responsibility to carry on the things he regarded as decisive. For who was there in American life who knew as much as he did through actual personal knowledge and experience of foreign affairs, which was the burden of interest in which the country and he, as its Chief Executive were engaged. Much of this was not a matter of the written record, but of personal understanding with other world leaders. For his was a personal diplomacy carried on by face-to-face meetings and over the telephone. He could actually do more in five minutes by personal conversation than many another man could do through long ponderous memoranda and formal conferences. It was his charm, his wit, his good humor, his alert mind that was able to discern between the trivial and the essential, his rare gift to say the right word at the right time, which made him the greatest political realist and negotiator of our time.

How he will be missed now, when this particular talent of reconciling the irreconcilables, of implementing the imponderables is so essential. He was "personna grata" to Stalin, Churchill and the Pope, even though they were not personable to each other. In this respect, there is no one who can replace him. The "Big Three" are now in his absence less than the "Big Two" for in his passing each of the remaining two has lost something of himself.

I asked him, "Mr. President, what message should I take from you to the boys?" And, quick as a flash he answered, "Take them my love." "Tell them that I am concerned over their welfare now and when they come back—assure them that the America to which they will be returning one day is not going to let them down." He then told me of ideas and plans that were in his mind for the welfare of the veterans, some of which have already become the law of the land.

As I travelled over the world and mingled with the G.I.'s, I found that he was tremendously admired by them. They loved his fighting spirit. They were anxious to vote for him, and now it may be told that they were bitter and resentful that obstacles were being placed in the way of the soldier vote. He was a war casualty like a million others. He died in action, with his boots on—on the road to victory.

Much as he will be missed by "my friends," his fellow citizens at home, he will be even more missed by the great unwashed masses of the world, of all colors and creeds—from South America, to Africa, India and China. Millions and millions of these people regarded him as their great hope. The name of Roosevelt was synonymous with Redeemer. They felt that he would champion their rights to freedom and to independence. They regarded him not as a politician or even as a statesman, but as a Prophet, as a Messiah. This was true also of my own people all over the world and in Palestine. They knew that he was their friend and champion. To me, he said, "Don't worry, Rabbi, I will stand by your people in Europe and Palestine and see that justice is done them at long last, only be patient—arrangements are already in process." In innumerable ways Franklin Delano Roosevelt gave proof of his friendship to the Jewish people. He was our friend because he was a great humanitarian and the plight of all stricken people made a special appeal to him, and Israel was the most "stricken of the stricken." It was this sensitivity of social wrong, to injustice, that made him the champion of the little man and the under-dog. Though born, as it were, to the purple, he understood the man in overalls. They intuitively knew that he felt for them, and with them. That is why the workers of this country did not hesitate to elect him four times, a record that is not likely ever again to be repeated in American history. As I pondered over the crushing news, one refrain kept pounding within me: if he only could have lived a little while longer, then he could have witnessed the climax of his life's work—the fulfillment of the two things for which he strove the hardest—the downfall of Hitler and all that regime came to mean, and the laying of secure foundations at San Francisco for the better world order of justice and an enduring peace. He had travelled all the way to Yalta, despite his impaired health in order that he might come to the Golden Gate. He was on the verge of doing that when the Almighty, who has his own mysterious ways, took him from us.

Like Moses and every great leader in history, Franklin Delano Roosevelt could only approach the Promised Land, but not enter it. From Pisgah's heights, he could only look across the Jordan and see the Holy City beyond the horizon. No more fitting monument can be created to his memory than to dedicate the San Francisco Conference to the ideals and plans which he had for it; so that it may be known in history as the Roosevelt Conference—the Security Conference, which would make the next war impossible. As fellow Americans, we owe it to our fallen Commander-in-Chief, not only to dedicate ourselves to the quick winning of the war, but to rededicate ourselves to the carrying forward of that program of progressive social and economic legislation which he encompassed under the New Deal. We must not permit the forces of reaction, which have been under cover since Pearl Harbor and which are slowly regrouping for action, to take advantage of his absence and to force us from the path on which he placed America's feet toward the goals of a better American way of life.

Like the children of Israel, we are standing at the Red Sea. The hosts of Pharaoh, the hosts of reaction and of undercover fascism are behind us—the Red Sea is before us. And God said to Moses, "Why do the children of Israel cry unto me—tell the children of Israel to go forward!"

In Praise of a High Priest

RABBI ARTHUR T. BUCH

WE SHOULD pay our respects—our deepest, heartfelt respects to one of the greatest men who ever lived. That we should gather together today to pay this unique tribute is entirely fitting when we consider all that he meant to us in these trying times.

These are indeed "yomin noraim," awe-inspiring, fearful days. These are days when life and death hang in the balance. Every day is a day of atonement. The sanctification of God's name is made daily over a cup of tears. Whole families are being wiped out hourly. No case in history may be found to compare with the tragedy of our own times. Never before have so many people suffered so much for so long. This is an unparalleled tragedy to which you and I and the rest of the world have not only been witnesses, but in which we have been sufferers.

And in the midst of this tragedy, yesterday at four o'clock all Americans stood still and spent a minute in silence, silence except for the sound of tears within one's heart. America stood still because the heart of its great leader stood still. It was not only for Americans that the death of Roosevelt meant so much, but it was also for the people of every civilized land a most grievous blow. Russians, Englishmen, Frenchmen, Chinamen,—indeed, all civilized peoples—along with Americans felt that they had lost a personal friend.

Never had there been in history a man for whom so many felt that he was their protector and their friend. The familiar opening phrase, "my friends," was sincerely meant by the President and was sincerely accepted by all those who heard it. When the news reached us in America that Franklin Delano Roosevelt had died, each of us felt that we had lost someone dear and near to us. It was a heavy blow because we all regarded him as a dear friend who we hoped would lead us out of the dark tragedy, in which the world and we are now sunk, into the better and brighter days of a New World.

Because of his having left us, the question before us is, what shall we do now?

We would do well to follow the example of Franklin Roosevelt himself, who whenever he discovered that he was faced with special difficulties, would pray for divine guidance and help. This is what we should do at this point,—pray, pray sincerely and deeply that the influence of Franklin Roosevelt shall not be dissipated with his demise, but that it shall grow in power with the passing of time.

How shall we voice this prayer? Since these may be considered, "yomin noraim," the awe-inspiring days when life and death are decided, we could turn for a suggestion to our prayer books which are utilized on the most sacred days of the Jewish calendar. And there we might discover the beautiful prayer that revolves around the story of the ten distinguished leaders of Israel who became martyrs. One of them, you remember, wrapped the sacred scroll around his body as he was burned at the stake. When he was asked by his disciples what he saw when his soul was leaving his body, he answered, "I see the scroll burning, but the letters are flying in the air." Similarly, although the body of Franklin Delano Roosevelt is dead, his spirit is alive all about us—it is in the very air.

For Franklin Delano Roosevelt was also a martyr. It is significant, I think, that the last words he spoke were, "I have a terrific headache." His headache was due not only to his having to fight the avowed enemies of his country, but I believe that his headache was also caused by the many trials and tribulations into which he was forced by men who had a smaller conception of human values than he did. As Commander in Chief of the greatest army that our nation ever mustered, engaged in the greatest war that any people ever waged, it became his duty to think of, and work for victory day and night, yet he was sorely beset by jealous people who could not permit themselves to afford him cooperation and encouragement. It was they who forced him to ride through the rain in order to prove to them and to the world that his weakened body might stand the strain of leadership. In spite of them, he was eminently successful. Yet the strain of more than twelve years was too much for him, and so he was slain like any other soldier, killed in battle, protecting a strong point against the enemy. He gave his life so that his country might live.

But perhaps it would be ironic to remember him in the garb of the soldier, because it was he who said, "I hate war." I think we would do better if we were to turn to another section of the high-holiday prayer book in order to discover a different mental picture with which to associate Roosevelt in our prayers. In our high-holiday prayer book, we are told of the high priest who offered sacrifices in behalf of the people. Franklin Roosevelt really was a high priest in the service of God and country—a high priest who became himself a sacrifice for his ideals.

What happened in his life time? Franklin Delano Roosevelt became the first man in American history to be elected for four terms because he had proven himself to be great among all his fellow Americans; the glory of his people rested upon his shoulders. In his time, the House of American life was renovated while the Temple of American ideals was fortified. It was he who had arranged for the N. R. A., the W. P. A., the T. V. A.,—abbreviations of not only great governmental agencies but of a whole philosophy of government which meant that the government was destined to serve the people. It was he who took thought for his people to protect them from robbers—not only human robbers, but also those conditions of life which robbed men of the opportunity to work, to earn a living, to enjoy the blessings of home. It was he who as a true high priest of his people's interests fortified his country against its bitter enemies to preserve the American way of life.

And how did this high priest look? His smile will live in history because it won the hearts of literally millions of human beings. It is being told that one time when he was about to deliver one of his Presidential addresses he fell. When he was placed back on his feet, or better stated when he was helped to stand on his braces, his head went up and a smile covered his face, so that no one knew of his embarrassment or of his pain.

His voice was fitting for his smile. When American hearts were troubled, his voice would be heard in a fire-side chat, and strength and courage and comfort would come into American hearts. In spite of his physical deformity, he was a handsome man. His glorious face will be an inspiration in the generation to come.

And what was his special service? Perhaps many of you know of the great duty of the high priest in the ancient Temple in Jerusalem which was to pronounce the ineffable name of God that expressed the oneness of the Creator of the Universe. This, indeed, was the great contribution of Franklin Delano Roosevelt, namely—that he concerned himself with the spreading of the meaning of the oneness of God.

This unity of God led him to think of the equal rights of all humanity. It brought him to remember the forgotten man. It taught him that if there were only one God there must be really only one world,—and if there be only one God then all people are equal, then everyone is entitled to the Four Freedoms. It was this same philosophy of life based on the meaning of God that made him withdraw the American Ambassador from Germany when the Nazis insisted upon their anti-Semitic, anti-human behavior.

The blessing of the Lord was upon his lips and he spread that blessing with out-stretched hands to all the people of the world.

He recited the priestly benediction and lived its meaning. Because he believed the meaning of the phrase, "The Lord bless you and keep you," he could pronounce one of the great statements that will live in history:—"The only thing that we need fear is fear itself." He was intent upon spreading the second of priestly benediction, too, for he did all in his power to make for the realization of it, namely—"The Lord cause His countenance to shine upon you and to be gracious unto you." He was interested in all human beings wherever they might be, wherever the sun would rise and wherever there were the moon and stars, wherever there were human hopes and human ideals. It was for all of these people everywhere in the world that he wanted to bring the blessings of the light of freedom and of justice.

And finally, he gave his life in an effort to achieve the third priestly benediction—"May the Lord lift up His countenance to you and grant you peace."

Now what is there for us to do? It is part of the Jewish tradition to say, "May it be the Lord's will," following each of the priestly benedictions. This means that we ourselves must do something to achieve the benediction, if we pray for it sincerely. Thus, we should be devoted to ending this war as quickly as possible and doing everything within our community and nation to achieve the everlasting Peace.

And if we will do this, then we will find that the soul of Franklin Delano Roosevelt will rest in Peace. The Jewish tradition teaches that the righteous of every generation regardless of race, color, or creed has a share in the world to come. Franklin Delano Roosevelt was one of the righteous of the nations of the world and his place in the better world that is to be born is assured.

Indeed, in the future, when our children will ask us concerning this great man, we shall see him rise in front of our eyes, his head held high, and a beautiful smile on his face, for Peace his goal and his ideal shall have been achieved in the world he loved.

Roosevelt's Ethical Will

RABBI IRA EISENSTEIN

THIS was the address which he never delivered, fated to be the last written but never spoken words of our martyred, beloved, gallant President, Franklin D. Roosevelt. In a way, it becomes his final message to us, his parting words, embodying his hopes, his faith, his moral code, his life's ambition. In it, in brief, is the essence of his great state papers. In his posthumously published Jefferson Dinner Address, which was to have been given two days after his death, Franklin D. Roosevelt bequeathed his tsavaah, his ethical will to the children of men.

With tragic irony, it begins: "Americans are gathered this evening in communities all over the country to pay tribute to the living memory of Thomas Jefferson—one of the greatest of all democrats, and I want to make it clear that I am spelling that word 'democrats' with a small 'd.' " Little did he realize that those multitudes would be gathered now to pay tribute to him—worthy of that same description.

Jefferson, he went on to say, was "an American citizen of the world." Here, in a word, was Mr. Roosevelt's life-long ideal, to be an American citizen of the world. For those of little vision and less wisdom, this was a contradiction in terms. In their eyes, one could be only a citizen of a country; but in Franklin Roosevelt's eyes, to be a citizen of a country was not enough. All the passionate love one may have for his native land may be transmuted into gall, and hate, and blindness if it be not tempered with the love of Man. For Roosevelt, only he who saw America in the setting of the world was a true citizen of the United States, a real friend of our safety, our prosperity, our honor. This does not mean that one can be a citizen of the world alone, for a man needs roots and hearth and home; he needs the spiritual incentive of having his stake, small or large, in the future of his country. Like Jefferson, even more than Jefferson, Franklin D. Roosevelt was an American citizen of the world.

"Today," he went on to say, "this nation which Jefferson helped so greatly to build, is playing a tremendous part in the battle for the rights of man all over the world." Mark the words: the rights of man. Mr. Roosevelt gave deeper meaning and greater stature to those words. The rights of man, for him, were not merely the right to protection against violence. They did not connote the right of the strong to exercise his power unmolested against the weak. The rights of man meant the rights to life, to a livelihood, to security against old age and sickness, security against unemployment and the hazards of an unpredictable and unstable economy. For him, rights meant freedom from fear as well as freedom from want, freedom from that gnawing and disintegrating fear which drives the successful to greed and the unsuccessful to despair. The rights of man included the freedom of religion, a freedom which he took very seriously indeed. This was no empty and theoretical right, for he was a deeply pious man. Sophisticated, ultramodern in every fibre of his being, he was yet strongly attached to the historic faith into which he was born. He not only went to church—he prayed. He was not ashamed, even before the millions whom his voice reached, to utter those intimate and fervent prayers which his heart dictated. And he was prepared to fight to the death for the rights of others to the free exercise of their inherited or chosen faiths.

The rights of man: Mr. Roosevelt fixed no barriers to the fullest interpretation of the term "man." He truly believed in the brotherhood of all men, of all races and creeds and religions. Perhaps no leader of any nation ever conceived of man in broader, more inclusive terms. The worldwide mourning at his death is testimony to that. Statesmen, churchmen, taxi drivers and factory workers, in Australia, China, Russia, South America, from the greatest to the humblest, all loved him, because they knew in their hearts that he loved them. He gave the name to the "forgotten man," who has since been forgotten no longer. Lincoln too loved the common man, and, like Lincoln, Franklin Roosevelt found in him uncommon virtues.

He had faith in the common man, faith in his essential integrity and good sense; and the rights he sought for the common man were rights, therefore, based on no doctrinaire theories of nature, but on the hard, practical basis of the welfare of our nation and of the world. Franklin Roosevelt believed that when the common man achieved his rights, all his rights, most of the evils of society would wither away.

It is easy enough to mouth the words, "the rights of man all over the world." Any politician can pronounce them; but no one remains in our generation who spoke those words with fuller and more heartfelt connotations than he gave to them. He meant, literally, all over the world; in India, in China, in the farthest flung corners of the earth. For he truly believed in the indivisibility of justice. He believed that this was "one world." It is not surprising that Mrs. Wendell Willkie felt bereaved a second time when our President died. She wired to Mrs. Roosevelt: "I cannot help but wonder why men of vision are being taken from the world when we need them most." Willkie and Roosevelt are no more, but the world remains "one world," and waits for its salvation at the hands of those who must rise to the vision of these men.

In the unspoken Jefferson address, Mr. Roosevelt wrote: "Today we have learned in the agony of war that great power involves great responsibility." Here was another great truth articulated for the last time by the immortal statesman—the indestructible bond that ties power to duty. In the discernment of this truth, Mr. Roosevelt reached the heights of the great moral teachers of Israel and of all peoples, at all times. He was not one to disparage power, to look down upon it with disdain as inherently evil. He was no dogmatic pacifist. He did not interpret the verse, "Not by power and not by strength, but by my spirit," to mean the glory of weakness, or even the potency of non-violence. He was a fighter, who gloried in a real battle. But he was vigorous without being belligerent, strong without being a bully. Power, for him, was an instrument, to be used, in the hands of the righteous, for the triumph of righteousness over the forces of evil. He was a realist. He saw, long before many another, the rising and growing menace of fascism, that prototype of social evil, and he dedicated himself to its utter destruction. He knew that such evil understands only one language, the language of power.

He brought our nation to the completest fulfillment of its potential strength. But he saw the moral corollary of that power: the responsibility to use it, not for narrow defense alone, but "letakken olam b'malkut shaddai,"—to establish the kingdom of righteousness.

"We as Americans," he continued, "do not choose to deny our responsibility. Nor do we intend to abandon our determination that, within the lives of our children and our children's children there will not be a Third World War. We seek peace—enduring peace. More than an end to war, we want an end to the beginnings of all wars—yes, an end to this brutal, inhuman and thoroughly impractical method of settling the differences between governments. The mere conquest of our enemies is not enough. We must go on to do all in our power to conquer the doubts and the fears, the ignorance and the greed which made this horror possible." Thus, behind his passionate hatred of the enemy, Mr. Roosevelt saw the true causes of war: not the madness of this ruler or the fanatical dreams of that dictator, but the underlying greed and the ignorance and fear by which that greed is nourished. The peace he profoundly loved and sought was not, in his eyes, a peace attainable merely by military conquest, but more by the universal understanding of the causes of war.

In this, Roosevelt revealed his fundamental faith in the uses of intelligence. Here was the liberal speaking out in unequivocal language. "Today we are faced with the pre-eminent fact that, if civilization is to survive, we must cultivate the science of human relationships—the ability of all peoples, of all kinds, to live together in the same world, at peace." The science of human relationships—Mr. Roosevelt was charting a new, uncharted sea. Only a great liberal could perceive that the scientific method, so long used to make tanks and ships and planes, to perfect bombsights and flame-throwers, had to be turned to the solution of man's inhumanity to man. A brilliant coiner of slogans, he mad no fetish of slogans, of fine-sounding battle cries. Peace, for him, was a problem, a challenge to human ingenuity, human skill, human intelligence. He believed that, if people knew the truth, the truth would make them free. But, like a true social scientist, he recognized that we still do not know the truth, the whole truth; that only if men made a sober, scientific study of wars, could they hope to achieve peace.

Finally, in this tsava-ah of his, he called upon us to have faith. "I ask you to keep up your faith. I measure the sound, solid achievement that can be made at this time by the straight-edge of your own confidence and your resolve. And to you and to all Americans who dedicate themselves with us to the making of an abiding peace, I say: The only limit to our realization of tomorrow will be our doubts of today. Let us move forward with strong and active faith." Yes, Mr. Roosevelt was a believer in science, in intelligence; but stronger was his belief that, ultimately, the difference between success and failure lay in the realm of will, in that mysterious human equation. The human will must not falter, nor diminish in power or intensity. And it can be strengthened only by faith, faith in the inherent rightness of the right, faith in the doctrine that the intuitions of Jewish and Christian ethics are more than useful hypotheses, that they do indeed constitute the basic laws of God. Without that faith, there is hesitancy, doubt, confusion, defeat. With that faith, no human power on earth can stand in our way.

May his last words never cease to echo in our hearts: "Let us move forward with strong and active faith."

In This Hour

RABBI ABRAHAM J. FELDMAN

IN THIS hour I recall something I read recently that was written by the late L. P. Jacks in his book called The Challenge of Life. Let me read it to you:

> "Both in his mind and in his body man is adapted for enterprises of great pith and moment, for the acquisition of astonishing arts that seem impossible till he has practiced them, for dangerous expeditions into the unknown, for stern and anxious battles with the powers of darkness, for standing

up to tremendous shocks, for enduring heartbreaking reverses, for rising up when he has been wounded and beaten to the ground, and for dying, if need be, sword in hand. To a being so splendidly equipped it is no hardship, no cause for whining, when he finds himself 'upon an engagement very difficult': he does not complain of his Maker for that. He praises his Maker, and goes into battle singing psalms. 'Here am I,' he cries, 'with my aptitudes and versatilities; yonder is the universe offering me the very problems, the very tasks those aptitudes and versatilities are made to cope with; here am I, Lord, send me.' "

I recall this passage now as being particularly apt with reference to the life and the spirit of the incomparable leader whose death has cast the pall of sorrow over the whole world. It applies to him as it does in the case of no other man in our times.

Politics and partisanship are now adjourned.

Note what it is that we remember as we think of this man.

Here was one born into the ranks of what is popularly called "the aristocracy." He was born into wealth and comfort and economic and social security. And yet we do not speak of this at this hour, as we evaluate the man or the significance of his life.

Here was a man who was one of the most skillful politicians of his day. And yet no one speaks of his magnificent skill in dealing with people and with situations.

Here was a man who was one of the greatest orators and most eloquent men of his generation; he of the winged phrase; he of the glorious voice. None speaks of these as we think of Franklin Delano Roosevelt at this moment, because these are all superficial, external aspects of manhood and all that is superficial, all that is external, is now ruled out. We are thinking rather of the spirit. We are thinking of the great generous heart. We are thinking of the magnificent vision. We think of the sterling qualities of character as we evaluate the great President whose life ended so suddenly.

It appears to me that in this point of emphasis in this hour,

America reveals her own heart. America declares what she believes permanent and worthwhile in individual and in national life. And as I consider this fact, it seems to me that it gives hope that America will come through greatly and nobly and will be worthy and great.

Standing figuratively at his bier as we do now, there is no true American, no decent human being but bows his head sincerely and in genuine grief because this great American, this great human being has fallen in the midst of the battle, and as victory over the world-foe is in our grasp. America, indeed, the world of today and tomorrow, could ill afford his going. As was said of Lincoln, so with equal appropriateness is it already being said of Franklin Delano Roosevelt, "Now he belongs to the ages." His immortality in history is assured, and long after the tocsins of wars are silenced and the smoke of battle is gone, he will stand as the greatest American of his generation, one of the greatest Americans in our history, one of the towering giants amongst men.

He came to the presidency of the republic at a time of hopelessness, of confusion, of despair. He came to his great office and great responsibility when the dread word "Revolution" was being freely used throughout this country. But when he appeared in the national arena he brought with him into our national life a contagious faith in America, an infectious fearlessness. You remember, do you not, that already classic sentence in his First Inaugural: "We have nothing to fear but fear itself"? He sounded the call to resistance. He led the counter-charge. Gallantry was his characteristic. Confidence in America, in the American people, and a superb confidence in himself, radiated from him, and a frightened, confused people rediscovered its capacities, its vitality and vigor; rediscovered its soul and went on from that point to the then undreamed of miracles of creativity.

He was sorely stricken of body whilst in the prime of young manhood, but his spirit was never injured.

I remember an occasion when Lord Marley (the Deputy Speaker of the British House of Lords) occupied our pulpit here.

After the service he was a guest at my home. He told us then that he had the great privilege of being a house guest of the President and Mrs. Roosevelt at the White House for several days. As was natural, we inquired about his impressions of the President and he told us then that there was never an hour of the day when the President was not in pain! And yet—he carried burdens, he bore responsibilities with a brightness, almost a gaiety of spirit which would have broken most men!

I think it is because he knew the meaning of suffering that he understood the heart of others who suffered in whatever way, and it is because of such understanding that he dedicated himself to the task of alleviating and preventing suffering everywhere in this country. I think it was his suffering, perhaps, more than any academic philosophy which taught him the significance of the dignity of human personality and responsibility for it. I think that it is out of such understanding and his sterling Americanism that there flowed that intense hate of injustice, that intense concern for the underdog, that superb understanding of minorities—economic, religious, social minorities.

His enemies accused him of being a friend of the Jews. It is one of the glorious boasts of modern Jewry that Franklin Roosevelt was our friend. But I am convinced that his stalwart friendship for our people was not the result of a particular affection for Jews qua Jews. Rather was it because he saw injustice, grave injustice being done to this people, and injustice he hated with all the fury of righteous indignation, with a blazing prophetic earnestness and zeal. Here is the source of his friendship for our people.

Long before most leaders and masses, he saw the dangers of Fascism and Nazism. Let us remember that whilst others scorned him and scoffed at him, he it was who called for a quarantine of these dreaded diseases. Who knows, perhaps if the world had listened to him then, our boys might be home tonight. He saw the handwriting on the wall, and against tremendous odds he prepared us psychologically and militarily for the conflict which the people refused to do anything to avert. And when the sword was finally forced into our hands, he, as Commander-in-Chief, proved himself not only a man of vigor, of dynamic force, of supreme faith in our cause, but also one of the supreme strategists in history. You see, to every task he brought "amazing aptitudes and versatilities" and fearlessly he gave himself: "Here am I, Lord, send me!"

And now he has fallen in the midst of the battle, "sword in hand," and we, all men, decent men everywhere, stand bereaved and shocked.

In this tragic hour we do not surrender to our grief. Rather we catch fire from his spirit and we thank God for his radiant life, his challenging life; and although for the moment we are stunned, we must immediately proceed to reform our ranks and under a new leader, for whom we pray, must loyally carry on.

When Job was stricken, he was told to "curse God and die." His answer was: "Shall we receive only the good from God and not the evil as well?", and then added, "The Lord gave, the Lord took, the Lord's name be praised."

This must be our mood and our attitude in this hour. With courage, with confidence, with faith, united as never before, as soldiers of freedom and knights of democracy, we must—go forward!

Franklin Roosevelt saw the promised land from the heights of Nebo. He was denied the thrill, the compensation of leading the world into it. Under Joshua, then, we must prepare for the morrow and loyally, unitedly, we must cross over the Jordan, a people, a world, indeed, united and disciplined—in our hands the sword, in our hearts courage, our souls on fire.

This is the hour. In God's name, then, let us "be strong and of good courage," and go forward to achievement and to triumph both in war and in peace.

"Both in his mind and in his body man is adapted for enterprises of great pith and moment, for the acquisition of astonishing arts that seem impossible till he has practiced them, for dangerous expeditions into the unknown, for stern and anxious battles with the powers of darkness, for standing up to tremendous shocks, for enduring heartbreaking reverses, for rising up when he has been wounded and beaten to the ground, and for dying, if need be, sword in hand. To a being so splendidly equipped it is no hardship, no cause for whining, when he finds himself 'upon an engagement very difficult': he does not complain of his Maker for that. He praises his Maker, and goes into battle singing psalms. 'Here am I,' he cries, 'with my aptitudes and versatilities; yonder is the universe offering me the very problems, the very tasks those aptitudes and versatilities are made to cope with; here am I, Lord, send me.' "

PRAYER

OUR God and God of our fathers, heavy laden we appear before Thee, heavy of heart and grieving of spirit.

In Thy wisdom, to us inscrutable, Thou hast summoned our chosen leader and commander out of our midst. Bereaved we stand. Alarmed we are.

In this hour we lift our anxious hearts unto Thee and pray for the continuance of Thy protection and inspiration. Hitherto have Thy mercies helped us and sustained us. Forsake us not now or ever.

Heavenly Father, we pray Thee receive in Thy compassion and great loving-kindness the soul of Thy servant, Franklin Delano Roosevelt. Have mercy upon him. Pardon his transgressions, for there is not a righteous man upon earth who doeth good and sinneth never. Remember unto him the righteousness which his life manifested and reward him according to Thy graciousness.

O Thou in Whose hand is the soul of every living being, shelter the soul of Thy servant, Franklin Delano Roosevelt, in the shadow of Thy wings. Vouchsafe unto him the abounding happiness which Thou hast treasured up for the righteous.

Our Father, send the healing balm of Thy love unto the stricken wife and children of Franklin Delano Roosevelt. May Thy love and the fragrant memory of his life sustain them, and the sympathy of the world comfort them.

O Lord, Who healest the brokenhearted and bindest up their wounds, grant Thy consolation unto the people of this country. Put into our hearts the fear and love of Thee that we may unitedly serve Thee with a perfect heart.

O Father of all men and nations, like one whom his mother comforteth, so we beseech Thee comfort Thou the grieving people of this world who share in our loss, and weep with us in our sorrow. Grant unto them and us strength of heart, unity of purpose, the wisdom of determination that the battle for justice, for liberty, for opportunity unto all the children of men in which Thy servant Franklin Delano Roosevelt gave his life and to which he gave his complete measure of devotion, may be crowned with victory.

And O Lord, in this hour of anxiety and concern, we pray for our new leader, Thy servant, Harry S. Truman. Endow Thou his spirit, protect him, inspire him, and assist him in the difficult task and the heavy burdens now placed upon his shoulders.

And even as we pray Thee for comfort and strength, so do we thank Thee O Father for the life and service of our departed leader, for his example, his gallantry, his courage, his triumphant spirit. Grant it O Father that in the days to come we may prove to be worthy heirs of that spirit and loyal servants of Thy will.

Thou hast given, O Lord; Thou hast taken away. Praised be Thy holy name forevermore. Amen.

Roosevelt Memorial Tribute

RABBI LOUIS FINKELSTEIN

UNTIL the moment of his death, Franklin Delano Roosevelt stood at the head of the millions of his countrymen in their struggle for peace; today, he stands at the head of the many millions of martyrs of all peoples who have given their lives that freedom may live. He achieved much as the commander in chief of our armed forces and as the supreme architect of both victory and enduring peace. But an ancient sage taught that the righteous can be even greater in their death than in their life; and it undoubtedly will be the destiny of Franklin Delano Roosevelt to serve America and mankind even more effectively as the symbol of martyrdom for civilization, than he did as the wise counsellor and courageous leader during his life. The works of mortal men are inevitably evanescent; the struggle for righteousness, for civilization, and for freedom must be renewed in each age. But there is one service to mankind which never perishes; and that is the service which is offered by the martyr. The crown of martyrdom is thus the highest crown of all; and it was of the grace of God to His devoted servant that he should be enabled to serve in the moment of death as he did in life, bringing, not only to us but to all future generations, inspiration, devotion, a renewed determination to see to it that human liberty, international peace, and justice for all shall prevail.

The Talmud teaches that the Torah, the just life, cannot survive except through the efforts of men who are ready to perish for it. This is equally true of human liberty and democracy. That democracy is today victorious on all fronts, and that we and our children have before us the prospect of living out our lives in peace, are the results of the arduous and incessant labors and thinking of President Roosevelt. Before the rest of us, he recognized the peril to freedom and justice which loomed in totalitarianism; and he rallied our forces to resist the invasion of human liberties everywhere, knowing that liberty is indivisible, that the destruction of liberty in one land would ultimately result in the destruction of liberty everywhere.

We were loath to believe that the burden of war would be placed on us; we sought to find some way in which we could defeat the threat to ourselves and mankind, without our entering the arena of battle. This was not to be. Thousands of Americans have had to make the supreme sacrifice; many more thousands are suffering wounds and impaired health. The man who called on us to give our all, did not spare himself. He himself has become a casualty of war as much as the soldier smitten in the field of battle.

He began his career as a brilliant and gifted American. During the struggle for freedom, he became the leader of our generation. He now has ceased to belong to any particular generation; he belongs to the ages, the ages that have gone by and that helped to mould his sterling character; and the ages which are to come, and which will benefit by his heroism and his defense of liberty in our time, and his inspiration which will endure for all times.

For us there remains to be grateful that in this time of crisis God granted us and mankind so noble and far-seeing a leader; to be thankful for our share in him, and for the fact that he had a share in us. The memory of the righteous is a blessing.

A World Humanitarian

RABBI G. GEORGE FOX

"Know ye not that there is prince and a great man fallen this day in Israel?"

THE world is stilled, and America stands with bowed head and heavy heart at the bier of one of its greatest sons. Only those whose souls are encased by a sordid selfishness that rises above national love and world welfare, can stand aloof from the deep mourning and heartfelt sorrow that at the hour, engulf us. The tears that well into our eyes are not restrained, nor is the poignancy of the soul lightened. Frankly, sincerely, unashamedly do we mourn.

The anguish that has gripped our beings is not alone the expression of a personal or national loss that we have suffered. It is not just the death of our President, our Commander-in-Chief, that brings forth our deep grief; other presidents have gone to their reward—others have died in office within our memory. We mourn not the loss of Roosevelt the President, only. We mourn the man who more than any other in our day and age and in previous ages, has been the symbol of the everlasting progress of mankind in its journey from the earthiness of the brutal that is human, to the heights of divinity that man can and must achieve, if humankind is to survive. We mourn the passing of the personality which was itself the reflection of our own abiding faith in a cosmic world which can become a Paradise, fitted for the sons of man. He has joined those who have become a part of the intangible Universal Will for a happier world, and like Abraham Lincoln, "He now belongs to the Ages."

Among those whose tears for the departed are among the most sincere, are the Children of the Household of Israel—not only the Jews of America, but the Jews of the world. They found in him a friend and a protector—a fearless battler for human rights everywhere. His early denunciations of the bestialities of Hitler when others held their peace; his courageous and forthright condemnation of Nazi inhumanity at a time when the rest of the world—even the officially religious world, refused to take note of them in a manner in which it should have noticed them; his overpowering drive to break the unholy yoke of Nazism and Fascism, have made the Jews throughout the world regard him as their outstanding friend; and he was their friend, when friendship for the persecuted in Europe was regarded as dangerous even in our own country. The uprooted, blasted, wounded lives, wherever they are, will never forget the tender concern for their welfare shown by the man who dared to challenge the jungle fury of the brutal beasts of Europe. The men and women who so courageously went down in their own blood in the Ghettos of Warsaw and other cities, were encouraged in their heroic sacrifices by the hopes and visions of the American President.

Like other Americans, there were Jews who did not see eye to eye with the dead. Many there were who thought that they detected in some of his theories, ideas that were contrary to what they regarded as the American Way of Life. They neither voted for him nor supported him. Many there were who publicly condemned him for what they termed his radicalism. But I know of very few who condemned him for his wide and idealistic vision of a better world; few who differed with him in his great hope for universal peace and a more just world; few who assailed him for his unmeasurable love for the common man. These ideals a Jew worthy of the name cannot condemn for they are the very substance of the religion of Israel's prophets and teachers, and their Christian successors. Jews could differ with him in local or national ideologies which affected economic, industrial and social relationships; on the cosmic truths and visions which affect the peace of the universe, Jews could hardly differ with him.

Roosevelt was one of the succession of great world humanitarians, without whose visions, faith and sacrifices, our world would perish for want of that spiritual force that gives it ethical values, worthwhileness and hope. He has taken his place by the side of other molders of the world, whose lives reflected the Will of the Divine and channeled His teachings into the hearts and minds of mankind. And Roosevelt's interest in our harried people, his concern with the great injustices heaped upon them, will entitle him to a place in one of the Niches of Honor which Jewish life has set up for those immortals whom it holds dear—Moses, and his successors in the ancient days, and Washington and Lincoln in these later days.

In the tradition of Jewish folklore, there is a special honor for the "Prophets of the Gentiles." These are the greatest and the best of those who were not of Father Abraham's household. These like the righteous of all nations, will have a share in the world to come. But special honors were reserved for these Prophets of the Gentiles, who also saw the Presence, felt It and helped to bring It to earth. Among these must he now be numbered, who but yesterday, dreamed the dream of universal peace as did Isaiah and Micah, who dreamed of a world fit for those on whose souls has been stamped the seal of divinity.

Like our Lawgiver Moses, Franklin Delano Roosevelt saw the Promised Land from afar, but into it, he did not enter. Throughout his mature life he dreamed of a world ideal, and he gave his life in the struggle for it. This ideal has now become the intangible inspiration for all mankind—the immortal hope of an immortal leader. His memory will be a blessing, forever.

Franklin Delano Roosevelt, 1882–1945 *

JUSTICE FELIX FRANKFURTER

"WHEN a great tree falls, we are surprised how meagre the landscape seems without it. So when a great man dies. We may not have been intimate with him; it is enough that he was within our view; when he is gone, life seems thinner and less interesting. . . . The happiest of us hardly can hope for a destiny so complete and fortunate as that which has just been fulfilled. We shall be fortunate enough if we shall have learned to look into the face of fate and the unknown with a smile like his." Said of another, it was prophetically meant for Franklin Delano Roosevelt and the world that mourns him.

Writings about Napoleon fill sizable libraries. Roosevelt will claim an even larger share of history so long as the civilization endures which he helped to save. Fluctuations of historic judgment are the common lot of great men, and Roosevelt will not escape it. What history will ultimately say, it is for history to say. Only one thing is certain: he will remain among the few Americans who embody its traditions and aspirations.

But if history has its claims, so has the present. For it has been

* With permission of *Harvard Law Review.*

wisely said that if the judgment of the time must be corrected by that of posterity, it is no less true that the judgment of the posterity must be corrected by that of the time. Franklin Roosevelt cannot escape becoming a national saga. It is right that this should be so, for such sagas guide and sustain the high endeavors of a people. But the saga must not swallow up the man, whose vivid friendship gave hope to millions though they never knew him, and whose death brought a sense of personal loss to those who never saw him. This deep identification with his fellowmen must be saved from the impersonalness of immortal fame.

This identification with his fellowmen was Roosevelt's profoundest characteristic and ultimate key to his statesmanship. He was a democrat in feeling and not through abstract speculation about governments. When he said, "we are all immigrants," it was not a phrase but a feeling. It was not merely gregariousness in a setting of charm. It was not an undiscriminating love of his kind. His friendliness was so inclusive that his discriminating and often uncanny perception of men's qualities was a more hidden trait. He was keenly aware of men's frailties and follies. But he identified himself also with their follies and frailties, and so the corrosion of cynicism never touched him.

This permeating friendliness represented true feeling. But equally true were deep recesses that were accessible hardly to anyone. From the time he was a boy, according to his mother, he had the self-sufficiency and the strength that come from a reserved inner life. Thus, while to outward view he was mostly debonair and of a gaiety at times easily taken for jauntiness, he had a will of steel well-sheathed by a captivating smile. His optimism was a phase of this resoluteness. For too many people optimism is an evasion, a Micawber's hope that something will turn up. In Roosevelt, optimism was not an anodyne, it was an energy—an energy to spur his resourcefulness in finding solutions, a force that gave creative energy to others. An official not given to idolatry was once heard to say, "After talking with the President for an hour, I could eat bricks for lunch."

There were thus fused in him, and to an extraordinary degree, qualities indispensable for leading his people out of a period of deepening economic and moral deterioration by invigorating the forces of democracy. The same qualities fitted him to serve as a symbol of hope for liberty-loving people everywhere, in resisting a seemingly invincible challenge to civilization. Franklin Roosevelt's sophistication gave him understanding of men, his simplicity gave him trust in them. His understanding enabled him to govern; his trustfulness made him the exponent of democratic government.

Public men, like other men, are moved by major and minor motives. And the art of government has its own logistics. Moreover, instead of being "after all a very simple thing," as one of our Presidents so tragically misconceived it, government is a very complicated enterprise, and democratic government the most difficult. Undoubtedly there were surface deviations and inevitable tacking from time to time in the course Roosevelt pursued. But one cannot read the first magazine article about Mr. Roosevelt as a public figure, written in 1911 by that discerning journalist, W. A. Warn, without realizing that during the thirty-five years of his public life he steered a true course—the course of his dominant impulses. When Roosevelt first came to the Presidency, he could not escape the truth of Burke's dictum that we must reform in order to conserve. Events demanded a leader of social reform, and Franklin Roosevelt had the prepared mind and temper for it.

Also, when Roosevelt became President, disillusionment about Europe, strong belief in disarmament rooted in idealism, preoccupation with domestic problems, and influential opinion in favor of economic nationalism, combined to produce a good deal of blindness concerning the extent to which the fate of this country was bound up with that of the rest of the world. A strange juxtaposition of history brought President Roosevelt and Hitler to power at the same time. By the law of his nature Franklin Roosevelt from the first felt revulsion against Hitler and his cohorts as individuals, and hostility to the resurgence of barbarism which they represented as a system. He clearly saw that the new barbarism, if unchecked, would be a menace to civilized society, not excluding that of the United States.

The function of statesmanship is to endeavor to forestall untoward events or to prepare adequately against them. The President had to do both at the same time. He worked with might and main to avert a war which was bound to be infinitely more destructive and agonizing than the last one, and to avert it by saving, and not surrendering freedom. Politics in a democracy means a continuous process of education. But education does not always mean exposition, and certainly not shouting. It involves much incubation. Not least of the arts of statesmanship is that of correct timing, of knowing what to say and when. The President was confronted with illusions highly creditable to men of good-will but steadily rendered invalid by Hitler. He was also confronted by pressures of every kind, of which democracy is an amalgam. And in his own political household he must often have encountered hesitations rather than vigorous encouragement. But there came a time when he could no longer doubt that he had to shift from the task of social reform to war leadership, in order not only to maintain our spiritual heritage but to assure opportunities for further progress as a free society.

There came a moment when President Roosevelt was convinced that the utter defeat of Nazism was essential to the survival of our institutions. That time certainly could not have been later than when Mr. Sumner Welles reported on his mission to Europe. Certainly from the time that the fall of France seemed imminent, the President was resolved to do everything possible to prevent the defeat of the Allies. Although confronted with the obvious danger of attack by the Axis upon us, there came that series of bold and triumphant measures which Mr. Churchill authoritatively summarized in his recent moving speech to the House of Commons—the shipment of arms to Great Britain, the stab-in-the-back speech, the base-destroyer deal, lend-lease, the smoothing of the difficult ways of the Allied purchasing missions, the encouragement of Mr. Willkie's trip to England, the assistance in a hundred ways of

British economic warfare, the extraordinarily prompt and cordial support of Russia. Moreover, while engaged in this series of complicated moves, he so skilfully conducted affairs as to avoid even the appearance of an act of aggression on our part.

And so, in the hour of national disaster on that Sunday afternoon after Japan had struck, when the President had gathered about him his Cabinet and his military chiefs, the most experienced statesman among his advisers, after watching the President's powerful and self-possessed control of the situation, could say to himself, "There is my leader."

His silver voice is stilled but the pitch he struck in others will gather volume. For while his death comes as a cruel and monstrous loss, the creative energy which his life released throughout the world will continue, and one is justified in believing will even enhance his influence. He now joins the select company of those whose "home (is) in the minds of men, where their glory remains fresh to stir to speech or action as the occasion comes by. For the whole earth is the sepulchre of famous men; and their story is not graven only on stone over their native earth, but lives on far away, without visible symbol, woven into the stuff of other men's lives."

The ultimate mysteries of life are merely renewed. They always remain the same. Franklin Roosevelt knew this well and he chose to express it at the Harvard Tercentenary Celebration in the words of Euripides:

"There be many shapes of mystery.
And many things God makes to be,
Past hope or fear.
And the end men looked for cometh not,
And a path is there where no man sought.
So hath it fallen here."

A Great Heroic Soul

RABBI SOLOMON B. FREEHOF

SINCE last Thursday evening this great country of ours has gone through an unprecedented emotional experience, one that was much beyond the normal grief at the passing of a public man. There is something extraordinary and profound about it. Historians will look back to these past three days in order to try to analyze our strangely deep reaction, and we ourselves shall think back upon these days in wonder and surprise. What happened to us spiritually in these three days?

We are a commercial people. America makes its living from manufacturing material goods, buying and selling and hawking the goods through the newspapers and over the radio. But suddenly, as if wiped out by the recording angel sponge, all advertisements disappeared from American newspapers and all commercial cries were silenced on all of America's radios. This happened too in a democracy, where there is no one in absolute charge of all communications to give an order:—Cease to do this, or cease to do that. Spontaneously the whole country stopped conversation about buying and selling and removed its soul from the market place.

We are a pleasure-loving country. But suddenly Thursday night all triviality disappeared. There was not a single song of light-hearted romance, not a single bar of dance music. For three days there were hymns, hymns of all faiths, hymns by all types of singers. And there were addresses, obituary statements by every type of public figure in America. For three whole days we have been conducting an unbroken religious service. This has never happened to us before. Evidently we have been stirred beyond ordinary expression, much beyond our own anticipation. Evidently we have delved below the level of ordinary sorrow and have reached the profound depths of the religious mood. We were very close to eternity during the last three days.

Therefore, it is not sacrilegious nor is it surprising that so many of the speakers all over the country thought of the obvious parallel between Franklin Roosevelt and Moses, the first of the prophets, who died before he could set foot into the Promised Land. Why should it be sacrilegious? Moses was a man, a human with human faults, hot-tempered and stubborn; but all his humanity was infused with the inspiration of divinity. Indeed, the parallel is more exact than the average speaker indicated. Moses, raised in a royal palace, brought up in luxury, somehow discovers in his heart a bond with the oppressed; and before he can fully express the sympathy in his soul, he is torn away from Egypt and isolated in the desert of Midian; and there in the flame of a burning bush he receives his true inspiration. He returns to lead the people through the desert of hunger, through the blazing danger of war, to the edge of the Land of Promise. The parallel needs no clarification.

The last few verses of the Book of Deuteronomy read as follows: And Moses walked upward from the valley of Moab to Mt. Nebo, and there God showed him the land from Gilead to the portion of Ephraim and Manasseh up to the further sea; and God said to him, "This is the land which I promise to give to Israel. Gaze upon it with thine eyes, for thou shalt not set foot in it."

Therein lies the tragedy for us. The promised land of victory is very near. Franklin Roosevelt saw it with his eyes. We hear the reports of the disintegration of the German armies, of the rapid capture of a succession of German cities. Reports which would have filled our soul with delight now have very little meaning. They do not touch us. What is victory without the architect of victory? If Franklin Roosevelt could have lived only another week, two weeks, and we should enter Berlin, and his grand, clear voice like a silver trumpet would sing the world song of triumph—that would be victory; but without him, a certain splendor has gone out of our world, a radiance has faded. We all know it now. We are a generation that has been bereaved. The American people is a nation that is orphaned.

There is a strange harmony of dates in the events of these days.

This is April the fifteenth. Exactly eighty years ago Abraham Lincoln died. It was April 15, 1865. When Lincoln died, many of the leaders—kings and potentates of other nations—sent their messages of condolence. These were formal courtesies, though some of them must have been sincere. But when Franklin Roosevelt died, great nations decreed national mourning and their people have wept. Wherever people have loved freedom and longed for the overthrow of tyranny, they know that freedom has lost its greatest champion. They well may weep in every land; they have a right to mourn.

But it is different with us. He is not just freedom's champion to us. He is ours. We have quarreled with him; we have loved him. We voted against him; we voted for him. We have disliked some of his actions; we have deeply admired others of his actions. He is one of us. He is like an older brother who came back in a time of family crisis to rescue the family in its trouble. Do we not remember—shall we ever forget—the March of 1933, that tragic March when all the banking and industrial structure of our country seemed to be in ruins? He spoke and our nation was resurrected. Who dares forget that he was our will power, he was our courage, he was our national revival?

From that time on he began that great process of social advance in behalf of the suffering portion of our American people. He has been praised by no less a judge than Churchill for the immortality that he will attain because of his friendship of the causes of the oppressed and the unfortunate.

I believe that that statement, true as it is, is only a partial understanding. It is true that Roosevelt understood the suffering and the unfortunate and devoted his life to ameliorating their lot, and that therefore the masses of the people loved him. That is true. But those who understand his social action merely on that basis understand only half of it. What he did was much more far-reaching. What he accomplished for the poor redounded also to the welfare of the rich and the middle class and the whole country, because he saw that we had come to a turning point in world history, a time of revolution. The great masses in every country were convinced that the respective governments of the nation no longer belonged to them but belonged to the few and the powerful. The dangerous time had come when explosive forces had piled up in every nation and no country was secure. The tide of history was due to turn; and it was Franklin Roosevelt who knew that our country would never be safe nor its Constitution secure unless we took giant strides towards social progress, so that the masses of America, the humbler folk, would feel again that this is their government, that they may give it their allegiance as of old.

He did more than benefit the poor. He saved our democracy by his social program. Yes, for all the NRA and its failure, for all the Supreme Court dispute and its bitterness; for all the WPA and its extravagance—what remains, what is firm is a new allegiance on the part of the many millions of Americans for this, their country. Patriotism is more real and widespread. Democracy is more genuine and on firmer ground because he led this country out of a swamp and put our footsteps upon the road, the American road of comfort for the average man and human advance.

Roosevelt's great achievement, even if there never had been a war or a prospect for permanent peace—his great achievement was that he was our conscience. He represented the best in us. He spoke for the unselfishness in our hearts. There was hardly an address of his but exalted us to be better than we normally are. He was our better self. He was the prophet of our social advance. He was not merely the friend of the poor. He put America back upon the road of progressive history.

No American president ever calculates for war as a regular part of his plans. War is never a normal thought for an American leader because it is not a normal thought for the American people. We always are a peace-loving people, and our apparent isolation confirms us in our belief that no one will bother us if we leave them alone. So Franklin Roosevelt counted on an era of continued strengthening of America through social progress when he was interrupted by Adolf Hitler. This interruption in a sense changed his relationship to the American people. His social program was unpleasing to upper class people but pleasing to the masses. He intended it for neither exclusively; he intended it for the country. But his war program was understood sympathetically by upper class people who had international contacts and, naturally, a wider world-view, but was contrary to the feeling of the American masses who believed that America need never get into war. Thus, just as in his social program he had to fight against the dislike of comfortable people, so in his war program he had to fight against the millions who had learned to love him.

But he saw more clearly than most of us. He knew we were not at peace, even though war had not been declared. He knew that the Nazis were merely waiting to conquer England before they would put into effect their plans for conquering the world with our country as the greatest prize. So when almost nobody was with him, Franklin Roosevelt started in peace time to do what no American president ever successfully had done:—to rearm the country. He gave the fifty over-age destroyers to England; forced through the Congress a repeal of our Neutrality Act, so that beleaguered England could buy war goods. Then, in peace time he established Selective Service. Most presidents would have retreated in horror from a proposal to have Selective Service in peace time; it would be political suicide. But he was resolved. He also rebuilt the Navy, beginning its rebuilding in peace time—a dangerously expensive undertaking.

Thus, when war came, if we were not prepared, we were at least not unprepared and on the road to being prepared. When the war came, he saw that this is a new military era and that, therefore, the Air Force and the Navy and the Army must now cooperate as never before. We know now that it was he who soothed away the jealousies of the separate services and brought unity in the military forces of our country.

He achieved even more. He brought unity between the military forces of England and the United States, so that the Joint General Staff functioned more effectively than ever allies had cooperated before. And as for the strategy, while he left the working out of the second step in strategy to the generals and the admirals, he had the courage to make the great decisions himself, and he made them intelligently.

Hence the tragedy of what has occurred! Much of what he has done now shows its results. No matter how much we complained, no matter how half-willing we were to follow him in his pre-war preparations for war, which he knew to be inevitable, we now know that he was right, because our road is emerging out of the dark valley into the sunlit plateau—while he has left us to walk alone in the valley of the shadow of death. Alone? No. He joins the hundreds of thousands of his comrades who have already given up their lives for the future which their eyes will not be privileged to behold.

He loved the Navy so. Perhaps what Walt Whitman said of his beloved Lincoln applies even better to Franklin Roosevelt: The ship has weathered the storm; it is entering the harbor now; but on its deck the captain, our captain, lies dead.

In 1919, May 30, Memorial Day, Woodrow Wilson left the wrangling of the peace conference in Paris and went to the little French village of Suresnes to dedicate a cemetery for American soldiers. His heart was heavy. He knew how he was being set upon by various forces to scale down the high idealism which he had held up before himself and before the world. Feeling the weight of his official responsibilities as commander-in-chief, Woodrow Wilson on that Memorial Day in 1919 stood amid the graves of American soldiers and said: I sent these boys here to die. Can I possibly utter a word which will not be in harmony with the assurance which I gave them? They are gone, but they have left me bound to them in eternal comradeship.

Franklin Roosevelt was a Wilsonian, an ardent follower of that great and spiritually martyred President. He resolved, from an understanding of what had happened to Woodrow Wilson, that he would try to succeed where Wilson had tragically failed. Wilson's great difficulty was with his allies. They had very little interest in his far-flung schemes of a united world. They wanted immediate, practical military alliance. Wilson fought them and was largely defeated. Franklin Roosevelt, confronting the same problem of the great powers of the world wanting primarily alliances, brought to them the vision of American idealism. Making use of the practical power of his influence, he gradually persuaded the leaders of world empire to accept the American ideal of a united world.

Wilson, being defeated abroad, was then subjected to defeat at home. Franklin Roosevelt avoided this second calamity. He made the peace effort non-partisan. Next week he would have seen the fruition of his achievement at San Francisco. May God grant that those who take his place in San Francisco will be privileged to build the mansion of cooperative humanity. If they do, we shall never forget Franklin Roosevelt, who was the architect—the architect who drew the plans for the world's mansion of enduring peace.

The Episcopal bishop of Washington, Angus Dun, must have expressed the thought that was in many hearts when he said at the funeral services that the President's first public phrase as President, "We have nothing to fear but fear itself," should be also his final word to us. How right the bishop was! When Franklin Roosevelt spoke of fear he spoke of something that he understood very well. He knew the fear of helplessness. He knew the fear of the stab of pain. And he fought against it and achieved courage, as courage can be achieved only through struggle and the conquest of fear. Having conquered fear, he became the bravest man we ever knew. Nothing daunted him, no difficulty, no entrenched power. He thought the country needed a great step forward socially; he fought all the entrenched powers for it and became our pioneer of social progress. He saw that our country needed military preparation for an inevitable attack from overseas; he fought the complacency of the whole American people for it. He saw that the world needed a permanent structure for peace; he fought the selfishness of empires and the isolation found in our own country, and he laid the foundation for that great structure.

We shall never meet a braver man, a more heroic soul. May

God grant that he live forever in the consciousness of this country, as he will be revered and loved by all of us who have been privileged to live in his generation.

We can but end with these words of prayer:

> Heavenly Father, in whose hands are the lives of men, receive in the shelter of Thy loving arms this Thy son, Franklin Delano Roosevelt. Grant that his courage may outlive his earthly career, that it may infuse vigor into the actions of his successor and give strength to the heart of the nation which he loved so well.

His Vision Lives On

RABBI ISRAEL GERSTEIN

DECEMBER 7 and April 12 will go down as the two blackest dates of this tragic war era—December 7, marking America's humiliation at Pearl Harbor, and April 12, when our beloved President was taken away from us by death. But while December 7 has been redeemed, the ships and planes the Japs destroyed have been replaced by many times their number—December 7, by serving as an alarm clock to awaken America to its danger has been a blessing in disguise—April 12 will remain a sad day, for we shall not look upon his like again. A Roosevelt appears only at a certain point in history.

Roosevelt dead—it is hard to put the two words together, for Roosevelt had become synonymous with life, with energy, with faith, hope and victory. Roosevelt was the symbol of victory. Whenever any doubt crept in about the outcome of the struggle, the words of Roosevelt were enough to restore our hope. And so when it was announced that Roosevelt is no more, people were seized with despair. Rarely has one seen such universal mourning, men, women, and children weeping unashamed. The heart inwardly bleeds and weeps. The voice which brought confidence, faith, hope, and courage into our hearts and homes is no more. He was more than President, he was commander-in-chief, but he was more than that—he was father to this nation, and not only to this people but to all men everywhere hoping for a better day. And the heart of this father is beating no more, the father who had given all his rich gifts to his people, whose vision had prepared us and enabled us to beat back the enemy, and bring the victory so near —he will not be here to celebrate that day with us—the day for which he had worked, prayed, and given his life. That is why 130 million people stand today with bleeding hearts and sad spirits as the body of this father is lowered into its last resting place. The Commander-in-Chief is now with the thousands of boys who have given their lives in this struggle, and perhaps he is leading them in a celestial army.

"Oi lo lasefino sheovdo es kvarneto"—"Woe unto the ship that has lost its captain." This tribute was paid to Abraham at his passing, and similarly we can say of our loss today: Woe unto the ship that has lost its captain. Roosevelt was the great captain of this ship called America. Great is the captain who can pilot his ship in a storm, but greater still who can foresee the tempest coming and warn others of it. When Roosevelt warned his countrymen of the coming storm, many of them denounced him as an alarmist. And finally when it did come, when the Nazis broke loose with a fury that shattered all illusions about our safety between two oceans, defeatist voices were heard, that said there was a "wave of the future," that there was nothing that could be done to check the Nazis, so powerful were they. It was then that the great captain brought us his boundless faith in the ultimate victory, and thus did he steer this ship, within sight of triumph.

Woe unto the ship that has lost its captain—will our ship be safe with any other captain at the helm? That is the question of paramount interest at this moment. Will the new president stand up under the load, will he be able to carry out the great plans of Franklin Roosevelt to build a permanent peace? These questions are natural. The new President himself has said that when the news of President Roosevelt's death reached him, he felt as if the sun and the stars and the whole sky crashed down upon him. But I think that doubts about the future while understandable are not justified. Our faith in President Roosevelt should bring us the certainty that he had laid sound foundations, that his blueprints were clear enough to be realizable. So well did the captain steer his ship that men of lesser genius can take over the helm.

In addition, I have faith in America, as I have faith in God. As we look back upon the past we cannot help but realize that God is, after all, the Commander-in-Chief, and that Franklin Roosevelt was his appointed deputy. We can now see the hand of God in the history of this stormy period. Roosevelt came into the White House at about the same time that another man was elevated to power, namely Adolph Hitler. This man who was to let loose forces of barbarism, who wanted to turn the clock back to the dark ages and almost succeeded, found his match in Roosevelt. It is fortunate for the world and America in particular that there was a Roosevelt throughout this period. His appearance is an evidence of Divine providence. And therefore, I am confident in the future.

This applies as well to our own position here. We have lost a wonderful friend in Roosevelt, but let us remember that Roosevelt was the spokesman for the majority of Americans who elected him four times. His life and thoughts reflected America, and prove that its heart is sound and incorruptible.

Roosevelt has been aptly compared to Moses. Both men were slandered and derided during their lifetime. Neither Roosevelt nor Moses was privileged to enter the Promised Land. Both were the servants of men but not their slaves. Both served their people with supreme devotion and sacrificial loyalty, but neither submitted to whims and the weaknesses of the men whom they led. Both Moses and Roosevelt remain the unsurpassed examples for all time of the triumph of men over nature, over heredity, over environment, over the handicaps of life.

The prophet dies but his vision lives on. Moses died a lonely man on the top of Mt. Nebo; Roosevelt died on top of a mountain in Georgia. But the ideals of both of these great leaders have outlived and will outlive their poor and tired frames. Their ideals they bequeathed to mankind as a precious legacy. God be thanked for giving unto his children in their hours of bewilderment and danger, leaders of the type of Franklin D. Roosevelt, so marvelously endowed with faith and courage and conviction and love to lead them through the darkness of the world to the open places of a freer and more beautiful life.

Roosevelt, Friend of Zionism

RABBI ISRAEL GOLDSTEIN

AMERICA has lost its foremost leader. The United Nations have lost their keystone personality. The postwar world has lost its architect-in-chief. The Jewish people have lost an understanding friend. Zionism has lost an avowed supporter.

At a time when Nazi Germany is all but finished and Japan is headed for defeat, Roosevelt died upon the mountain-top of his career beholding the promised land but not privileged to enter it. His vision must be fulfilled in a world order of peace, security and justice.

The Zionist Organization of America is in deep sorrow.

We hope and pray that the spirit of Franklin Delano Roosevelt will go marching on. He will rank in American history with Washington, Lincoln and Wilson. A world order of justice and of international accord will be the monument to his memory.

On Pisgah, the topmost height of Mt. Nebo, like our teacher Moses of old, our President, our leader, our friend fell by the Eternal's inscrutable will within sight of the promised land—victory, freedom and peace.

To say that we mourn Franklin Delano Roosevelt, as Americans, as Jews, as Zionists, is to say far too little.

The cause of Israel and the cause of Zion have been made by the development of history itself the central moral problem of the Western world. Our President knew that with his mind; he grasped it with his great heart; he proclaimed it for all men to hear, his noble and wise friendship for all mankind, and so for the people of Israel he was the luminous center about which gathered all yearning for justice, our hope for a better world, all the aspirations of good and just men everywhere.

Franklin Delano Roosevelt's name will be a blessing to Israel and to all mankind through all the generations to come. We stand bowed and stricken and the one prayer on our lips is this, that for the sake of America, of Israel, of the world, his successor may be sustained to follow closely in his footsteps and to be ever mindful of his incomparable example.

Man, Creator of God's Kingdom

RABBI ISADORE GOODMAN

THE unexpected and sudden death of President Roosevelt is an act of God. This act is beyond human understanding. It is as the Psalmist declared: "This is the doing of the Eternal—We can but watch and wonder." (118.23.)

When President Lincoln was stricken dead, suddenly and unexpectedly, Walt Whitman burst forth with a grief laden cry of:

> "Exult O shores, and ring O bells
> But I with mournful tread,
> Walk the deck my Captain lies,
> Fallen cold and dead."

Within sight of a new social order, like our own Moses on Mt. Pisgah in sight of the Promised Land, Roosevelt when he reached the farthest heights ever attained by man, was taken to a world beyond our powers to describe. With a vista before him that must have reached beyond the furthest sight of any human in modern ages, Roosevelt passed into history.

That the Commander-in-Chief should have fallen at a similar moment when Lincoln fell, on the threshold of victory, is just one of those phenomena that are the secrets of God, not revealed to man. Nor do we propose to ponder this imponderable problem.

I have looked to the skies, as all of you have, times uncounted. I never thought that clouds could be designated and marked off by distinguishing names. Clouds were just clouds to me. When one day I read the interesting fact that though clouds have been seen by man since the dawn of history, it was only in 1803 that some one observed the very plain fact, that there were clouds and clouds. There were long low clouds heavy and forboding; there were light silvery clouds lined with pink and white; there were black clouds pregnant with rain, there were white clouds full of wind and thunder with not even a drop of rain.

We all have observed death at one time or another. There are deaths that come like the unclouded sun, sinking into rest, at the close of the day. There are deaths that come in the peacefulness of the night with the unexpectancy of a falling star.

Not until I was a boy of fifteen did I observe death and henceforward I discovered that there are varying sorts of deaths. Then I learned in the Talmud that the Rabbis spoke of death not as equivalent happenings but "To die at fifty is a premature death; at sixty it is the act of heaven."

"To have died suddenly is a hurried death, to have lingered and slowly passed on was the way of all flesh"—

Do we not all know that a full four score is a life more to be desired than is the span that snaps in mid-stream or as a day whereupon the sun sets at noon time?

Not all deaths are to be bemoaned. In fact, Rabbi Meir, a Sage of old, viewed death, in instances, as a blessing, a relief from torture, a merciful act of God.

In Rabbi Meir's Torah Scroll, there was a note on the verse:

> "And behold all was very good"—
> "And behold even death."

We can't view all instances of death with a similar attitude. Our emotions are influenced by the particular circumstances. With President Roosevelt's sudden death it is like some one dying in your own family. You feel like the lad of fifteen when his great father falls by the way, without notice, like a noble tree struck down by lightning. You feel as if the mainstay of the craft you are sailing, the one stout pole from which there swings the heavy canvas sails, snaps and you see only water and sky and no safety ahead. You feel as one lost in the dark damp fog of London Town, when you've slipt off the pavement and you move about the open roadway with none to direct you, none to guide you. In the morning we were hopeful, confident, secure in our minds, for the leadership was certain; in the evening there was fear in our hearts, whither shall we go—will we steer into port, or will we drift on to the rocks?

With Roosevelt there passed a father of men and as a father we mourn his death. Like the Patriarch of old so the President:

> "He breathed his last, he expired, and was gathered unto his people."

Our faith in God's judgment is not questioned; even though we cannot fathom the deep meaning of God's supreme will in this instance, when victory in Europe is at hand and the evil is being extirpated from the earth. Yet there is a lesson and this lesson I wish to teach.

Declares our Sage: "Everything is in the power of heaven except the fear of heaven"; everything is in the power of heaven except the establishing of the Kingdom of God on earth; That depends on man. When God created man, God furnished him with the gift and the power to create veritable worlds. And the "Kingdom of heaven" is not an act of God, it is the one act left to man, by man's deeds of goodness, by his misdeeds called evil, that Kingdom is created or it is postponed.

Viewing Roosevelt's public life there is the undeniable fact that he sought to establish the Kingdom. The well-being of his countrymen was furthered in his conception of the New Deal, and the well-being of all mankind was his aim through the United Nations activities.

The New Deal in America, which raised America out of the catastrophic depression of 1929–33 and put our country ahead, socially, economically and politically, many, many stages, will be Roosevelt's monument. The Square Deal which was planted at Dumbarton and cultivated at the Conferences and is yet to become a fruitful tree meant for all nations, will be accounted as the undeniable contribution to a better world by Roosevelt, the friend of the forgotten man and the friend of the forgotten nation.

Among the harried harassed persecuted nations is the Jewish nation which was never forgotten in Roosevelt's scheme of things to come. The claim of Jewry for a Jewish Commonwealth in Palestine found a deep understanding in Roosevelt's mind and a warm echo in Roosevelt's pronouncements on many occasions.

As Jews and as Americans we shall cherish the memory of this *"Chasid Umos Haolom."* This Saint among the Nations—we shall remember, unto the end of time. I wish to conclude on a note of hope. "Ours is a government of laws and of men," said Stanton as he stood by the bedside of the martyred Lincoln. And today the

American ship of state goes sailing on. If the commanding officer of the Army falls, is the battle broken off? Never. We shall continue to press forward until that vision seen by Roosevelt will be the vision seen by all God's children.

Now, President Truman reports to the leadership, at a moment such as did Joshua bin Nun, the Successor of Moses. Unto Joshua it was said: "Only be firm and brave." So we say to President Truman: "Only be strong and of good courage!"

Wracked in body, burdened with mental responsibilities the man Roosevelt has slipped away. But the spirit of Roosevelt goes marching on to victory for all mankind.

Why has this occurred at this climatic moment in history let the Psalmist tell us:

> "This is the doing of the Eternal—
> "We can but watch and wonder.
> *"Thee Nofsho Z'rura Bizror Hachyim."*

And may Franklin Delano Roosevelt's soul, be bound up with the immortal ones!

Design for Great Living

RABBI ROBERT GORDIS

TO SEE Franklin Delano Roosevelt in the light of the ages is beyond our power today. Our generation, which was privileged to be his contemporary, knows that he is one of the immortals, but we are still too close to him to be able to evaluate his precise position in the ranks of the great liberators of humanity, who include such diverse figures as Moses, the Roman Gracchi brothers, Washington, Lincoln, and many others. It is, however, significant that the lives of nearly all these great heroes of mankind tend to follow a pattern that seems more than the result of coincidence. This pattern, almost symbolic in its clarity, is graphically exhibited in the Biblical narrative of the life of Moses, the redeemer of Israel. It is suggestive that many a detail is repeated in the life and career of Franklin D. Roosevelt. A few elements in the design may be noted.

The great champions of the masses, the advocates of the people's cause, generally come from the upper classes. On the one hand, the members of the aristocracy, with the bearing and prestige of their origin, seem able to command the respect of those whom they seek to liberate. On the other, these idealistic leaders possess the courage and the assurance required to oppose the oppressor. The aristocratic provenance of the Gracchi and of George Washington comes to mind at once. Moses, too, was a prince in Egypt, who could have lived in ease and comfort all his days, but he could not rest in his luxury. So, too, Franklin Delano Roosevelt lacked for nothing to gratify his needs and desires. Born into a family of wealth and prominence, he was a scion of aristocracy in our democratic society. But a more powerful impulse beat in his heart. He had to learn how the other half lived. When he discovered the ill-fed, ill-housed, and ill-clad, he had found his war and had enlisted for the duration.

These tribunes of the people may or may not win the love and veneration of the masses they seek to serve. They are sure, however, to earn the undying enmity of their former associates. According to the Bible, Moses was hated and cursed by the Hebrew overseers who saw in him an agitator and a trouble-maker: "The Lord look upon thee and punish thee because thou hast brought us into ill repute with Pharaoh and his servants, giving them a sword to slay us." How closely the President's experience parallels this is well-known. Deep-seated hatred was visited upon him by members of his own class who regarded him as a traitor to his own group. But President Roosevelt knew a higher loyalty—to mankind, to those whose lot is the real touchstone of civilization: the underprivileged, the exploited, the poor.

His career as President was marked by the two greatest crises that have ever faced our nation, both symptoms of the profound disorder of our society. He came into office when America was deep in the throes of the worst depression in history. Courageously, he grappled with it when others were content to sit idly or helplessly by.

Before this blight of poverty could be removed, there came the menacing threat and finally the dread actuality of war that had to be fought against the most dangerous foe ever let loose against humanity. With much of the country not aware of the peril, and the remainder understandably eager to postpone the day of decision, his was the difficult task of seeking to maintain an increasingly precarious peace while preparing for war.

Franklin Delano Roosevelt was not merely a great leader but a peerless spokesman, voicing man's deepest hopes and aspirations. Thirty-five centuries before, Moses had lived, not only a statesman who built a nation, but a prophet with a vision for all time. Not all the liberators were seers as well. But President Roosevelt, too, had this double gift, not only for action but for the inspired word. Clear, trenchant, unforgettable were his phrases: "the good neighbor policy," "the abundant life," his assurance that "the only thing we have to fear is fear itself," his enunciation of the Four Freedoms, and the Economic Bill of Rights.

Immeasurably practical and politically astute, FDR was at the same time deeply spiritual. He knew and loved the Bible as no President since Lincoln. Like Lincoln, too, his style reflected the simple and majestic cadences of Scripture, as in his moving description of war, which he hated. His allegiance to a spiritual interpretation of life was attested to time and again.

Greatness is far more human than perfection. Even Moses is pictured as imperfect. There is only one way to be sure to do nothing wrong—to do nothing. Of this the President was incapable. Quite naturally, his career was marked by errors of omission and commission. What human being could grapple with all the world's problems in its most critical hour and never err in his judgments, techniques, or objectives? Naturally he was influenced by his associates, he had to depend upon experts, and relied for execution of his plans upon his subordinates. More than once, disappointment came to those who counted, and justly so, upon his effective aid in the fulfillment of their ideals, which they knew instinctively he shared. But however keen their disappointment, there could never be any doubt about his deep humanity, his hatred of cruelty, his love for justice, his yearning for peace.

That pattern of greatness which seems to have characterized the lives of the great liberators followed Franklin Delano Roosevelt to the end. Sometimes the leader offers up his personal happiness and even his life for his ideal without avail. But even the successful leader, whose sacrifice is not in vain, may see the prospect of success and yet be deprived of the fruits of victory. Moses was able to bring the people he had freed and recreated to the threshold of the Promised Land, but was himself denied the privilege of entering it. Abraham Lincoln led his country through a bitter civil war until he knew that the union was safe, but he, too, died before he could taste the blessedness of peace. President Roosevelt fought the cruelest enemy in history, until the decision was no longer in doubt, however bloody the cost. But like Moses and Lincoln, he was not fated to know the rapture of final victory and the rewards of peace.

Finally, the trajectory of his career followed the pattern in death as well as in life. Moses, tradition tells, died alone with only God at his side, taking his soul with a kiss. In the midst of a crowded and busy world, President Roosevelt passed away almost alone, and far from home—but God was with him and called him with a kiss, without long torment and pain.

A great philosopher declared a thousand years ago, "God does not leave His people at any period without a leader whom He inspires and enlightens that thereby its condition may be ennobled and improved." Franklin Delano Roosevelt bequeathed a living heritage to the people he loved.

Like Unto Moses . . .

RABBI DAVID GRAUBART

"And the Lord said unto him: 'This is the land . . . I have caused thee to see it with thine eyes, but thou shalt not go over thither.'"

FRANKLIN DELANO ROOSEVELT, our lamented President, was a modern Moses, who, like Moses of old, led the people of our generation out of the wilderness of war and despair to the Promised Land of Peace and Victory. Like Moses, President Roosevelt was not privileged to enter the Land of Promise. Moses died on Mount Nebo, on the top of Pisgah, having caught a mere glimpse of the Land. "I have caused thee to see it with thine eyes, but thou shalt not go over thither," God tells him. Franklin Delano Roosevelt labored to the end in behalf of peace and victory, but he himself did not live to see the glorious end.

Mysterious are the ways of Providence; it is not given unto us to fathom them. God in His wisdom took Franklin D. Roosevelt unto Him.

There is a mystical dialogue in the writings of our sages. King David discourses with God, asking Him when his end would come. God tells him that he would depart this world on the Sabbath; David insists that he would pass away on the first day of the week. . . .

There is meaning to this quaint discussion. God tells David that his labors will be completed, the Sabbath rest will come, when he will be gathered unto his fathers. David, on the contrary, thinks that he will pass on without completing his manifold tasks—at the beginning of the week.

President Roosevelt's Sabbath had come: his life-work completed, a life of gigantic achievement at an end. He was gathered to his fathers.

There is much in the life of President Roosevelt that is reminiscent of Moses. Like Moses, he came from aristocracy, from wealth and affluence, but soon "Went out unto his brethren." He sought out the common man, and gave himself to the betterment of his lot. He sought out the common man in every land and clime, and contributed to his advancement. Like Moses, he was often "slow of speech and of a slow tongue," because he sought to express the will of the people, and the people were not as advanced as he was. . . . Like unto Moses . . .

Like Moses, he was fought bitterly by his opponents who were often vile enemies. "What shall I do unto this people? They are almost ready to stone me." They were often almost ready to stone him, as they took up their cudgels against him.

Like Moses, he was the unflinching champion of social justice. He was the prophet who can not help but give himself entirely to justice and righteousness. Was he a great warrior? Was he a great legislator? Was he a great orator and spokesman? Franklin D. Roosevelt was the prophet, the champion of justice par excellence. Like unto Moses. . . .

Like Moses, Franklin D. Roosevelt died a 'mitah bi-n'shikah,' the Divine death kiss. A prophet walked in our midst, and in a moment he was no more.

F. D. R. belongs to the ages.

He Scored Over Tyranny

CHAPLAIN SIDNEY GREENBERG

"Hushed be the camps today
And soldiers, let us drape our war-worn weapons;
And each with musing soul retire to celebrate
Our dear commander's death.

No more for him life's stormy conflicts
Nor victory, nor defeat—no more time's dark events,
Charging like ceaseless clouds across the sky.

But sing poet in our name;
Sing of the love we bore him—because you, dweller in
Camps, know it truly.
As they invault the coffin there;
Sing—as they close the doors of the earth upon him—
one verse
For the heavy hearts of soldiers."

Walt Whitman (Upon the death of
Abraham Lincoln)

SCARCELY twenty-four hours have passed since a thick mourning shroud enveloped our entire nation. We are still too stunned by the suddenness of our overwhelming loss to be able to cast our gloom into words which will adequately express the deep personal sense of bereavement in which we all share. With poignant relevance does the Rabbinic observation apply to the passing of Franklin Delano Roosevelt:

"When a wise man dies all are his relations." Our mourning today is not only intimately personal, it is also universal. We have each lost a close friend; our Armed Forces have lost their Commander-in-Chief; our nation has lost its President; humanity has lost its champion.

The tragedy of our President's death is deepened by its untimeliness. How sorely the United Nations shall miss his vision and his leadership during the coming months! How richly he deserved to taste the fruits of victory over Nazism—fruits of which he was the chief planter and which are now virtually ripe for the plucking. In millions of aching hearts there is a gnawing rhetorical question: "Why couldn't he have lived just a little longer?" It is almost inevitable that the painful Biblical analogy of the untimely death of Moses should insinuate itself into our thoughts at this moment. Moses too had transcended a physical handicap to assume leadership of his people. He too led them through critical, perilous years, inspiring them with courage and his leadership, battling their doubts, buttressing their faith and keeping steadfastly before them the vision of the ultimate, single objective—the Promised Land. When finally the Promised Land appears within view, when the threshold of realization is reached, Moses is permitted only a glimpse of the Promised Land from the distance before death rudely intervenes to claim him.

I recall the sense of rebellion that filled me when, as a child, I read this Biblical story for the first time. How cruel was the sense of frustration I felt for Moses. To have struggled so long for an overarching goal only to be denied its attainment at the precise moment when it was virtually within reach—Ah! that was too disheartening a climax to the story of a great human adventure. It seemed to betray the very faith which Moses himself had lived. It seemed to empty the vision which Moses had so resolutely championed.

With maturity however, the sense of rebellion was mellowed by the realization that in the apparently premature death of Moses the Bible was conveying an inescapable truth of human experience. The great always die too soon. For it is in the essence of greatness that it sets up for itself goals which are too all-embracing to be achieved in any lifetime however long, its objectives are too far-reaching to be realized in any single life-span. Every Moses inevitably leaves his final Jordan uncrossed and must rest content with only a glimpse of his Promised Land.

Franklin Delano Roosevelt could never have accomplished all his humanitarian tasks. As long as man hungered for bread anywhere, as long as man wore the shackles of servitude anywhere, as long as man suffered persecution or walked in the shadow of fear anywhere, his work would have remained undone. Whenever death would have claimed him, it would have found him in the midst of some unfinished human symphony. Let this thought temper our sadness tonight.

We may find additional comfort and at the same time better appreciate the great spirit that moved among us, if we dwell not upon the circumstances of his death, but rather upon the quality of his life. We are still too close to the scene of his momentous accomplishments to be able to evaluate properly their full import upon human history. A future historian equipped with the perspective that time alone affords, will record the full measure of President Roosevelt's legacy to man's spiritual endowment. But ours has been the unique privilege of being his contemporaries. As such we have had the opportunity to be his co-workers for a more abundant world. Under his inspiration, we fought against greed and selfishness at home so that the manifold blessings with which nature has so lavishly endowed America might be enjoyed by the many rather than the few. Under the banner of his leadership, we overcame our differences and welded this nation into a mighty fighting force which is now battling on a hundred battlefields so that Freedom and Human Dignity might be the common lot of all men. Through the magic of his eloquence we were aroused to the realization that Democracy, to survive, had to cease being a way of speaking and become a dynamic, purposeful way of living. Tonight let us be thankful that we were the America that President Roosevelt led. Let us mingle the grief over his death with gratitude for his noble life.

We find solace also in the dictum of our Sages who said: "The righteous even in death are called living." In a deep and noble sense, the great never cease to endure as a living influence among humanity. Moses does enter into the Promised Land with his people. Though physically removed from them, he enters with them in their hearts, in their hopes, in their strivings. He has become indelibly impressed upon their national and individual consciousness, woven into the very web of their existence.

President Roosevelt will live in the victory which we shall score over tyranny and barbarism. His spirit will be with us in San Francisco and at all conferences where men of good will gather to plot the lasting peace he worked for and wherever men assemble to build the world of simple justice, kindness and righteousness which he envisioned. His guiding genius will be as real to us in the Promised Land as his dynamic personality was in the wilderness through which he led us.

It is our human custom to insure against the failings of human memory by erecting monuments to perpetuate the great who stir among us for a few fleeting moments before they are claimed by the ages. Undoubtedly, we shall rear impressive marble figures to President Roosevelt. But the greatest and most enduring monument to his memory, he himself has already built not alone in the hearts of his countrymen but in the hearts of all men everywhere who aspire to life's blessings. He more than any other person symbolized the truths for which we fight. He more than any other person articulated the dreams of the underprivileged, the weak, humanity's common men who found in him their indefatigable champion. These shall ever gratefully kindle the flame of his memory in the fireplace of posterity.

If we would truly pay tribute to our fallen leader, let us do so not by words alone but by deeds as well. Let us first strive with a common and resolute will to hasten the end of the war which he waged with exemplary courage and determination. And when the furies of war are spent and peace is restored to a sadder but wiser humanity, may we prove capable of patterning America after those ideals which he held sacred. Let us make of it a better and more beautiful America which will lead in the search of a happier world—a world that will not have to pay for its mistakes with the lives of its youth, a world where all men shall be equal and all men shall be free, a world in which each man will lie under his own vine and his own fig tree and there shall be none to make him afraid. For only as these things come to pass shall President Roosevelt's visions be clothed with flesh, his dreams become living substance. In that better world his spirit will live and never perish from the hearts of men.

As we commit his sacred soul to the hands of God who loaned it to mankind, we pray in the words our President used in his message to the Armed Forces at the end of 1943:

> "We ask that God receive and cherish him who has given his life, and that we keep him in honor and in the grateful memory of his countrymen, forever."

F. D. R. of Blessed Memory

RABBI GERSHON HADAS

IT WAS a bleak March 4 in 1933 that Franklin Delano Roosevelt was sworn in as President of the United States. Millions of Americans were unemployed, the financial structure of the nation was tottering, fear and despair threatened to overwhelm the country. The people swept Mr. Roosevelt into office in the hope that he would lead them out of the fearful tragedy of poverty made yet more grim by the plenty all about them.

And Franklin Roosevelt did not fail his fellow Americans. Immediately after his inauguration he entered upon the herculean job of bringing order out of the chaos which was gripping our economic order. Very soon he demonstrated his magnificent capacity "to dominate and to control a supreme emergency, which is perhaps the rarest and most valuable characteristic of any statesman. With complete grasp of every development—the President never for a split second ceased to be master of the fate of his country."

Someone once said that when the President came into a room three people entered, the President, his love of a people, and his passionate devotion to his country. It was always a good committee, a trinity that gained the confidence of the great masses and endowed them with something of his courage, his fortitude, and his faith.

With rare vision he very early recognized the dangers which America faced because of the rise of totalitarianism, and with determined and unswerving consistency he labored to prepare us psychologically and materially to meet these dangers. The epic tale of the last thirteen years of our history is one that will stand out as the great monument to the genius of American achievement. The greatest single hero of that tale is unquestionably Franklin Delano Roosevelt.

We so often bear hatred toward the people to whom we are indebted. "I don't understand why he dislikes me. I never did him a favor," remarked a friend when we told him that a certain man resents him. So it was with our President. It was quite normal that his powerful and dynamic personality would arouse jealousies and bitterness and hatred. It is worth noting, however, that many of his most violent detractors were of those who were most benefited by his policies. The high tension under which we have lived during the past decade became more strained because of Nazi propaganda. The population of gutter misfits and dealers in social poisons wrapped in religious rags added their chorus of hate against the President.

Despite every attack upon him and his family, in the face of bitter opposition, he never faltered in his love for his fellowmen. Never did he waiver in his passionate faith in the American people or in the sacred worth of the American dream.

We Jews have always felt that in Mr. Roosevelt we had a very sympathetic friend. That is true; but not because he had singled us out of all peoples. He possessed a real understanding and a very deep sympathy for all those who are persecuted. He was eager to do what he could to alleviate and to obviate pain wherever he saw it. The plight of the Jew was for him the symbol of the tragedy of many minority groups.

When he appointed Jews to public office it was not because he sought to show to the world his particular interest in our people. Nor were such appointments made for political reasons. Mr. Roosevelt made his choice of aides simply and clearly and courageously as should an American, bearing in mind only the individual's capacity to do the job that needs to be done.

Mr. Roosevelt, like all our presidents since Woodrow Wilson, was a firm believer in the Zionist program. Only a few weeks ago he reaffirmed his determination to use his best efforts to set up a Jewish Commonwealth in Palestine. This faith and this determination stemmed from his eagerness to secure justice for those who have been so terribly wronged and to secure an enduring peace for all nations and all peoples.

A beneficent Providence blessed us with his leadership during these critical war years. The high idealism and the inspiration which was his have become a prime source of strength and hope to all Americans everywhere and to untold millions throughout the world who look to America for the attainment of victory and peace.

Mr. Roosevelt symbolized in his person and his character the glory of America. His gaiety and his grace, his nobility of mind, clarity of vision, kindness of heart, together with a brave and intrepid spirit endowed him with that glamour that is the America we love and revere.

Now Franklin Delano Roosevelt is no more. All that was mortal in him is gone. His body lies in Hyde Park, but his spirit is everywhere amongst us. "The unrighteous are dead even in life; the righteous are alive even in death." His spirit will unite our land and bring added determination to our citizenry to sustain our President, Harry S. Truman, in his resolve to attain speedy victory over our enemies, to secure a lasting peace and to carry on the building of an America firmly founded on faith in man, faith in democracy, and faith in God.

God bless the memory of Franklin Delano Roosevelt.

God bless our President, Harry S. Truman.

A Twentieth Century Prophet

RABBI FERDINAND M. ISSERMAN

THAT a prophet is never appreciated in his own country is an old truism. It might even be amended to read that a prophet is usually never appreciated in his age. Nor is this an aspersion of the people in whose midst he is, for prophets like other men are subject to human frailties. Even as they have great strength, so too they have great weaknesses. The age and generation in whose midst they live enlarges the weaknesses and minimize the strength. History with its clearer perspectives and with its distant views overlooks the weaknesses and marvels at the strength. To an ocean traveler, a ship on the distant horizon always seems majestic and stately. To a sailor on the ship, who knows its defects, it may be a worthless scow. That universal sorrow and universal praise for him followed Franklin Roosevelt's death is natural and normal. He was the head of a great state, the leader of the leading nation in the world and the leader of the United Nations engaged in a titanic conflict and about to emerge victorious over its Axis foes. He had been elected President of the United States four times, a record unparalleled in American history, which may never again be equalled. He had just returned from a momentous conference which he had made despite his failing health. He was at work preparing for the United Nations meeting in San Francisco, a meeting around whose outcome the hopes of men cling, and he was regarded a friend of the orphaned masses of humanity when he was suddenly stricken alone away from his family. All the circumstances of his death were such which would enlist universal sympathy. Never in all history did so many people depend for so much on one man. Their shock and grief was spontaneous and inevitable. Despite our proximity to the Roosevelt era, I have no hesitancy in hailing him as a prophet of the twentieth century, who walked in the way of the great prophets of Israel, who emulated their heroic example, and who saw to translate their vision into realities, who used the great powers that were his more than any other American in history to protect the weak, to safeguard the widow and the orphan, to strengthen the poor, to build ties of good will between religions, races, and nations, to disseminate freedom, and to eliminate wars. He possessed the virtues of the great prophets.

First, he understood the rights of the weak and battled to secure them. This was one of the revolutionary conceptions which the prophets of Israel introduced into the ethical and religious thinking of men. The rights of the strong had been taken for granted. Might makes right was the universal philosophy. Strong men lorded over their weaker brethren. Strong nations robbed weak nations, strong tribes exploited weak tribes. The right of the strong to rule, to dominate, to do what they will with the weak was unchallenged until the prophets of Israel with divine insolence asserted the rights of the weak. This notion marked a revolution in world thought and sympathy for the weak has colored the ethical values of all men, who have accepted the Jewish Christian heritage. Christianity like Judaism has acclaimed as its noblest sons those who have upheld the rights of the weak. No one will question where Franklin Roosevelt stood and where he ranged himself, and whose cause he championed. He was partial and he was one sided and he was partisan to protect, to uphold the rights of the weak. He did not lead for sympathy for the weak, he spoke of their rights. Judaism knew no charitable concept which meant that generosity and goodness of soul induces men to help the weak. It knew tsedokah, righteousness, not charity. Righteousness, means the rights of men. It was said that Roosevelt was partial to Negroes. So he was. They were the weak. It was said he was fair to Jews. So he was. They were a minority. It was said that he sided with the oppressed people. So he did. Sharecroppers, unskilled workers, tenant farmers, dwellers of slums, forgotten men, had first claims upon his concerns. He struck many a blow on their behalf and instituted many a reform, so that he is the hero and the idol of the common man of America and of the unwashed masses of the world. Like Isaiah of old, he was a child of wealth and like his prophetic predecessor he became a champion of the poor.

Second, even as Roosevelt shared the prophets' faith in the rights of the weak, so did he share the prophetic notion that all men were children of God and that the nations of the world were members of one family, between whom there could and there must prevail the laws of justice, the ties of fellowship and love. He re-echoed the prophets' cry, "Have we not one Father, has not one God created us all?" He loved to quote the prophetic truth that all men are made in the image of God and flung it as a thunderbolt in the camps of bigotry and of prejudice. When men hoped to insulate themselves in isolationism, he spoke of quarantining outlaw nations, of applying the laws of God to nations that transgressed them. His wisdom was ignored and condemned. When Mussolini pounced upon a prostrate France, like a prophet, Roosevelt condemned the assassin, who stabbed a dying nation in the back. When Great Britain was beaten to her knees and the last light of freedom was being dimmed in Europe, he declared America must become the arsenal of democracy, and began to create the pipe-line of life across the Atlantic to keep the flame of freedom burning. When we found ourselves engaged in the war, he created lend-lease and extended the philosophy of the good neighbor whom man must love as himself by planning lend-lease instead of war loans. The latter would be a crushing debt, the former a symbol of mutual aid and neighborly cooperation. He became the author of the Four Freedoms, freedom of religion, freedom from tyranny, freedom from want, and freedom from fear, which he sought to win for all. And as he was dying he wanted as the fruit of victory a union of nations which could "beat swords into plowshares and spears into pruning hooks." He had envisioned not merely a peace secured by force, but based on justice and equality of opportunity and faith of man in his neighbor. How well he walked in the prophetic succession.

Like the prophets of old, Roosevelt possessed great physical courage. To preach as they did, the prophets of Israel risked their lives. Jeremiah had to flee and it was believed that he was assassinated. Kings and the powerful men of their day arrayed themselves against the prophets, and sought to destroy them. One of Roosevelt's richest legacies, which will inspire men for generations for centuries was his personal courage. He should have been an invalid, nursing his wounds and lamenting over his sickness, instead of ministering to the hurts of humanity. After he was crippled, he entered the political arena, ran and served as governor and became president. What a lesson for every sick person for all time. Has it ever happened before? In the heart of the war he crossed the seas five times and each time risked his life. What a prize for the foe, his earlier death would have been, a foe whose spies were everywhere even in our nation's capital. Yet Roosevelt went to Casablanca and to Cairo, and to Teheran and to Yalta, to the Aleutians, and to write the North Atlantic Charter.

Like the prophets he also had moral courage. He was not afraid to offend the mightiest. As a young assemblyman, he fought a corrupt political machine. As a candidate for the vice-presidency, espousing the League of Nations, he fought for internationalism against provincial nationalism. He incurred the wrath by his social vision and daring, the wrath of the mightiest of his day. They hated Roosevelt as men hated Jeremiah. As Jeremiah said, "I am become a laughing stock all the day and everyone mocketh me." But as Isaiah said of the prophet, "He was despised and forsaken of men." Roosevelt had moral courage.

And Fifth, like the prophets, he had a deep faith in God. The justice they sought, the brotherhood they advocated, the prophets received from the lips of God. "Love thy neighbor as thyself, I am the Lord," said the Book of Leviticus. The prophets' faith in man, belief in justice, hope for world peace, came out of their belief in God. So, too, Franklin Delano Roosevelt. He was a deeply religious man—the lay leader of his church in Hyde Park, New York. He read the Bible. In one of his last letters to Temple Emanu-El he extolled the Old Testament. He believed in organized religion. He attended services regularly. He found religion sailing in the ocean, but also found it in the pew of his church. Through his faith in God, Franklin Roosevelt was moved to his prophetic ministry to all men. Like the prophets of old, he pleaded the rights of the poor; he rose above racial and religious prejudices; he sought to establish peace in the world; he was unafraid, even of the blows of fortune. He had moral courage, and deep religious faith. Verily, Franklin Delano Roosevelt was a twentieth century prophet. In closing may I paraphrase with the Torah's epitaph of Moses—"that Franklin Roosevelt died the servant of the Lord and his eyes were not dimmed nor had his vision abated. And the children of mankind wept for Roosevelt and there shall not rise a prophet like unto him who knew God face to face for many generations in all in the signs and the wonders which the Lord sent him to do in the land of the axis tyrants to the Pharaohs of our day and their servants and to their land and in all the mighty hand and in all the great terror which Roosevelt wrought in the sight of all men."

He Raised America

RABBI LEO JUNG

FRANKLIN DELANO ROOSEVELT has entered on his eternal reward, and has become part of the American tradition which he enriched and ennobled. His death stunned America, deeply grieved the Jewish people, saddened the world.

The usual interpretation of President Roosevelt's career reads thus: He came from aristocratic stock that offered him every opportunity. He was afflicted with the handicap of a grievous illness, rose above it and achieved outstanding success. The tragedy of his life was that of a leader who was granted a vision of the Holy Land, yet denied the privilege of entering it.

The poignant meaning of his history is rather this: He was born with the great moral handicap of a silver spoon in his mouth. But the Lord threw him on a sickbed, taught him for many weary years the abyss of hopelessness, the meaning of affliction, aroused in him a passionate understanding of what the poor and the sick have to face. "He prayed to the Lord out of the depth of his misery, and the Lord answered him with enlargement." His affliction made him a great man. He apprehended the trackless desert of human unhappiness and determined to advance the cause of "those who are crushed and of lowly spirit." America, he believed, was established to promote the welfare of every citizen by permeating the whole life of the nation with constructive help to the underprivileged. Above all, he was a warmhearted humanitarian who shed the warmth of his radiant personality upon his whole environment. Possessing true humility, he loved his fellowmen and included them in his plan of happiness. Their poverty aroused him to righteous indignation. He passionately espoused the cause of all minorities. He was both visionary and practical statesman. With Lincoln he shared the love for the common man, with Wilson the great ideals. But like Samuel of old, "he knew not only the course of the stars, but also the meanest alleys of the metropolis."

President Roosevelt possessed the courage of his vision. He saw a plague, made in Germany, afflicting large masses of our people. Compromise with that evil, he maintained, was treasonable. He taught Americans to fight bigotry and oppression within the country and without. He overcame selfish isolationism as he battled narrow sectionalism, by focusing the attention of the people on the danger confronting them. Out of a discordant congress and a divided nation our sainted President forged the mightiest instrument for the perpetuation of world justice and the re-establishment of world democracy.

He raised America to the height of her destiny, the championship all over the world of righteous democracy. To him truly apply the Psalmist's words: "Forever blessed be his name; sure as the sun itself his fame. All peoples envy his high bliss; all nations hail him as a happy man."

The Architect of a Better World

RABBI C. E. HILLEL KAUVAR

AS WE are still within the thirty days of mourning for our late President Franklin D. Roosevelt, I want to add yet another tribute and speak of him as the Architect of a better world, and I choose as my Text, these words from the Book of Isaiah describing an ideal ruler of his people,

> "And the Spirit of the Lord shall rest upon him, the spirit of wisdom and understanding, the spirit of counsel and might, the spirit of knowledge and of the fear of the Lord." (Isaiah 11.2.)

Surely the Spirit of the Lord rested upon our President; with wisdom and understanding, he guided the destinies of our nation; with counsel and might and the fear of the Lord, he prepared the plans for the new world-order.

The representatives of the United Nations are now in conference at San Francisco, and are holding the most important meeting in all the history of the world, to forge an association of nations to lay the foundations of a new world-order, a world of liberty, security, and peace; and the leaders of all the nations are inspired by the vision and the humanity of our late beloved Chieftain.

We, the children of an orphaned nation and a bereaved world, mourn him as a personal loss, and are made holy by his dreams for a nobler America and a better new world-order.

When the Patriarch Abraham died, the people of his day cried and said, "Woe unto the ship that has lost its pilot." Surely we who have lost our President can voice our lament, "Alas for the world that has lost its Captain." In his lifetime, the spirit of the Lord rested upon him; now he abides in the presence of God.

As President of the United States he reinterpreted the Bill of Rights, the fundamental law of the land, and he deepened, strengthened, and ennobled it. When history shall appraise his record, it will reaffirm the verdict of his contemporaries that his achievements will remain as everlasting as the eternal tides.

This great American loved all lovers of freedom. He visioned a Bill of Rights, not only for Americans but for all humanity, and he fashioned the frame-work for a new and better world-order. President Roosevelt wrote:

"In the future days which we seek to make secure, we look forward to a world founded upon four essential human freedoms.

The first is freedom of speech.

The second is freedom of every person to worship God in his own way.

The third is freedom from want.

The fourth is freedom from fear, which, translated into world terms, means a world-wide reduction of armaments to such a point and in such a thorough fashion that no nation will be in a position to commit an act of physical aggression against any neighbor."

These noble ideals formulated a new Magna Charta for a united world, and are now being discussed at the San Francisco Conference. They were visioned long ago by the Jewish prophets, Isaiah and Micah, who foretold that in the days yet to come, the Law that came from Zion would become the international code for all peoples. "On that day, nation shall not lift up sword against nation, neither shall they learn war any more. But they shall sit every man under his vine and under his fig-tree; and none shall make them afraid. For let all the peoples walk each one in the name of its god; but we will walk in the name of the Lord our God forever and ever."

Our wise and valiant leader, the radiant messenger of a happier tomorrow, was an ambassador of good will not only among the nations of the world, but also between man and man. Like the messenger described by the prophet Isaiah, our President proclaimed peace, and published good tidings and salvation for all men. "He achieved peace with justice in the industrial world," and urged fair play for capital and for labor alike. His influence "kept the coalition of the United Nations fighting side by side to Victory."

In a world aflame with injustice, brutality and hate, he yearned for peace. America's mission, like that of Israel, was to bring peace. The prophet said, "Thy Peace shall be like a river." Just as water does not rise higher than its source, so peace cannot be better than those who conceive it. This thought was eloquently expressed by Angela Morgan in these words,

"Man is the maker of his own defeat,
Man is the measure of his own despair,
And wars are making when the planners meet
To forge the chains the future race must wear.

"No greater than the minds that give it birth,
No purer than the hearts from which it springs,
Can be the peace imposed upon our earth,
Sharp with the punishments a conquest brings.

"No kinder than their prejudice or spite,
No deeper than their vision of the soul,
No saner than their arrogance of might,
Shall be the peace the statesmen shall unroll.

"On anvils where the 'peace' is hammered out,
The swords of future wars are hammered, too!
And 'peace' already is a battle shout
If men who make it 'know not what they do.'

"Ah, some day men shall frame a peace so pure,
So true to cosmic law and human worth,
Its noble principles shall all endure,
Broad as the bastions of the sky and earth.

"For God is active in his world this hour
As when the first great word of 'Light'! he spoke,
And peace shall come in majesty and power
When love of God is born in human folk."

Blessed indeed is our generation, that it produced a man of peace, filled with the spirit of the Lord, the spirit of wisdom, of counsel and might, the spirit of knowledge and of the fear of the Lord.

Our distinguished president, an ambassador of good will, was worthy to plan the better world. By birth, Roosevelt was an aristocrat; from his youth he was surrounded by all the advantages that birth and wealth and culture can bring; and yet his heart was touched by the plight of the struggling masses, and he made the cause of the common man his own concern. Like unto Moses, who, though brought up in a palace, yet championed the cause of the rightless slaves, young Roosevelt knew and felt the tragedy of submerged, suffering people.

When, in his prime, he was stricken with the dread disease of paralysis, his courage and his faith not only enabled him to conquer the ravages of disease, but spurred him on to mobilize America to bring healing to others similarly afflicted. His constant pain purified his heart; his suffering strengthened and sanctified his character. It was lovingly said of our Commander-in-Chief that his frail, feeble limbs could not carry his body, but his great, stout heart carried the burdens and sorrows of the world. Every outraged, uprooted people turned to him as its champion. In our hour of need, the Jewish people also turned to him for help, and he recognized Israel's historic claim to the Holy Land. He wrote to the Jewish citizens of America:

"We favor the opening of Palestine to unrestricted Jewish immigration and colonization, and such a policy as to result in the establishment there of a free and democratic Jewish Commonwealth. I know how long and ardently the Jewish people have worked and prayed for the establishment of Palestine as a free and democratic Jewish Commonwealth. I am convinced that the American people will give their support to this aim, and I shall help to bring about its realization."

He was equally concerned with the cause of all exiled, conquered peoples; he knew the problems of the Negroes and other minority groups and sought to improve their condition. Everyone looked upon him as a personal friend. All peoples came to him as to a 'hiding place from the wind, and a covert from the tempest.'

Franklin D. Roosevelt realized, from the very beginning of this war, that freedom, justice and peace are indivisible. As long as there is one single nation enslaved, one single people rightless, all nations are enslaved and rightless.

He was a man of action, of noble convictions, unflinching courage and indomitable faith. He knew that a Divine Purpose guides the destiny of nations, and that in the long run Democracy would prevail and truth would triumph.

A decade ago, in the darkest days of the depression, he reminded his countrymen, "We have nothing to fear but fear." In his last unspoken message to the American people, he wrote these prophetic words:

"The only limitation to the realization of tomorrow's dreams are the doubts of today."

Realist that he was, he could see the rising tide of brute force, and he warned this nation of the coming holocaust of war that would be let loose upon an unprepared world, and then he prepared us to meet that storm of war.

The artist Lillien portrays the prophet Isaiah standing upon the Mount of Olives in Jerusalem, gazing into the future. He sees black clouds over the City of Splendour; he sees the streets of Jerusalem crowded with young people, drinking and dancing, draining the cup of fleeting joy, unconcerned with the clouds over the mountains, clouds of war, of exile, of destruction, which will soon burst over them.

Like the prophet of old, our late President also saw the clouds over the mountains while our American people were growing rich, callous, selling to aggressor nations, oil, scrap iron and other tools of war. They were indifferent to the wrongs perpetrated by the Nazi-Fascist-Japan Axis, and deaf to the cry for pity and protection that came from Ethiopia, Korea, China and Nazi-occupied Europe. He tried to rouse the American people to rally to the side of freedom and justice. When we were attacked so treacherously and wantonly at Pearl Harbor, Roosevelt vowed that America would defend our way of life, until the sword of the foe should be broken.

Almost a year ago, our immortal Captain led our nation in a prayer to Almighty God to give strength to our armies, and to lead to victory our sons and daughters, the pride of the nation, now engaged in a mighty struggle "to preserve our Republic, our religion and our civilization, and to set free suffering humanity."

It was God's will in His Infinite wisdom, to take from us this mighty leader, this skillful military strategist, this man of understanding and counsel, the advisor and friend of all nations. Alas, he was not privileged to reap the harvest of his hopes. It was he who planned the San Francisco Conference, but like Moses, who was not privileged to enter the Promised Land, Roosevelt did not live to see the free and friendlier world of which he dreamed.

The artist who was sketching a portrait of the President, in the closing hours of his life, did not complete it. Is not that the parable of the President's life? He too did not complete the sketch he was making, the blueprint for the better world. And as we mourn and grieve for our friend, puzzled by the infinite plans of the Divine Architect, we are reminded by Rabbi Tarphon: "It is not thy duty to complete the work; faithful is thy Divine Employer to give thee the reward of thy labor; and know that the grant of reward unto the righteous will be in the time to come." A righteous man is likened to a precious pearl. When it is lost, it is lost only to the owner, but the pearl itself is never lost. "A great man," we are told, "is never lost to you, unless your heart forgets his greatness." The influence of good and noble men lives on, and the righteous are even greater in death than in their lifetime.

Of Abraham Lincoln it was said: He belongs to the ages. Of Franklin D. Roosevelt we may say, he belongs to the future; the ages not yet born will arise and call him blessed. His monument will be the better and happier world of tomorrow, and when we cry, "Alas for the world that has lost its Captain," we hear his friendly voice calling to each one of us, "Do you become a pilot, the Captain of your soul." Would that a double portion of his spirit rest upon us, so that every one of us may be filled with the spirit of God, the spirit of wisdom and understanding, of counsel and might, of knowledge and of faith!

He Made the White House a Lighthouse

RABBI ABRAHAM KELLNER

"IT IS good to give thanks unto the Lord." With this quotation from the Book of Psalms did our late lamented president introduce his first war-time Thanksgiving Message in the very uncertain days of November, 1942. Surely we could do no less in this solemn moment when we gather to honor the memory of Franklin Delano Roosevelt, than to register our grateful appreciation that by the grace of God, he was at the helm of our country during the twelve most momentous years of its history. The personal grief that we nevertheless feel is too deeply etched in everyone's soul to require elaboration, and we must be careful lest in the moment of overpowering sorrow we forget to offer our bountiful thanks for having been permitted to bask in the vivid glow of his personality and to live securely in a Democratic society which prospered under his fearless leadership.

Though it may sound presumptuous on my part, none the less I am convinced that if the man of the kind heart, of the infectious smile, of the warm generous disposition, could speak to us now, he would no doubt assure us that he wants us to honor the day of his departure from our midst with Tennyson's immortal lines:

Sunset and evening Star
And one clear call for me
And may there be no mourning at the bar
When I put out to sea.

The historian of the future who will write with cool detachment and calm deliberation will be best equipped to sum up his enduring achievements and lasting accomplishments. Even we can readily enumerate, however, that he brought us through the most critical depression in our history, led us successfully toward victory in history's most devastating war, and he brilliantly demonstrated that the free will of a Democratic people can cope with the sharpest crisis in a world ridden with baneful dictatorship.

To those who mourn that he did not see us through to complete victory, I quote King Solomon's picturesque assurance:

K'shoshano Ben Hachochim
"He was like a rose between the thorns."

Well we may quote the philosophy of Alphonso Carr: "Some people always find fault with God for putting thorns on roses; I always thank Him for putting roses on thorns."

That both President Roosevelt and those who believed in him had a thorny road to traverse, nowise lessens the exalted fragrance of his magnificent qualities which were symbolized by the majestic rose. One of his greatest tributes will be the realization that though the vituperative cannibalism of politics snapped at him at times with insane fury, and though the mounting disasters of humanity shook the very foundations of the earth, he remained serene while others grew tumultuous, clear of vision while others were confused, undeviating while others were erratic. He was secure in his democratic faith, while others doubted, certain in his orbit while others floundered hopelessly in the treacherous mire of politics and diplomacy.

In the Biblical selections read in our Synagogues yesterday, we were acquainted with the functions and purposes of the Kohen, the Priest in ancient Jewish Rituals, who had a special responsibility when the dreaded plague of leprosy made its appearance.

These plagues were generally classified in three categories: those of Nigei Odom—Assailing people, Nigei Bais—those attacking human residence, and Nigei Beged—those encroaching upon the clothing and habiliments of people. Many of our commentators interpret these to be manifestations of moral leprosy where the physical rehabilitation that followed in the wake of the Priest's ministrations, was coupled with spiritual regeneracy. That these plagues were conspicuous in our days need not be argued, but that Franklin Delano Roosevelt saw them in their full horror will forever remain his greatest tribute. We remember that significant expression in his classic Second Inaugural when he spoke with concern over the fact that "One third of the nation was ill-housed, ill-clad, ill-nourished," thus attacking boldly all three classes of *NEGOIM* which were gnawing away at the very vitals of our people's existence.

Our rabbis significantly comment that a great benefit redounded to our ancestors who set themselves earnestly to the task of destroying the homes thus plagued: for in so doing they discovered untold wealth hidden by the former owners of Canaan. Similarly can we gratefully recount that because our great erstwhile president had resolutely set himself the obligations to eradicate these modern plagues, he left unto us an untold legacy of physical wealth and spiritual gains.

He gave new hope to a desperate people and at the same time enriched the nation with a magnificent network of roads, a wonderful development of parks, a splendid expansion of schools, urgently needed hospitals which carried over and became the blessed results of a wretched depression. He, like our Master Moses many centuries before, found the people murmuring because of the bitter waters and, like the Hebrew Law-Giver, he cast the trees over the expanse which sweetened the bitter waters.

The future will adequately recount that the marvelous program of reforestation, soil control, and civilian conservation, not only changed the physical landscape of America, not alone did it give several million young people a new hope, but it considerably sweetened the bitter waters of adversity which plagued our people in the early thirties. This courageous leader, who had the makings of greatness in his fibre, rose to the full stature of his greatness when the times demanded it, and electrified a moribund people with winged words of storied hope. In this hour of America's great grief, we, his countrymen whose proud champion he was, take heart from the inspired realization that the courageous leadership of our great president not only made him the symbol of humanity here at home but that with his all-embracing love for his fellowmen he succeeded in making the Whitehouse a Lighthouse for human hopes *everywhere.*

There is a final thought which is especially timely today and compels articulation. Eighty years ago on this day of April 15th, Abraham Lincoln breathed his last after a night of agony and a life of suffering. There is much in common between the trials and tribulations of these two martyred presidents. To quote from the Gettysburg Address is therefore most timely. The words, "That these honored dead shall not have died in vain," certainly take on meaning when we must dedicate ourselves to the sacred obligations for putting into reality the blue-prints for peace worked out by our late president. Then too, "From these honored dead, we take increased devotion." The honor to Franklin D. Roosevelt's memory will be best expressed if we accept his martyred life as a new source of devotion from whence we draw the inspiration to give meaning to his faith in Democratic processes.

It was symbolic of his great love of the outdoors, of his dogged attachment to the land he loved, that the end came to him under God's blue heaven, while he was looking at far horizons, basking in the glow of his coming sunset. Behind him stood the clear silhouettes of the paths he trod—before him stretched the unknown mysteries of Life eternal, as if in his last conscious mortal moments, he wanted to cast one more lingering look upon the country for whose welfare he sacrificed so much and for whose benefit he too offered his best years, to make sure the promise of former days which effectively holds that, "Government of the people, for the people, and by the people, shall not perish from the earth," would remain true.

When the News Came to France

CHAPLAIN MORRIS N. KERTZER

IT WAS midnight in France when the radio flashed word of our great loss. An officer called me on the telephone and asked whether he and a fellow-officer could come to my quarters; they wanted the comfort of talking to someone, to share their grief with their chaplain.

A soldier rushed in to the Headquarters mess hall and cried out, "There's a rumor that Roosevelt is dead!" Several GI's were violent in their reaction: "It's a dirty lie, a Nazi propaganda trick!" For these youngsters, Roosevelt could not die; he was a permanent landmark in their experience. They could no more conceive of America without him, of a world without him, than they could imagine the Rock of Gibraltar disappearing into the sea.

When the emblazoned headlines in the Stars and Stripes brought bitter confirmation of the tragic truth, an overwhelming mood of grief prevailed. It was more than the Commander-in-Chief who was gone; it was also the symbol of the principles that moved us to sacrifice and to struggle.

Our telephones rang all day as French friends called to offer their words of consolation, to soften the blow in the loss of one near and dear to us. The mood of the Jewish community was not only sorrow, but also fear—a compelling dread that the stilling of freedom's most passionate voice would dash forever their hopes in Zion and their confidence in a just and enduring peace. Men and women in Marseilles wept like frightened children. It was a paradoxical situation for us Americans. In our own moment of despair, we were called upon to assure the Europeans that the flock would somehow find a new shepherd.

I was present at two moving synagogue services in Paris: a military service, conducted by American chaplains; and a civilian service, led by the Chief Rabbi of Paris.

At the first service, a tremendous crowd of American troops stood in silent tribute before the colors. A Jewish WAC officer and enlisted girl, a Navy officer and enlisted man, and two Army representatives stood motionless at attention while Chaplain Nadich and Hyman read the memorial psalm, our abiding faith that "The Lord is my Shepherd, I shall not want. . . ."

An overflow congregation attended the civilian service. We saw the United States Ambassador Jefferson Caffery, British generals, French admirals and Russian officers rise as one man when the Chief Rabbi came to the pulpit. What an inspiration for these liberated French Jews to witness this token of esteem to their rabbi, who only a few months ago had been hounded as a common criminal by the Nazi rulers of Paris! In that one moment they must have felt that this great and good American had not lived and labored in vain.

As I left the Grand Synagogue of Paris, the beautiful tribute penned by Israel Zangwill at the grave of Theodore Herzl flashed before my mind: "Death has but transfixed him to immortal life."

He Walked with God

RABBI MAX KLEIMAN

WITH bowed heads and contrite hearts have we gathered in bereavement over the crushing news of Franklin Delano Roosevelt's sudden death. Americans of every creed, of every religion and those without religion, the poor and the rich, black and white are praying and paying homage to the beneficent life of our beloved leader.

Never before in the history of America has this nation reached so heartrending a point; never has the world cried and mourned so deeply and faithfully the tragedy that has befallen the family of America's Commander-in-Chief. Out from the depths of pain that is sensed in the hearts of the children of the earth, there comes a flowing sympathy and thanks for the great heroic life that was Roosevelt's.

His long office of Presidency has left a very deep mark upon the life and destiny of our people. His career on earth is marked with experiences of common good that he sought to bring to the common men of the earth. Men the world over will ever be grateful to God that it was this man who stood at the helm in a position to give leadership to the American people in the dark hours of ruthless Nazi barbarism seeking to destroy the work of the ages.

Never will I forget the inspiration, hope and faith in America that was conveyed to me by that magnetic personality as I stood on the Eastern Lawn of the White House before the President, back in 1939, as a student representative of American Colleges.

More than anything else, this Statesman and beloved leader of mankind has been lost as a dear friend. It is most peculiar how the world in its divided categories claims him as their friend. For the aged he was a source of security; for the ailing, the sick and maimed he was the world's greatest symbol of courage and hope that all will be well again; to the poor, the ill clad, the ill fed, the ill housed, he was a messenger of God, a prophet in the world, seeking and promoting human happiness and warmth. To the men on the field of battle he was a front line general risking and giving his life for freedom and liberty. To the world he was a banner of glory and a flag of unstinting devotion to the principles of peace on earth and goodwill toward mankind.

To America he pledged himself body and soul that it would get a new deal, a square deal and a happy contented home life. Out of the chaos and devastation of 1933 he emerged as a world figure bringing old age security, unemployment insurance, a shorter work week, social legislation, a strong economic policy, a national physical rehabilitation and an international spirit of friendship that was characterized by a policy in which he dedicated himself and this nation to the doctrine of the good neighbor, the neighbor who resolutely respects himself, and because he does so, respects the rights of others. Back in 1937, almost eight years ago, our president in a bold statement recognized the slow movement of Fascism and Nazism as an epidemic of a physical disease which was starting to break down all international law and order, which had to be quarantined to protect the good health of ninety-eight percent of the community against the spread of the disease.

One brief statement which he made before Congress in 1941 seems to typify his entire philosophy of life when he said, "In the future days which we seek to make secure, we look forward to a world founded upon four essential freedoms: The First is the freedom of speech and expression—everywhere in the world. The

Second is freedom of every person to worship God in his own way—everywhere in the world. The Third is freedom from want—everywhere in the world. The Fourth is freedom from fear, which translated into world terms, means a world wide reduction of armaments to such a point and in such a thorough fashion that no nation will be in a position to commit an act of physical aggression against any neighbor—anywhere in the world." "We are not citizens of America," he declared, "we are citizens of the world, members of a human community."

Now the body of Roosevelt rests in the quiet of his beloved Hyde Park. Prayer and mourning is spread as a holocaust over America.

The world is now turning to the late president and the voice of destiny is declaring, "Well done, well done, faithful servant of mankind." Roosevelt lives today and shall continue to live in the hearts and minds of the world as the great Lincoln lives today and is enshrined in the hearts of civilization forever.

As Moses, Commander of the Israelites, ascended the mountain and witnessed the promised land, as our Commander-in-Chief rested on the hilltops of Warm Springs, Georgia, he too must have smiled as he witnessed the eclipsing of Victory and an international society of nations dedicated to peace and human happiness.

O Heavenly Father, Creator of all mankind, in this hour of crisis and tragedy, sustain us with courage and grant us a continued successful leadership. Imbue our new President, Harry Truman, with vision, with determination to carry upward and onward and with good physical and mental vigor. Grant Thy consolation and Thy peace to the mourners, to the family of Mrs. Roosevelt.

Grant us, O Lord, peace, genuine peace, for us, for our children and children's children, for mankind and for the whole world.

Lament for Our Dead Leader

RABBI EUGENE KOHN

OUR Chief is dead . . .
From farm and factory, from shop and home,
From sun-drenched deserts and from wind-swept mountains,
From teeming cities and lone wildernesses,
From ships at sea and planes afloat in air,
Rise mourning voices.

They all remember him now whom he remembered,
All the forgotten men, the lowly folk,
The Oakies from the dust-bowl whom he saved
From a life of vagabondage, sharecroppers
Redeemed from endless serfdom, wage slaves freed
From sweating away their lives for others' gain,
Negroes emancipated but not free,
Whose cause he championed, outcast Jews,
Homeless and haunted by memories of horrors,
For whom he sought a haven and a home—
They all remember him and sob and weep.

O Lord, what shall we do? Where shall we turn?
So long we laid our burdens on his shoulders.
So long we counted on his shepherding
To save us from the ravenous beasts of prey.
When he but beamed upon us with that smile,
That gay and gallant smile we knew so well,
We were ashamed of all the fears and doubts
That plagued our hearts. And when he spoke to us,
His voice so warm and vibrant, calm and steady,

More than his words, assured us we had naught
To fear but Fear, that in us lived a soul
Inviolable, which no demonic fury,
No frothing madness of raving wolf-men could
Intimidate or subdue.

Lord, Thou didst test and try his mettle well
Ere Thou didst charge him with the task to be
Defender of Thy throne against Amalek.
For Thou didst send to wrestle with his flesh
The mighty angel of that dread disease,
With whom, through a night of many nights and days,
He grappled. Yet no anguish and no terror
Could make him curse his God and die. He fought
Pain and despondency, and with the dawn,
Though lame and limping, made the angel yield
And bless him, saying, 'A valiant wrestler thou
With God and man, be thou victorious.'

Thus was he tested and thus was he blest.
Well known to suffering and at home with pain,
His heart was tender and compassionate.
A lover of life, God and his fellow men,
He laughed to scorn all promptings of self-pity.
Grown strong in struggle with his own weak flesh,
He lent his strength for weaker men to lean on.
He served his neighbors and they trusted him,
Seeing in him a servant of the Lord,
A scion of the Messianic line,
Who ever judged with sympathy the poor,
With equity the needy of the land.
The bent reed never feared that he would break it;
The flickering flame that he would quench its light.
He never raised his voice in strident orders,
Nor shouted raucous slogans to the crowd.

But malefactors smote he with his words;
And tyrants fell before his eloquence.

Little we knew, the day we made him chief,
To what titanic tasks, what epic conflicts
God had appointed him. That wicked plot
Of warped and twisted spirits to dethrone God,
And take to them all power, all dominion—
We doubted it could be, so weird it seemed.
But he, our chief, alert in our defense,
Unmasked it to our sight, stirred us to action,
Imbued us with his strength and resolution,
Summoned us to the service of the Lord.
In those dread hours when we were near disaster,
And when we reeled under the treacherous blows,
Of the aggressor, and our strength ebbed from us,
His steadfast faith rallied our drooping spirits.
The tide of battle turned. The enemy
Grew weak as we grew strong. Our Chief's commands
Were leading us to victory, and then,
With victory in sight and all but grasped . . .
How say the bitter words? . . . Our Chief fell dead.

Why was he snatched so suddenly away,
Leaving us all bewildered and distraught?
Pond'ring this question with a heavy heart,
As though transported from this world of sense,
Entranced, I gazed, and lo! I seemed to stand
In that high hall in which the Lord of Hosts
Holds council with his staff of archangels
And plans his stratagem of war against
Amalek and his cohorts of the damned.
I heard an angel speak and tell his tale
Of the struggle on man's earth. 'The foe,' said he,
'Seems all but vanquished on the battle field.

He is in full retreat, while they that serve
Thy Kingdom have advanced and overrun
The land but lately subject to his vile
And blasphemous rule. Yet is our cause in danger.
For he has strewn about poisonous seed,
And hatches subtle plots to breed dissension
Between united peoples and to set
Race against race and nation against nation.
Villainous men who had incurred the wrath
Of our brave champion the foe has armed
With sly deceits, insidious innuendoes,
And on that day when the united peoples
Will meet to plan the peace that is to be,
These deadly weapons all will be released
And work their havoc. Something must be done
To shield the leader of our hosts, or else,
The foe when routed may more dangerous prove
To our Kingdom's cause than when he took the field.'
He ceased, and a sad silence filled the hall.

Then spoke another of that heavenly council:
'One way remains to foil this dark design.
At any cost, our hero must be protected
Against the shafts of slander aimed at him.
He must be placed forever out of reach
Of all such secret weapons, be transported
Here to our heavenly fortress, and be raised
To a position of command among
The heavenly hosts that battle for the Lord.'

Then a protesting voice, plaintive and sad:
'But what will then befall his hapless folk?
They look to him for faith and confidence,
For sage and prudent counsel. Should he leave them,
Will not the people all, bereaved, bewildered,

Sunk in dejection, slacken in their struggle?
How can we take their trusted leader from them,
Now when they know their destiny for ages
Hangs in the balance?'

To him the High Command,
'Fear not; he still will lead them. They will know
That his translation to the heavenly spheres
Means not that he no longer dwells with them.
His presence will be felt and manifest
Wherever freedom's banner is unfurled.
In reverent awe, they will convey to rest
The worn-out body that so long in pain
He forced to do the bidding of his will.
They will recall his deeds, his legacy
Of noble thoughts and holy purposes.
His spirit will pervade and strengthen them
Making them all immune against the poisons
Which are the last foul weapons of the foe.
Imbued with immortality the leader
Will be more potent in his leadership
Than when he dragged his pain-wracked body on earth.
His gay and gallant smile will be reflected
On the bright faces of children in every land,
Children of white, black, red and yellow skins,
For whom my world will be a merry playground.
The warm and vibrant accents of his voice
Will find an echo in the speech of lovers,
Founders of faithful homes, brave simple folk,
Bound each to each in fellowship, and to Me
In pious fealty.

Then the vision faded.
Again the world of sense closed in on me.
The poignant sadness stole into my heart

Again, but mingled now with exaltation.
I felt my leader's presence filling me
With faith and courage, bidding me take heart,
Assuring me that victory was at hand,
And that he had not lived nor died in vain.
An end to weeping then, to sobs and sighs!
Lead on, immortal champion; we follow.

The President's Message to Congress

RABBI MORRIS S. LAZARON

(As I listened and later read the complete text, I did not think of economic, political and social theories and programs. I thought of a man, one human being standing at the very center of the mad forces of our time. I tried to project myself imaginatively into his mind and heart.)

"RETURNING from my journeyings
I must confess to a sense of let-down. . . ."

I often wonder
What is in the President's heart
As he starts the last year of his third term,
Walking where no man ever walked before.

It might be well
If men would put themselves in his place.

A sobering thought
Even for the confident and self-assured

And perhaps a salutary, humbling contemplation,
If partisanship and hate
Have not too completely seized the mind
And left no room
For calm, objective judgment.

"My friends,
It's been a grievous but a glorious task,
A fight from the moment I took office.
Remember—?"

Do we remember?
Harding, Coolidge, Hoover preceded him.
Mellon, "the greatest Secretary of the Treasury since Alexander Hamilton."

1929–1932
Millions unemployed,
Strong men selling apples on street corners,
No adequate relief,
Foreclosing of homes and farms,
Bank failures,
Gangsters, racketeers,
Hesitation and despair,
Social unrest,
In some places rioting
And all the gloomy portents of
Angry disaffection.

Into the picture
One man walked
One voice was raised,
Sure, confident.
Help—
Reform—
Regulation.

"The government has obligations to its citizens,
The government is not the possession of any one group,
It is the protector and guarantor of the rights of
all citizens—"
The rich as well as the poor were lifted out of
The slough of despair
The country got on its feet.
He had given the nation not only a conscience
But a vision!

How soon men forget.
The very ones he saved from their own failures
Now raise their voice in condemnation or abuse.
From both sides, capital and labor,
Snipe at him, distort his words, misrepresent his program.
States' rights!
Centralization!
Dictatorship!
As if the trend of life
Were not in the direction
Of more state regulation and control.
Who's not blind can see.

1933–1935
Gathering storms in Europe and in Asia.
Angry clouds on far horizons
Mad potencies held in leash
Till one day they would break loose against the world
To enslave it.
The country calm, innocent abroad
At home serenely unconscious
Of the morrow's peril.
Chicago. The "quarantine" speech.
"The free nations cannot hope to face the foe alone
They need to stand together

And the destiny of our country is bound up with that
Of all the free peoples of earth."
Then—
Shrill cries of native isolationists
Little men in big places,
And propaganda from across the seas
Joined with the dark evil forces in our own land
To play upon our prejudices and fears.

"I saw it coming,
But it was not an easy task
To make the people see it."
The persistent fight for appropriations for defense.
"War monger," "Interventionist"—
To the last moment.
So—on the very eve of war
One single, solitary vote
Kept the training program going.

Pearl Harbor. . . .
The epic mobilization of all our resources—
Guns, tanks, planes, ships,
Supplies, material, weapons,
The trickle across the waters
To the far ends of the earth
Became a stream of flowing might. . . .
America on the march with
The forces of freedom
For the redemption of the peoples
From the slavery of dictators.
What a story for future Americans to read.

"It is not easy to lead a peaceful people into war,
Take its youth from school and office, farm and factory
Break up life plans and hopes

Intrude in happy homes
Scatter families. . . .
It had to be done to protect and to defend
Our freedom and our future."

The swift flowing pageantry of events
Runs through his mind.
Atlantic Charter, Oran, Cairo, Teheran, Moscow.
United Nations
Poised in Europe for the final deadly stroke,
In Asia growing power tensile,
Near ready for the spring—
Everywhere dear youth
Pouring out its life with its ideals,
Testimony to the deathless nature of man,
Guarantors of a better, happier, freer world!

"Returning from my journeyings
I must confess to a sense of 'let-down' . . .
Faulty perspectives. . . .
A noisy minority maintains an uproar
Of demands for special favors for special groups.
They have come to look upon the war primarily
As a chance to make profits for themselves. . . .
But the overwhelming majority of our people
Have met the demands of this war
With magnificent courage and understanding."

"Of course I've made mistakes,
Chosen badly at times,
At times yielded when I should have been firm.
The record is there.
History will appraise our times, my work and them who
oppose me.
I've done my best

Shall strive to do so to the end
As long as strength be mine.
I do not ask that my enemies
Should hate me less.
I understand I've trampled on
Their privileges, threatened
Entrenched power, overrode
Their prejudices.
Strange irony that lies at the heart of life—
One must often destroy
Before he can build.
Man will not relinquish voluntarily
What he has enjoyed, without a struggle.
I've fought two battles at the same time—
Fight them even now,
To keep the social vision, the larger horizon,
Greater hope for greater happiness for
The greatest number of my fellow citizens;
And
To beat down and destroy
The ruthless brutal power of the tyrants of the earth,
So that men may live out their lives
In greater freedom."

Of course they will hate you, Mr. President.
Can you expect a different fate
Than that which has befallen
All the benefactors of mankind?
Not only hard days are ahead for you
But cruel days,
More cruel than any your dream
For your countrymen and the world
Has yet brought you.
They will continue to lie and slander,
Ridicule, misinterpret and abuse you,

Distort your words,
Look for subtle, hidden meanings,
Selfish implications.
Bitter are the years ahead for you and all you love.

But
They can't wipe out the vision you have given.
They can't destroy the healing you have brought,
The hopes you have kindled;
The fires you have lighted
In this land and in all the world
They can never quench.

"I do not ask that they should hate me less,
Rather I pray that
They should love our country more,
See it as I see it,
Have it as I would have it."

Stand firm, Mr. President,
Speak out
The truth as you see it.
Millions now call your name with reverence
And pray God keep you in strength
To see the day of victory—
The millions returned to useful labor,
Work for all, for all
Opportunity for education and leisure;
A nation of freemen
Where not race or color, creed or gold
Are the basis of its aristocracy
But intelligence and integrity, energy and social usefulness.
May you live to see
The captives' chains removed,

The naked clothed
The hungry fed
The weary wandering hosts of the disinherited
Led to pleasant stable habitations.

Great heart, courageous spirit,
Prophet of the nobler day
That is to be,
The children of the world
The millions of innocents
Who will live in the happier tomorrow
Will link their gratitude with ours
As they rise up and call you blessed!

"Each and everyone of us has a solemn obligation
Under God
To serve this nation in its most critical hour—
To keep this nation great,
To make this nation greater
In a better world."

I often think
What is on the President's heart.
The burden of the times?
The deathless future hope?
Surely it would be well
If men would put themselves
In his place—
A salutary, humbling contemplation.

The Lord Hath Taken

RABBI JOSHUA LOTH LIEBMAN

I AM heartbroken, as all true lovers of humanity are, at the passing of our incomparable leader, Franklin Delano Roosevelt. Our age can hardly hope to witness another like unto him for he was strength and compassion uniquely blended, a gay and courageous humor mingled with world-embracing vision. All the humble people of the earth have lost their Commander-in-Chief. Yet a fragment of his spirit will live in the hearts of decent men and women everywhere. He belongs with Washington, Jefferson, Lincoln and Wilson, among the heroes and fathers of our American way of life. He has immortally woven himself into the fabric of our highest hopes for peace, our common struggle for justice. Wherever and whenever in the future children breathe a free air and young men and women live and work in peace, Franklin Delano Roosevelt will be in their midst for his efforts on behalf of a juster social order at home and a permanent peace throughout the world shall have been the foundation-stone of the better civilization in the bourne of time. He has been our refuge in the raging storms of this century; the shadow of a great rock in a weary land, the stream of living waters to the parched and hungry of the earth.

May all Americans now loosen the bonds of prejudice and self-centeredness and break the chains of injustice and greed as our only true memorial to his memory. We dare not fail his dream. We dare not fail to struggle to finish together the building of hope and serenity and peace that this master architect has left unfinished when he fell asleep. May we, the humble contemporaries of one of history's titans, prove ourselves worthy to have lived in his time and great enough to carry to fulfillment his luminous plans for a free humanity. The Lord has given, the Lord has taken away, blessed be the name of the Lord.

He Drew from Deep Waters

RABBI MENDELL LEWITTES

STILLED is the familiar voice, cold the warm handshake, gone the genial smile, passed into eternal life the living symbol of the nation's ideals. Stunning in its suddenness came the grim tiding that our President lives no more and has passed along into the ages and the immortal history of our country. His untimely death has plunged the entire nation into grief and mourning. And Americans of the Jewish faith, in their synagogues and in their homes, from their hearts and upon their lips, join their fellow citizens of all creeds in lamentation and tribute. We give expression to our personal bereavement and profound loss in the words of David wailing over the death of Jonathan. "How is the mighty one fallen. Beloved and dear in his life, even in death not separated. How is the mighty one fallen in the midst of battle."

Yea, in the midst of battle, on the eve of its victorious climax, he fell, to pass on to others the responsibilities of war and peace which he shouldered so courageously. The blessings of peace for which he so earnestly prayed and strived were beginning to appear in the not-too-distant horizon. But God spoke to him as He did to Moses of old. "Get thee up unto this mountain, and behold the land of Canaan, and die on the mount whither thou goest up and be gathered unto thy people, for from afar shalt thou see the land, but thither shalt thou not go."

For twelve long and fateful years he guided our nation through the wilderness of our times, through the decade which witnessed the greatest political and social upheavals in the history of Western civilization, through the years which saw the rise to power, and the inevitable decline, of Nazi barbarism and Nippon treachery. These were years which required of the leaders of the forces of righteousness and humanity great vision and still greater determination. These were times which truly tried men's souls and imperiously demanded unstinting sacrifice and unswerving devotion. Franklin Delano Roosevelt was not found wanting when the challenge of his times came. His eye was not dimmed and his force had not abated. To the very last, he gave to us and to the world his prophetic vision and unshakable faith in human progress. His indomitable courage and the manner in which he overcame his physical affliction, served as an unfailing source of inspiration. Far beyond the confines of his own country did his beneficent influence travel. His name was a symbol to millions throughout the world. People terrorized by a most brutal foe, subjected to the most cruel forms of enslavement, kept their spirits free and their hopes high because of his words of encouragement. Americans are not alone in their grief and keen sense of loss. From every corner of the earth sincere professions of sympathy are true testimony to the universal esteem and love which he so richly deserved.

Franklin Delano Roosevelt drew from the deep waters of religious teaching his faith in democracy and his concern for the common man. His program of social legislation, his passion for economic righteousness, stemmed from the teachings of the Hebrew prophets and their place in Christian doctrine. The Fatherhood of God and the brotherhood of man was his basic creed. He believed in the dignity and sanctity of all human life, without distinction of race or color or religious faith. His human sympathies and understanding reached out to all classes of men. His warm friendship and happy personality kindled love and understanding in the hearts and minds of those with whom he worked. He realized full well that the foundation of international peace must rest upon the bedrock of mutual respect and willingness to cooperate with others. He labored much to remove mistrust and suspicion among the members of the United Nations. The crowning glory in a life full of achievement is his forging of the tools of international co-operation with which those who carry on will build the structure of lasting peace and universal justice and freedom.

Americans of the Jewish faith, and Jews throughout the world, have truly lost a genuine friend and benefactor. The years during which Franklin Roosevelt was President of the United States were tragic for the House of Israel. When he assumed the office of Chief Executive in this country, the most diabolical enemy of the Jew seized the reins of government in Germany. That year marked the beginning of the Nazi program whose ultimate aim was the annihilation of the Jewish people. And each succeeding year of Nazi rule brought fresh decrees against German Jewry, and the dangerous spread throughout democratic countries of the poison of anti-Semitism. Jews turned to the world professing the Christian doctrines of love and mercy, expecting outspoken condemnation of Nazi racism and havens of refuge for its victims. Few and far between were the voices raised in behalf of suffering Jewry. Still rarer were the responsible leaders of government who were ready to open the doors of their countries to the Jews dispossessed from their native land. President Roosevelt was one of the outstanding few who were forthright and unambiguous in their denunciation of Hitler and his insidious propaganda. It was President Roosevelt who cabled American consuls in European capitals to facilitate the granting of visas to German Jews seeking to escape their doom. It was he who by message and personal pledge furthered the realization of Zionist hopes for a free and democratic Jewish commonwealth in Palestine and encouraged American Zionists in their task to mold public opinion in this country in behalf of Eretz Yisroel. It was he who warned the leaders of the Axis that they would be brought to full account for their horrible crimes against the Jewish people. Yes, indeed, he was a champion of the rights of the Jew as he was a champion of the rights of all the oppressed and underprivileged.

We shall not have fulfilled our obligation if we but confine ourselves to these words of tribute. Our sages tell us that the compensation of a eulogy is uplifting. We must be uplifted in our firm resolve to complete the task which he so nobly began. The Jew at the dark moment when his near and dear one is placed in the dark earth to eternal repose, unbends his back and with firm faith intones the Kaddish, dedicating himself to the establishment of God's kingdom on earth. Great and hallowed be the name of God. May abundance of peace be bestowed upon us. We offer this prayer to Almighty God.

Now He, Too, Belongs to the Ages

RABBI LOUIS L. MANN

FOUR score years ago today, a great President closed his eyes. A member of his official family uttered the unforgettable words, "Now he belongs to the ages." It is with indescribable sorrow and unspeakable sadness that we must record the passing of our immortal President. God and history will find a niche among the immortals for Franklin Delano Roosevelt. Now he, too, belongs to the ages.

Without detracting one iota from the Founders of our Republic and without diminishing from the brilliance of those who preserved our Union, and without the superlatives which flow so easily in time of great emotion, it is safe to say that no President ever faced problems of such magnitude, or faced them with greater singleness of purpose, loftiness of vision and unflinching heroism. Of course he was misunderstood—great men always are—but he had faith in the vindication, the verification and the justification of history.

What a combination of contrasts and seeming contradictions!

He was an aristocrat who was truly democratic. He was aristocratic in the original sense of the word—"aristos," a seeker for the best—democratic in thought, in feeling and in action.

He was a rich man who really cared for the poor. Franklin Delano Roosevelt's solicitude for the poor was not the lip-service of politicians, but the real service of love, devotion and consecration. He was the attorney general for the ill-housed, the ill-fed and the ill-clad.

He was handicapped and yet more active than any not the victim of a dread and paralyzing disease. His handicap became not an alibi, but an incentive. Like Demosthenes, Milton, Beethoven and Helen Keller, he rose above his personal liability and converted it into a public asset. The tragedy of 1921, when infantile paralysis overcame him, was so transformed, transmuted and transfigured as to become an example, an incentive, and an inspiration—sublime beyond words!

Our martyr President fell heir to a depression full of doubt for the future; this he lifted by an expression of faith to visions of a new world. Fear and anxiety haunted and hounded the hapless, the helpless and the homeless. Poverty stalked the land like a dread spectre. Despair, despondency and disenchantment were depressing the dispositions of men. He faced this "city of the dreadful night" with these first words: "We have nothing to fear but fear itself." In the depths of depression, he lifted people to the heights by a faith that was as contagious as it was creative. It was literally contagious. It was profoundly creative. It was truly re-creative.

With his own freedom of movement hampered, he vowed that all men everywhere should be free. He realized all too well what limitation of freedom meant. He sublimated his disability by liberating others. The Four Freedoms are both individual and social. They are both national and international. They are based on the dignity of man, on the inviolability of personality and on the sacredness of individuality. Freedom of expression! Freedom of religion! Freedom from fear! Freedom from want! These were necessary to implement the inalienable rights of man, "among them life, liberty and the pursuit of happiness."

He gave intimate, personal, confidential, helpful fireside chats not only to the 130,000,000 of his fellow citizens, but to the whole world. To the peace-loving everywhere, to the liberty-loving everywhere, to the fair-play-loving everywhere, to the democracy-loving everywhere—personal, intimate talks, with the whole world listening in! To sympathizers who were lifted to the heights! To brutalitarians who saw their destiny in the depths!

He was the most controversial figure in our entire history. He was not all things to all men. He was all that God gave him, to be so true to himself that he could not be untrue to others. Neither the threat of Wall Street nor the opposition of politicians in both parties, nor the insinuations of reactionaries and stand-patters, nor the labels and libels of the radicals could turn him from following his vision, his gleam. Though misunderstood and misinterpreted, and frequently maligned, he followed what he believed to be for the best interests of his country—our country—and for the best interests of all mankind. These interests never conflicted. By serving America, he served all mankind. "We love him for the enemies that he made."

Like another great leader before him, he was given a glimpse of the promised land but not allowed to enter. History seems to have repeated itself. Moses stood on Mount Nebo and saw the Promised Land only from afar. Franklin Delano Roosevelt followed in the footsteps of Moses not only in the liberation of the masses but also in being vouchsafed only the vision of victory and the fruition of his principles.

Though I am not swept away by the intense emotionalism of this hour, and the depths of sentiment that have caused strong men to weep unashamed on the streets, and the personal tragedy that is in every heart, and the moral climate of intense grief and mourning to a degree that no one could have envisaged or predicted, I weigh my words carefully as I say that no one man has contributed as much either to the winning of the war or to the winning of the peace as has Franklin Delano Roosevelt. Yes, the people expressed themselves by breaking all traditions in electing him for a third term, and then the miracle of miracles, the fourth term! Statisticians a decade ago would have said the chances against such an event were a thousand to one. Such precedent-breaking is significant beyond words. Even so, not until his untimely passing could anyone have had an idea of the real love and deep personal affection that people had for this man. How all the petty differences have been swallowed up by the greatness of his life!

We are altogether too near to Franklin Delano Roosevelt either to appreciate or to evaluate his place in history, his contributions to America and to the world. Some achievements, however, stand out above all others. I shall enumerate a few that, in my judgment, will live on and become part of the warp and woof of American ideals and aspirations.

The New Deal was one of them. It was and is, and doubtless will continue to be, strongly controversial. Franklin Delano Roosevelt realized that the depression was not an accident. It was inevitable. It was not "just another economic cycle." He understood that when "rugged individualism" becomes ragged individualism, social concern for the individual must come to the rescue. He appreciated that mass production without mass consumption is economic suicide. He was determined that the economic blood transfusion from the anaemic masses for the over-red-corpuscled classes must cease. He appreciated that the monopolization which led to pauperization and hence to the degradation of man and the degeneration of personality, must be halted. He saw that freedom to starve in the sight of plenty is not freedom at all—but serfdom. Lincoln said "This nation cannot endure half slave and half free." So Roosevelt, living in an era in which science had annihilated time and space, proclaimed in no uncertain terms, that this world cannot endure half slave and half free. Lincoln once said that "no man is good enough to rule over another." Roosevelt made it known everywhere that no nation is good enough to rule over another. He insisted that a nation capable of over-production must not suffer from under-consumption. He saw the tragedy of a "prosperous America" with one-third ill-clad, one-third ill-housed, one-third ill-fed—prosperous on the surface, but diseased within. He put meaning into the adage "the laboring man is worthy of his hire." He determined that labor should earn enough to buy back what its brain and its brawn had produced. Labor will never go back to pre-Rooseveltian days! Hours must be reduced; conditions of health, sanitation and ventilation must be assured. The New Deal means all this—and more! True, the time was ripe for it. It had to come. But Franklin Delano Roosevelt gave it direction, vision, fellow-feeling, and consecration. It needed but to pass through his great mind and heart, and, because of the alchemy of his spirit, became an expression of justice and a help for humanity forever. Details may be changed! Contents will be altered! The principles, however, of social justice and fair play, of broad humanitarianism and of human decency are there—to remain! Reactionaries will not like this. Stand-patters will feel their blood pressure rising. Like Ibsen's "Master Builder," they would stabilize and deify the status quo. To the imperishable glory of our martyr President, he saw the vision of social justice and never turned from the gleam of human well-being and of social righteousness. "Where there is no vision a people perish." Where there is vision, a people become brothers. Franklin Delano Roosevelt was not "the indispensable man," but because of self-chosen consecration, he became the expendable man!

The Good Neighbor Policy will also receive the sanction and commendation of history. It included all nations even though it was focused on the South American governments. This policy began with the very first month of his first administration. Franklin Delano Roosevelt saw clearly that the Monroe Doctrine was imperiled. He also realized that aggressor nations, through the techniques of propaganda, had established moral and spiritual beach-heads in South and Central America. He appreciated that they ultimately hoped to take the Panama Canal, come through Mexico and endanger the freedom of the United States. It was necessary to win them. This he did, not by methods of conquest, such as would have been natural for Hitler, Mussolini and Hirohito, but by fair play and service. In this way, he won not only their respect and their confidence, but also their cooperation for peace on this hemisphere. He did not wait until a moment of life or death for the United States, until the pistol was pointed to our hearts or the noose was around our necks. His Good Neighbor Policy was equally to the advantage of the South American governments as it was to our own. Roosevelt knew that a friend is better than an enemy—anywhere, everywhere, especially so close to our shores. All but Argentina yielded to this humanitarian approach toward the solution of an age-old problem. Argentina recently crawled in like a worm. We now know that Germany counted on the South American government in all of her plans. But the best-laid plans of mice and men—! This Good Neighbor Policy saved millions of lives, billions in treasure and years of indescribable anxiety. This insight and foresight are part of the imperishable glory of Franklin Delano Roosevelt, the voice of the inarticulate masses everywhere, the prophetic conscience of the under-privileged, and the most beloved man in the world!

Franklin Delano Roosevelt anticipated the aggressor. Long before most of our people knew what was going on, and long before they appreciated what it was all about, Franklin Delano Roosevelt knew that sooner or later we must come to grips with the aggressor. History, with which he was so well acquainted, revealed that no aggressor or potential conqueror can ever be satisfied. Roosevelt saw it when Manchuria fell. He was not surprised with the long succession—Austria, Ethiopia, Czechoslovakia, Poland, Norway, Belgium, Holland, France, Jugoslavia, Greece—the roll call, aye, a toll call!

I sat beside him when he dedicated our bridge in Chicago in 1937 and advocated the "Quarantining of aggressors." I shall never forget the grim determination engraved upon a countenance whose eyes seemed to look so far, far into the future. Had we followed him then, millions of lives might have been saved. From the time that Roosevelt instructed the late Ambassador Dodd to protest to Hitler against his fiendish treatment of the Jews which aroused the conscience of the world, the President understood that the threat was not against Jews alone but against the Judeo-Christian civilization, against the principles found in the Ten Commandments and in the Sermon on the Mount, against the Golden Rule and the Beatitudes, against justice, love and mercy. Roosevelt saw in Nazism the resurrection of barbarism and the resuscitation of paganism. But the Chicago Bridge speech gave isolationists the opportunity of calling him a "war-monger," and nothing happened until Japan united us at Pearl Harbor.

May I digress for a moment and tell you of the first time I stood beside Franklin Roosevelt. It was here in Chicago in the summer of 1932 when he flew to our Stadium to accept the nomination. It was my privilege to have pronounced the invocation on that day. When they lifted him to the platform, his sun-tanned face and beaming countenance, in a world depressed by unemployment, brought confidence and courage to all who were privileged to look upon him.

Another digression of a personal nature may be of interest. Mrs. Roosevelt and I were the speakers at a national gathering held in Washington. When her time came to speak, she begged for my watch, saying that her little fleur de lis watch did not keep time but that Franklin gave it to her for an engagement present and that she wore it at all times "just the same." I noticed by this morning's paper that the same fleur de lis watch was pinned on her bosom as she stood by the grave. We parted late that evening from the banquet. I had said some drastic things, having been re-enforced in some of my opinions by what I had heard the night before at the home of Mrs. Carnegie in New York. It was a meeting of one of the Carnegie Foundations of which I am a member. The morning after my speech in Washington, when I came down for my breakfast in the hotel, there was a letter in my box. To my surprise, it was a long letter from Mrs. Roosevelt. It began with words of praise for my efforts the night before, and then added, "What you said kept me awake last night. This morning I discussed your remarks with my husband and he was very anxious for me to give you his point of view and that of the administration." I cite this not because of the personal compliment implied, but because it is typical of both Franklin Roosevelt and Eleanor Roosevelt to care about what even the humblest of 130,000,000 citizens think about national issues.

To return now from these digressions, permit me to point to the obstacles our beloved President had to overcome in anticipating the aggressor. These obstacles can be epitomised in three words which were not only used, but misused and abused. Through the technique of propaganda, they were made not to reveal but to conceal meaning. These three words are sovereignty, neutrality, and isolationism.

The first is sovereignty—absolute national sovereignty. As commonly understood, it means that a nation may do what it wants, when it wants, as it wants, so long as it has the power to carry out its wishes. Small nations, therefore, have little national sovereignty, if any. Roosevelt understood, as did John Dewey, that "absolute national sovereignty is but another name for international anarchy." The big truck always has the right-of-way over the run-about whether the light be green or red. It ultimately speaks in terms of the arbitrament of force. Anarchy leads to chaos and chaos is a challenge to civilization. Jean Jacques Rousseau pointed out that civilization begins when men give up some of their liberties for liberty. Absolute national sovereignty must be modified and qualified.

The second of these obstacles was found in the word neutrality. It meant sitting in the world's grand-stand watching the human gladiatorial contest go on. As the aggressors were armed and the victims of aggression were pacifistically unarmed, neutrality meant helping the aggressor and harming the aggressed. Neutrality on such terms meant being used as an instrument of brutality. No moral being can remain neutral when the decencies of life are being ruthlessly violated. Neutrality under such conditions is immorality.

The third of these words used as obstacles is isolation. A world in which science has annihilated time and space makes isolation an impossibility and if it were a possibility it would be both futility and imbecility. Germany wanted each nation to believe in isolation while one after the other was being conquered by her. With a worthless promise after each conquest, she said, "Now I want no more." Motivated by wishful thinking, nations were willing to believe Hitler. Some lived in a fool's paradise and others in a coward's hell. Be it said to Roosevelt's eternal glory that he lived neither in a fool's paradise nor a coward's hell, but on a courageous man's earth. He insisted that isolationism at best was repudiationism, a repudiation of religion's greatest teaching: "I am my brother's keeper." Isolationism says "I am not my brother's keeper." When we refuse to be our brother's keeper, we become our brother's killer. We have refused to be our brother's keeper. We have become our brother's killer.

After brushing aside these skillfully laid plans of the propagandists, how did Roosevelt anticipate the aggressor? With a genius as uncanny as it was inexplicable, he found a way to circumvent the Johnson Act which forbade us to sell ammunitions to any nation that was indebted to us from World War I. With all of Europe at the mercy of the aggressor—who always has the initial advantage—with no money to pay, with no credit available, with both the Senate and the House unwilling to repeal the Johnson Act, came Lend-Lease! A stroke of genius! That was a horse of another color. It wasn't selling, it was lending; it wasn't giving, it was leasing. Like Portia in Shakespeare's "Merchant of Venice," it was granting the pound of flesh—but, without a drop of blood! A technicality, to be sure! But a technicality that saved America—and the world. Only on such a pretext were we able, while "at peace" technically—as if anyone is ever really at peace with the aggressor abroad—to retool our factories to prepare for the inevitable conflict by accelerating the production of munitions. All of this happened a full year before we were treacherously attacked at Pearl Harbor. A full year. How easily these words are spoken! But when we realize how, later on, a month or even a week meant the difference between victory and defeat, life and death, a full year before Pearl Harbor turned the tide of history. Later on Lend-Lease was extended by only a narrow margin in the Senate.

With equal statesmanship and genius, Franklin Delano Roosevelt convinced our Congress of the need of peace-time conscription, a full year before Pearl Harbor. Pearl Harbor was tragic enough. It was possibly the blackest day in our entire history. Unprepared as we were, we had at least begun to make preparations for the preservation of freedom. From the "arsenal of democracy" to the defenders of democracy, we became the creators of the United Nations which, in the near future, may and should pave the way for a United States of the World. To this end, no one contributed as much as did Franklin Delano Roosevelt. For this alone he will remain immortal for the ages unconceived in the womb of time.

Among the achievements that stand out even now like mountain peaks on the horizon of history, our President realized that political democracy without economic democracy is a sham, a deception and a mockery. He not only saw; he acted. For the first time in history, in his discussion of freedom he included freedom from want and freedom from fear, its psychological concomitant. Franklin Delano Roosevelt knew how futile religious freedom and freedom of speech—the opportunity to say "Oh God, don't let me starve" or to pray "give us this day our daily bread"—would be without proper implementation. Through his dynamic leadership, his passion for justice, and his solicitude for the poor, this implementation was realized in legislation. This man born wealthy was rich not only in money but in character, in qualities of heart, in gifts of mind, and in fellow-feeling for the disheartened, discouraged and the dismayed.

How was this implementation accomplished? Through unemployment insurance. The unemployed should no longer be looked upon as a leper to be shunned. There must be continuous employment and ultimately, continuous pay. When the rich shut down the mill, the poor should not be shut out of food. How was this implementation achieved? Through old age security. Untold thousands have read and prayed in the words of Scriptures, "Cast me not away in my old age," but they were cast away over the hill to the poor house. Poor people were thrown upon the human scrap heap in shame and ignomy through no fault of their own. How was this implementation accomplished? Through labor legislation, from which we dare not recede. Through slum clearance. How often have I recited the facts to you—slums cost twice as much in fire protection, five times as much in police protection; instead of a financial asset to the city, they are a financial deficit on the city; the death rate where you and I live is ten per thousand per year; in slums, as high as forty-seven per thousand per year; the crime potentiality where you and I live is one half of one per cent, in slums, eighty times as large. Equally staggering figures have been gathered about disease, corruption and perversion. Franklin Delano Roosevelt knew that slum people do not create slums. Slums, however, do create slum people. Had you and I been born in the slums, we too would have been victims. "There but for the grace of God go we." How was this implementation achieved? Through public works programs. If well planned, it need not be an object of ridicule. Only when there is political corruption will public works as such be held in scorn. A democracy in which planning is impossible sinks either to mediocrity on the one hand, or to mobocracy on the other. How was this implementation achieved? Through TVA. Nature's abounding energy and wealth should be used for the good of all rather than exploited by the few. As democracy ultimately is the leadership of the wisest and best for the good of all, so must it use the bounties of nature wisely for the good of all. How was this implementation achieved? Through encouraging medical care for the poor. It is not true, as is so frequently said, that the very poor and the very rich get the best of care. Even if it were, the seventy per cent in between, and especially the white collar class, would be neglected. It is known that poor people are sick three times as often and call in a physician one-fourth as often, making their predicament twelve times as great from the health point of view. Such things should not continue to take place in the most prosperous country on the face of the earth. Franklin Delano Roosevelt changed the moral climate of our generation. Because of that, we may apply to him the words from the Book of Daniel: "They that be wise shall shine as the brightness of the firmament and they that lead many to righteousness like the stars forever and aye." The memory of Franklin Delano Roosevelt will shine "like the brightness of the firmament" and his achievement in leading many to righteousness will "shine like the stars" for generations as yet unborn. "The righteous are alive even after death—alive in influence" says the Talmud.

Among the achievements that even now stand out is his vision to see beyond the arbitrary, artificial man-made distinctions that so frequently divide, to the overwhelming number of God-made resemblances that can, should and must unite man to his fellow man. He envisaged civilization in its various stages. He saw how domination had outlived its usefulness and become outmoded even though Hitler, Mussolini and Hirohito attempted to resurrect it. He realized that competition, ruthless competition—"each for himself and the devil take the hindmost"—was passing. He looked forward to the third stage, cooperation, when law and order, justice and fair play, self-imposed rules and regulations would distinguish the civilized man from the barbarian. Franklin Delano Roosevelt insisted that unless and until these same principles were applied to nations as well as to individuals, anarchy would hold sway, and death, destruction and devastation would reign supreme. He knew his Bible. He recalled the words, "Let nations remember they are but men." How clear this becomes if we read any of the official documents to which he contributed so greatly. Take the Atlantic Charter as an example. Countries should seek no aggrandizement; no territorial changes should be brought about contrary to the freely expressed wishes of those concerned; the right of people to choose their own government and to restore it to those forcibly deprived of it; equal access to raw materials to nations large and small, to victor and vanquished; economic collaboration of nations to improve labor conditions and social security for all; freedom from fear and want for all, a peace that will enable all to traverse the high seas without hindrance; for spiritual as well as realistic reasons, nations must abandon force.

This is true not only of the Atlantic Charter, which I have outlined, but also of Casablanca, Bretton Woods, Dumbarton Oaks, Teheran, Moscow, Yalta and—San Francisco! No, I haven't made a mistake. I deliberately said San Francisco. Roosevelt's spirit will hover over and guide that epoch-making gathering. According to the Talmud, "Great men are even greater in death than in life." Our President has planted the seed. A world that has become smaller physically must become larger spiritually. Once upon a time the loftiest words in any language were "the Declaration of Independence." In the not too distant future, there must be a Declaration of Interdependence, and when this time comes, the name of Franklin Delano Roosevelt, like Abou ben Adam, will lead all the rest. In this vision of a united mankind, he was the sworn enemy of prejudice. He believed that the accident of birth should neither be a help nor a hindrance. A man should be evaluated by his motives, his achievements, his character and his integrity—by his vision and his aspirations.

So frequently during my life, in reading the pages of American history, I have wondered how it felt and what it must have been like to have experienced a national shock and to have lived through the inexpressible calamity of Lincoln's death. I turned to the papers of that day and read the story and relived the tragedy. But even so, I wondered how it felt. I know now. I was sitting at a banquet for the Salvation Army in evening attire when I was literally picked up from the table and taken to the radio station to speak words of comfort to a mourning nation. Some two hundred and fifty-six stations listened in. Our Sages said that when a truly great man dies, everyone might feel as if he had parted with the nearest of kin. May I confess to you that while I thought that I knew what these words meant, I never did until the passing of Franklin Delano Roosevelt. Each of us has lost the nearest of kin. In psychoanalysis, the patient must be capable of "transference" in order for the analyst to achieve the best result. The analyst under those conditions becomes the patient's psychological prop for the time being. Franklin Delano Roosevelt was the object of our transference. We had supreme confidence in him. We feel just a bit shaky without him. The nearest of kin has gone. On my way to the radio station, I saw what one might carelessly designate as "hardened men" with tears furrowing their cheeks. My taxi driver was so overcome that he went through the red lights and almost struck a number of other machines. My announcer was sobbing copiously and unashamed. The elevator girl had eyes that were red from weeping. The scrubwoman on the floor where I alighted was sobbing bitterly, and between her moaning one could make out the words, "I lost my best friend." What was it like when Abraham Lincoln died? Now, I know.

"The only limit to our realization of tomorrow," said Franklin Delano Roosevelt in his last written words a few hours before he entered the realm of the immortals, "will be our doubts today. Let us move forward with strong and active faith."

It is for us the living to dedicate ourselves to the unfinished tasks which he so nobly began. We pray for America. She is orphaned. We pray for the world, poorer for his passing even as it was richer for his having been. We pray for the new President. He needs our prayers. He needs our help. Of all the thousands who have spoken, no one said it as well—no one could—as Mrs. Roosevelt: "I am more sorry for the people of our country and the world than I am for us."

The cynic cannot be right in a world that produced a Franklin Delano Roosevelt. The skeptics are undermined when we point to him. Pessimists are refuted by his buoyant faith. The fearful have found new courage because of his confidence. The handicapped have been inspired with new enthusiasm by his triumph. Democracy has new hope because of his achievements. Faith in human nature has been restored by his passion for social justice. Not only we who were privileged to call him our President, our Commander-in-Chief, but the liberty-loving everywhere, the justice-loving everywhere, the peace-loving everywhere, and the democracy-loving everywhere, have lost their champion, have been deprived of their prophetic voice, have been robbed of their courageous soul, have been disassociated from their social conscience—have been parted from their better selves!

Franklin Delano Roosevelt was a war casualty. He died for his country. So to live is not to die. To die for an ideal is to live for eternity.

Now he, too, belongs to the ages.

Man of Faith

RABBI C. DAVID MATT

MINE is the sad duty, at this time, to pay tribute to our immortal President. It is difficult indeed, to make an adequate appraisal of the life and achievements of one of the greatest men produced by the greatest crisis in the world's history—that outstanding leader of men, the lover of his fellows, the great conductor of war and the outstanding worker for peace, Franklin Delano Roosevelt.

We shall single out a few of the many traits of his character and phases of his career. Roosevelt was a man of courage, as was manifest throughout his life by the causes he championed, by the forces and interests he was willing to challenge, by the ability to follow the course he had chosen and see it through to the final conclusion, regardless of the opposition he expected to meet.

But Franklin Delano Roosevelt was also a man of faith. Himself a deeply religious man, he did not hesitate to admit his dependence upon God. His deep religiosity found expression in his frequent calls for nation-wide prayer. He wanted his people re-enforced by the belief that God was with them, and again and again he urged them to pray for strength and guidance, no less than for victory and peace. The importance he placed upon religion was highlighted by his invitation, for the purpose of consultation, to the representatives of the three main religious groups of our country, the Protestant, the Catholic and the Jewish. As representative of the Jews and Judaism, he had selected our late distinguished townsman, Dr. Cyrus Adler, whose successor is Dr. Louis Finkelstein, head of the Jewish Theological Seminary of America.

Roosevelt's faith explains his passionate idealism which found its expression in the efforts to help the underprivileged. To him, the dividing lines of race, color and creed were artificial barriers. He considered all men as brothers, the children of one Father. As the great humanitarian, he sympathized with all who suffered, especially with those whose sufferings came through no fault of their own, but who were victims of those who had gained power over them and were using that power to hurt, to oppress, to crush. Some of his most powerful utterances were those which denounced this oppression of the victims of persecution, and the bestial treatment of the weak and helpless by the arrogant and heartless warlords.

His belief in God and his conviction that Justice would ultimately prevail probably explain his liberalism. The social legislation of the last twelve years, the amelioration of the condition of the workers, the translation of the ideals of social justice into concrete legislation, was due in great measure to Roosevelt's efforts. Though less spectacular than the war effort, it will be remembered side by side with his accomplishments in the international scene. He had a passion for championing the cause of the underprivileged. The individuals, the groups, the nationalities that most needed help, were the ones most sure to win his sympathy and support. His pleas on their behalf will remain classic expressions of humanitarianism and of the desire that justice be done to those who had been sinned against by society and by the world.

He was a marvelous strategist and much of the clever and inspired planning of the war effort of the United Nations which already has brought us so close to victory, and the tremendous and priceless contribution of America's resources to the successful conduct of the war, were due to Roosevelt's initiative and marvelous insight. Yet though realizing that military force was necessary, if human freedom were to be regained and safeguarded, he hated war, and abhorred its inevitable methods and the toll it must take of everything valuable in civilization. He loved peace, and the very vehemence of the war efforts which he sponsored was in order to bring a speedy end to war and to make peace permanent and assured. It is no paradox in the thinking and methods of Roosevelt that he was the more militant leader in war because he wanted to safeguard peace. He envisaged peace not only as the immediate successor of war but as something that would be assured in the decades to come and that would really permit our children and their children to live in a world that would not know the scourge of war any more.

I need not dwell on the opposition he had to overcome in carrying out the program which he saw with such prophetic clearness. To have accomplished all that Franklin Delano Roosevelt achieved as humanitarian, as idealist, as head of the world's greatest democracy, as war leader and as crusader for peace might well have taxed the health and vitality of the strongest. How much more remarkable is the record of Roosevelt's accomplishment in view of the physical handicap under which he had to labor all these years!

He was able to surmount his disability by sheer willpower and even made of his affliction a source of help, blessing and healing for countless unfortunates. Who knows how many thousands have been given a new lease on life and hope because of what Franklin Delano Roosevelt was able to do for, and through, the Infantile Paralysis Foundation and the annual President's Birthday Ball!

This, our tribute, would of course be incomplete without a reference to what Roosevelt meant to the Jewish people. As far as his attitude to his Jewish fellow-citizens is concerned, we wish to emphasize this thought: That he appointed Jews to public office is not to be considered a mark of special favor. It was rather eloquent testimony of his sound American belief, that any special gifts and talents with which citizens are blessed should be put at the disposal of the community, for the public welfare. That he saw fit to appoint to various public offices within his gift such men as Secretary of the Treasury Morgenthau, Justice of the Supreme Court Frankfurter, former Governor Lehman as head of the UNRRA; that he availed himself of the counsel and help of Bernard Baruch and Judge Rosenman, not only resulted in untold blessing to our country but also emphasized that here in America all are permitted and encouraged to serve their fatherland, regardless of creed or race. Also it was another evidence of the broadmindedness and the courage of our great leader. As to the Jews in Europe and the Jewish aspirations in Palestine, Roosevelt was a powerful and sympathetic friend and spokesman. His passion for justice and his innate, over-mastering desire to aid the underprivileged, those who were most in need of help, explain his great interest in the welfare of the Jews of the world, who were the first, and the greatest, sufferers from Nazism and Fascism.

Roosevelt's passing at any time would have been a great loss to all the causes which he sponsored. His death at this time is a tragedy of the greatest magnitude. His loss to America, where many of the projects he initiated and championed are beginning to attain their full development cannot yet be appraised. His absence from the councils of the war will be keenly felt. The influence of his sturdy, dominating personality surely was still needed. His planning for what was to follow the war and the implementing of the charters of peace would have been most valuable, if not indispensable. The battle he was waging for domestic welfare and universal well-being still require most determined backing. Surely we Jews can feel that his sympathetic understanding of our problems and the needs of our co-religionists who live in less happy lands would have made the post war adjustments infinitely easier and more grateful.

Yet all Americans, and indeed all mankind, can find solace in this thought: It is tragic that Roosevelt was not permitted to enter the Promised Land of his ideals. Yet when the end did come, he was so close to the attainment of his hopes and he could envisage so much of the ultimate picture that, we believe, he was as nearly content to go as it is possible for a human being to be. Above all, we can be thankful to God, whose plans are beyond the questioning of us mortals that the end did not come earlier. A few months ago, the impending victory that now seems so imminent, was still far beyond the horizon. Had Franklin Delano Roosevelt been called away from his earthly labors before the most recent victorious sweep of our army and navy and air fleets, he might have had reason to worry about the ultimate outcome.

May I quote several lines of a sonnet by a venerable Philadelphian, Felix N. Gerson, which he composed in memory of Theodore Herzl, founder of modern Zionism:

> Such men are rare—they tow'r above mankind
> And on the scroll of life their names are signed
> In characters of flame. The great and wise
> Know them afar, and at their bidding rise
> To nobler conquests of the heart and mind.
> Thou, too, hast dreamed a world compelling dream—
> With glance prophetic and unfalt'ring soul.
> If thou were dreaming, Herzl, sleep content—
> A dream like thine, God unto Moses sent.

Let me paraphrase these last two lines:

> If thou were dreaming, Roosevelt, sleep content—
> A dream like thine, God unto Moses sent.

Let us thank God that Roosevelt was granted at least the preview of the success of his plans and dreams for the world's betterment. In that better world to which he has been called, may he enjoy the bliss that is granted to those who have labored faithfully and earnestly here on earth. May we, who have been blessed by his efforts and by the inspiration of his sincerity, his love of his fellowmen, his abhorrence of evil and godlessness and his devotion to the establishment of freedom and safety in a free and peaceful world, be granted the vision, the strength and the ability to walk in his footsteps and to do whatever we can to help bring his hopes and dreams to realization.

PRAYER

OUR God and God of our fathers; Creator at whose behest life begins and ends, shelter beneath the wings of the Shechinah the soul of our beloved leader, Franklin Delano Roosevelt. Grant him the reward Thou hast treasured up for the righteous.

Bless, guard and guide, we pray Thee, him who has been summoned to step into the breach. Upon our new President, Harry S. Truman, we invoke Thy blessing. Give him strength and wisdom to fulfill his task. Send permanent and victorious and righteous peace. Grant the fulfillment of the benediction of the priests of old: The Lord bless thee and keep thee. The Lord make His countenance to shine upon thee and be gracious unto thee. The Lord lift up His countenance unto thee and grant thee peace. Amen.

Prince of Righteousness

RABBI MOSES MESHELOFF

THE most revered word in the Hebrew dictionary, *HASSID,* we lay in tribute at the feet of our departed president tonight. No better description can we find for this great, noble, generous soul than that of Hassid.

The Hassid is he who seeks the welfare of others. Our departed president devoted his life to the forgotten man. The Hassid of old spent his life seeking to heal the sick, to supply the needy, to help the crushed. Franklin Delano Roosevelt opened his heart to the needs of his people. His great heart bled with the knowledge that a third of his country was improperly housed, clothed and fed. So much of the legislation that he initiated was that of the ideal Hassid who sought the welfare of the lowly, the meek, the forgotten! We mourn tonight the loss of that soul which was so attuned to the needs of the "little people."

Franklin Roosevelt was more than a great leader seeking the welfare of all his countrymen. He was one of the *Hassidei Umot Ha-Olam*. His great heart embraced all nations. He fought against bigotry and prejudice, hates and barbarities, not alone in his own land, but wherever they revealed themselves upon this earth. He dreamed of the betterment of the condition of the Chinese and the Indian as well as of the backward areas in his own blessed U.S.A. His vision was as great as all the earth. His plans and vision included the men of all nations. All men, he believed, of all origins and fealties were entitled to a place in the sun and a share in the bounty of the earth. It was this conviction that helped create the Atlantic Charter. This was the foundation of the struggle for the Four Freedoms. He stood gallantly in the forefront in this global fight for justice and equality, for humanity and peace for all.

There are those among us who mourn twice tonight. They mourn at having lost their great leaders, the friend of all peoples. They mourn too that he should have died at the eve of victory. He died unprivileged to see the triumph over the mighty foe who had been considered unconquerable, and for whom he had raised an army which had been considered fantastic.

But Roosevelt did not die without a taste of victory. What he lived for, believed in and gave his every energy for had triumphed before his death. The world which he helped plan, the world of the future, the Olam Haba, will bear his unmistakable stamp. It has already been moulded by his genius and his humanity. He has already gained his immortal share in the world to come. That post-war world cannot but be established in keeping with his utterances and acts on behalf of humanity, brotherhood and peace. The beginnings of such a world he foresaw before he left this earth. They will remain his contribution to a brave and lasting new world. They have become part of the thinking and acting of all civilized men. This contribution to the development of mankind is the enduring tribute which towers over that of a mere military victory.

Of Franklin Delano Roosevelt it may well be said in tribute: *Hassidei Umot HaOlam Yesh Lahem Chelek L'Olam Haba!*

But one more word I would say to you tonight. Our president has his undeniable share in the world-to-be. But it is only a share, tremendous as it is. We, you and I, each have our shares too. We must each contribute our share to that world if it is to be complete.

Ours is the task of helping build through devotion to his ideals and through the same burning passion for humanity that world which he believed could, would and must be established. Our tribute cannot be given in mere words, nor at a single public ceremony. Our tribute must be given through the dedication of our lives and those of our children and of generations yet unborn to the establishment of that world which he founded on equity and humanity, and whose structure is one of freedom and peace for all men and all times.

Such a world will be the living, eternal tribute to one of the greatest men in our times, President Franklin Delano Roosevelt.

We Were Enriched by His Life

HENRY MONSKY

THE world and its people—all of them throughout the universe—have suffered an irreparable loss. The foremost champion of human dignity, Franklin Delano Roosevelt, who will be recorded in history as one of the great immortals of all time, has been called from his labors to eternal rest. We were enriched by his life as we have been bereft by his death.

He was the friend of man—eminent and humble—of every race, creed, and color. He was the symbol of justice, and the champion of freedom. He was the enemy of tyranny, oppression, persecution, and of all the evil forces of reaction.

He inspired a new world order, calculated to insure enduring peace, buttressed by the full enjoyment of the freedoms so essential to the happiness of mankind. He was not destined to see the full realization of his great and inspired vision.

As Americans, in common with the people of all nations, we are bowed down in grief. As Jews, we have suffered especially the loss of a great-hearted humanitarian who, in the tragic period of our history, shocked by the inhuman treatment of our people, and in line with his concept of morality and justice, has been our friend and protector.

We must rededicate ourselves to the high purpose for which he gave so much. We must be steadfast in our faith in the ultimate attainment of his program. We resolve to help uphold the hands of President Truman, and pray for divine guidance that he may bring to fulfillment the ideals of President Roosevelt.

"In essentials, unity. In non-essentials, liberty. In all things, charity." This quotation from a statement made by President Roosevelt on the occasion of the dedication of the Sara Delano Roosevelt Memorial House, is symbolic of his philosophy and consonant with his whole pattern of life.

Farewell, O Prince

RABBI LOUIS I. NEWMAN

FRANKLIN DELANO ROOSEVELT was uniquely a classic American type. Buoyant, vivacious, good-hearted, generous, practical, he represented many of the finest virtues of our national character. He was in a real sense a member of the country-esquire group; he was an aristocrat to his finger-tips. But even more than his famous cousin, Theodore Roosevelt, Franklin Roosevelt transcended his class and his economic group. He realized that America must belong to no one group of individuals, however favored by circumstance, whatever the date of their forefathers' arrival on these shores. He appreciated the place and the right of the "common man," the "forgotten man," the "man at the base of the economic pyramid." Like his illustrious master, of whom he was a faithful disciple, Woodrow Wilson, he sought to channelize the major currents of American life into fruitful and helpful activities for the national good. Hence though not of the people, he was for the people, and throughout his entire career he sought to work with the people, for their advancement.

Mr. Roosevelt's greatest victory came in the early days of his political career, when he was stricken with infantile paralysis. Emil Ludwig has given a graphic account of the effects of this terrible misfortune upon the young statesman. He had been able to climb a four-thousand foot mountain just to win a bet; to make many speeches a day, and to show the reckless indifference to over-exertion, of which so many vital young people are guilty. His very love of life had led him into tragedy; he rejoiced in sea travel, in fishing, in sociability, in being ever-ready to help others, in the eager curiosity which typified his nature. Now at the very peak of his career, he had received a cruel, and apparently, insurmountable blow at the hands of circumstance.

A radio commentator has told of a conversation with a friend who had seen Mr. Roosevelt lifted from a train to a wheel-chair two decades ago. "What a pity," he lamented. "He had so much to anticipate, but now he's through." Ten years later he was present at the first Inauguration of Mr. Roosevelt as President. In the presence of the bearded Chief Justice, Mr. Roosevelt seemed rugged and roseate with health. The same friend said to the same commentator, recalling the scene a decade before: "What a lot of courage some men have stored up inside of them." In the presence of his affliction, Franklin Delano Roosevelt showed the true mettle of his character. He might have become soured and embittered; he might have sought escape along the easy way that weaker men have taken, in rebellion, in self-indulgence, in frivolous amusement. Instead, he began truly to live, as he had never lived before.

He was able to receive friends, for whom previously he had had insufficient time. He was able to maintain a large correspondence. He was able to read, to prepare himself for whatever the future may bring.

Instead of repining and pitying himself, he declared: "I'll beat this thing." "It's ridiculous to tell me that a grown man can't conquer a child's sickness." The doctor has said to Mr. Roosevelt's close friend, Louis Howe: "The only thing that can help now is a struggle maintained daily and hourly, but only in the rarest instances has the patient the energy for it." Howe quoted his chief as replying: "All right, when does the cure begin, and what have I to do?" Mrs. Roosevelt has given a further view of the manner in which her afflicted husband met his trial: "We didn't do anything except treat him as a perfectly normal, able-bodied man, which was what he made us all feel he was. He never let anyone intimate to him that he was trying to do too much. Once when he was planning to go South, he said it would be easier for him to go by boat than by train. That was the only time I ever heard him acknowledge that he was not just as he had been before. You know he never has said he could not walk."

And this was the man who carried himself from the valley of despond to the heights of the Presidency, and to world leadership in its hour of travail. During his early speaking campaigns, Mr. Roosevelt once lost his balance and fell; but he was lifted again to the rostrum, and went ahead with his speech, as if nothing had happened. The only reference to his affliction I can recall, occurred in his final address on returning from Yalta before the combined Senate and House. This heroic, unquenchable spirit, by his very power of will, impressed himself upon the soul of our republic and upon humanity. In our time of tribulation, when the Fascist and Nazi menace became more acute, he displayed that "vision without which the people perish." How puny and empoisoned seems the judgment of those men who opposed his endeavours to warn America with respect to the Fascist danger! How wisely he fulfilled his trusteeship as the Commander-in-Chief of our nation, when he sought to do the utmost to safeguard the overseas bastions of freedom, until the attack of the Japanese made our entrance into the War imperative. America, Britain, France, China, and other freedom-loving nations will long remember Mr. Roosevelt's wisdom in making possible lend-lease aid until we stood at their side as fighting allies.

Perhaps it may be said that Mr. Roosevelt, like Mr. Wilson, was the "Talleyrand of a dying order." Whatever the criticism directed against him with a ferocity unparalleled in our history, Mr. Roosevelt espoused the system of free enterprise and private initiative within the orbit of a voluntary collectivism. Except for a crucial action in Chicago last June, we might now have a leadership, zealously committed, not merely to the successful prosecution of the War, but also to provision for the 60,000,000 jobs our country needs in peace as well as in battle. Mr. Roosevelt had faith in the skill and resourcefulness of the American business man and industrialist, but he was determined that no one group should dictate the economic destiny of our nation. He sought to keep the scales of justice evenly balanced as between capital and labor, management and workers, yielding to unwarranted pressure neither from the right nor from the left. He shattered the generalizations of opponents by saying that our institutions were safe as long as free elections and the two-party system prevailed in our political life. In retrospect his proposal to raise the number of Supreme Court justices from nine to fifteen does not seem so revolutionary, but Mr. Roosevelt was more concerned with the spirit than the letter of his proposals, and the sound liberalism of American courts, with respect to social welfare legislation—as in the days of Theodore Roosevelt in 1912—is due in great measure to the "pitiless publicity" which Franklin Roosevelt turned upon the backward looking elements in our judiciary.

To the everlasting honor of Mr. Roosevelt, let it be said that he appreciated talent whatever its origin and creed. Men of all denominations and ethnic origins were called into national service. Though made the target by the hucksters of hate for vilification, Mr. Roosevelt went forward unswervingly to summon to his side helpers and co-workers whose judgment he trusted and whose abilities he believed the country needed. Whatever may have been the questions raised concerning Mr. Roosevelt's attitude towards the problems of some of the small peoples, including the Yishub in Palestine, he could be counted upon, as always, to do the right thing at the right time in what seemed to him the right way. Whether in the betterment of city government or in the conduct of other reform measures, Mr. Roosevelt was satisfied, if need be, to move slowly and with adaptability, following, as he said, the tactics of a quarterback in a football game, using new plays if old ones did not succeed. The result was that he was admired, respected and loved, though his critics condemned him with an equal intensity of feeling.

And now his magical voice has been stilled. Like Moses on Mount Nebo, he could behold the promised land of victory and peace, but it was not granted him to enter it. We are still wandering in the wilderness, and not merely a Joshua is needed, but wise statesmen and, above all else, far-seeing and forthright Prophets, who can carry forward his message. There has been a fateful nexus between the career of the demon Hitler and the saint Roosevelt; they came to power in January, 1933, and they have remained in power, one for deviltry and destruction, the other for goodness and service. And now the righteous man, Job amid his afflictions, has been called into the great silence. Hitler, the Satan, the Adversary, still lives, but it will not be long before he and his evil partners are obliterated from the earth. To be sure, it is a tragedy that Mr. Roosevelt could not have been granted a few more years to witness the coming of complete victory over Germany and Japan, and the advent of a long era of peace, with Woodrow Wilson's dream of a League of Nations fulfilled.

If Henry Wallace, like Hannibal Hamlin, had been granted the designation as Vice-President in his Chieftain's later term, the spokesman for "the century of the common man" would be in the White House today. Franklin Roosevelt, by sheer power of will, wished at Chicago and in the driving rain and wind of his New York visit in 1944, to impress upon the electorate his resolution to live, and to finish his mission. Now we have a President who has distinguished himself in an important Senatorial task, and who, at the parting of the ways, has been summoned to sit in the councils of the nations by the side of Stalin, Churchill, de Gaulle and Chiang Kai Shek. Let us remember that America is greater than any one man, and while Franklin Roosevelt is dead, America lives. The obligation of everyone who loves liberalism and espouses the American way of life, to stand on guard, is greater than ever. Now the people, as an aggregation, as a vast community, must share the responsibility for making the era of justice and peace a reality. Our nation is only as strong as the humblest citizen, to whom Franklin Roosevelt spoke in his fireside chats. If we are disposed to dissension, to bickering, to backbiting, to unwarranted suspicions and hatreds, we will be called to remember the words of Thomas Jefferson: "I tremble for my country when I reflect that God is just."

With President Truman in the chair of Franklin Roosevelt, we must give him the same devotion, cooperation and counsel, which we, the citizens of this democracy, who loved his predecessor, sought to furnish. And as for our Captain, who like Abraham Lincoln, lies fallen on the deck, while the Ship of State must still sail on, we say, in the words of Israel Zangwill concerning Theodor Herzl:

> Farewell O Prince, Farewell O sorely tried,
> You dreamed a dream, and you have paid the cost,
> To save a people, leaders must be lost,

By foe and follower be crucified;
But yet it is your body only that has died,
The noblest soul in Judah is not dust;
But fire, that works in every vein and must
Reshape our life, rekindling Israel's pride.

So we behold the Captain of our Strife,
Triumphant in the moment of eclipse,
Death has but fixed him in immortal life,
His flag uphold, his trumpet at your lips,
And while we weeping, rend our garments' hem,
Next year, we cry, next year Jerusalem.

First Citizen of the World

LOUIS NIZER

THOSE terrible words, "Roosevelt is dead." They are sharp words with piercing edges. They stab the heart. They cause numbness and disbelief.

His voice—it will never spill music over us again. His smile—it will never warm us with its radiance. His heart—it will never beat again. That handsome head—we shall never see it again.

Our shock dissolves in tears. We cry unashamedly. Not for our Commander-in-Chief; not even for our President. For him we would have only deep sorrow. We cry for our personal friend; for a near and dear member of our family; that is what he was to each of us.

As he is carried in his coffin on his last journey to the White House, our hearts ache. The poignant fact strikes us that he will never sit behind that desk again; never thrill the world again with his fireside chats; never keep the White House lights ablaze as he works on the architecture of peace.

And then we see his noble wife emerging even greater in her tragic grandeur. There she stands at the grave clutching the flag which has been taken from his coffin as it is lowered forever underground. And when the military ceremony is over and everyone is gone, she returns alone to stand over the grave in a long, silent and final farewell. We stand with her—all of us. Prayers emanate from our hearts for him and for her.

Throughout the war, homes have been darkened here and there by news that henceforth a gold star must substitute for the presence of some beloved son. But now our whole nation is suddenly old with grief. We have all lost a father and America has lost its greatest son.

It is a national tragedy. But of what nation? Not only America, but England sorrows in equal measure. Its humblest worker and its heroic Prime Minister sob for England's loss. They have recognized the greatest of English characteristics in this American: unconquerable persistence and a love of liberty. Gratitude is the memory of the heart. And England's heart is filled with memories of her rescue by him who loved liberty.

The people of England know that adversity is sometimes the rain of spring. A merciful rain fell upon them in their most desperate hour and now a harvest of friendship and love for our President—yes, for their President too—makes them equal mourners.

And in France, the simple farmer leaves his plough untouched. He sits with bowed head in his liberated home, sharing with his wife and hushed children the new loss for France. They admired the great French qualities of the President; his gaiety akin to courage, and his graciousness akin to humaneness. Yes, joy and courage make a handsome face, and what artist could have conceived a nobler one? It bore grim determination—highlighted by wit, and made forever young by enthusiasm. The heart of France is heavy and tears dedicate his memory. The French people, too, have lost a President.

And over the vast plains of Russia a winter of grief suddenly envelopes the people. Millions of peasants and workers bow in despair before their great loss. They understood the President's indomitable will in overcoming disaster. They understood his leadership which encompassed military gifts as well as statecraft. These were Russian qualities—and since he embodied them, he was one of them. Not the learned but the one who suffers most is wise. He knew suffering and he worked that others might never have to endure all that they could learn to bear. He knew how to turn helplessness into hope. He infused the world with his spirit. He who could not stand raised a stricken America to her feet in 1933, and a shattered Europe to her feet in 1943.

The Russian soul is draped in black. Russia has lost a President, too.

And so has China. Word spreads to the farthest corner of that ancient land, that the great American has slept away. In millions of families there is the painful silence of personal tragedy. The Chinese understood and recognized the great man's endless patience. It is the philosophy of their ancestors. Patience—in time the grass becomes milk.

They understood his simplicity. They knew that a truly great man never puts away the simplicity of a child. He was their idol—their friend. Yes—their President, too.

For the first time, all the peoples of the world are united in sorrow. Never before has the death of a statesman of one nation been so profoundly and intimately felt by all civilized nations. It is a new phenomenon in international relationship. His own life is the bond of amity among the nations of the world. It is a triumph in personality which exceeds any in the history of statesmanship. He stormed the ramparts of national suspicion and transformed them into faith. Faith in humanity. Faith in neighborliness. Faith in one another. Faith in peace. The international structure now to be built is a great mechanical adventure. He has created the spirit which impels the builders. He has inspired the peoples of the world to demand its successful completion. Never in history has there been a greater personal achievement by any man.

There are many echoes in the world, but few voices. His was the great voice of mankind. He will stand alone like some peak that has no fellow in the mountain range of greatness.

This is our comfort. In this realization our burdened hearts will be joyous again. Our eyes will be dry again. For in saying farewell to our President, we know that the ages will welcome him. Their peace will be his lasting monument. Its inscription will be written in the hearts of millions yet unborn: "To Franklin Delano Roosevelt, first citizen of the world."

Humanity Is Bereaved

RABBI D. DE SOLA POOL

OUR heads are bowed with grief. The citizens of this stricken country are stunned by the tragedy that has overtaken us all. It is too soon, far too soon, for us to realize how grievous is our loss. We know that we have lost our leader. We know that it was our President, Franklin Delano Roosevelt, who with his brave spirit and encouraging smile, strengthened and upheld our spirits in the darkest days of the war. We know that it was he who unfailingly held before us the great vision of human brotherhood, justice and peace as the ends for which we are waging this war.

His marvelous human sympathies and love of his fellow men of every race and every creed gave him that human touch which has been so saving a blessing to us in our world of mechanized warfare, organized mass techniques and vast impersonal administrative operations. With Mr. Roosevelt, our Commander-in-Chief was not the main cog in an army machine, but a man, warmhearted, vivid, human. With him, the President of our country was less a symbol of executive functions than of the living human people of America to whom he spoke so simply, so naturally, so warmly in his fireside talks. He was one before whom "all Nature might stand up and say to all the world, this was a man."

But it is not only our own beloved land that is stricken. All of freedom loving humanity is bereaved. All the untold millions of the peoples of the United Nations are mourning the loss of this premier citizen of the world. To them he was the very symbol of America. To them Mr. Roosevelt was the embodiment of our American tradition of love of freedom. To the exploited, downtrodden, suffering and crushed masses of ravaged Europe and Asia, he was the symbol of hope of the better and happier day to come when oppression would be crushed and all mankind might know that liberty in which the United States of America was born and in which we live.

I speak as a citizen; but I speak also as a rabbi. I recall that infinite human sympathy which so characterized our President that to him there was truly no Jew or Gentile in his public and personal relations. I recall his burning indignation at the unspeakable atrocities committed by the Nazis against the helpless Jews of Europe. I recall his far-visioned understanding of the historic role of Palestine in the life of the Jewish people, and of the great part which destiny is setting upon Palestine for healing their wounds. This he understood and for this he consistently labored. To him it was unthinkable that righteousness and justice could be established on earth without righting the ancient wrongs of the historic people of the Holy Land, the birthplace of those ideals of humanity, righteousness and justice.

We thank God for a life such as his. Our country and the world have been richly blessed by his great heart and soul. We mourn that he has not been spared to see the fulfillment and the complete fruition of his life's work. But we are deeply grateful to God that like Moses he saw the approach of mankind's entry into the Promised Land.

God grant that we be worthy of his abiding faith in us, and that through our courage, steadfast high purpose and unwavering faith we may pay him the sole tribute for which he would have asked by carrying through to completion his great work for brotherhood, justice and peace on earth.

Architect of World Organization

TAMAR DE SOLA POOL

A WORLD stood still at his bier, galvanized into a unity that transcended all frontiers. The high born and the lowly—ministers, kings, generals, GI's, free men, slave laborers—all mourned as in personal bereavement.

April 12 will be remembered as the day when Franklin Delano Roosevelt left this mortal scene. And it will be remembered as the day when the prophetic spirit of a fearless fighter and builder passed into the souls of countless millions of his fellow beings the world over. It will be remembered, too, as the day when the world was united in reverence and sorrow and yearning for peace. The soul of Franklin Delano Roosevelt was translated into the soul of mankind on April 12.

It is Hadassah's hope that that day will be made forever memorable in the lives of men. We urge that April 12 be designated as Franklin Delano Roosevelt Day and be established as the first international, legally recognized and publicly observed day—a day dedicated to peace, justice and international goodwill. We call upon the United Nations to create that symbol of world unity and preserve the solidarity which electrified mankind, thus paying tribute to the valiant architect of world organization who served unto death that his fellow men might be free.

To Mrs. Roosevelt, Hadassah turns with hearts full of understanding. More than any one else, she expressed in her life the ideals common to her and her illustrious husband. She made herself part of our lives in an intimate way. When we say "our," we mean every member of the great American family—poor and rich, colored and white, Jewish and Christian. She has sought out the GI Joe's in waste islands and in the shadows where Purple Hearts beat. In the years of our war on depression, she made herself the great mother of youth and of workers wherever the dikes against want were being built. In this hour of greatest test and infinite pain, she stands a tower of strength, an exemplar to the world.

"How can we help you?" she asked. We answer that she go forward as in the past, to be a standard bearer of the highest principles of our democracy and the spirit of human equality; that she appraise not too modestly her place in American life. The story is not finished. For her and for us, it is only begun, born anew out of her grief and ours. We turn to Mrs. Roosevelt with trust and, indeed, with assurance that she will lead in our common determination to keep faith with the future, a future that demands so much from all of us for the fulfillment of our hopes.

In some ways President Roosevelt's task was done. He knew that victory was assured and that a new world order was marching on—Atlantic Charter and Four Freedoms, United Nations Declaration, International Food and Agricultural Commission, UNRRA, Bretton Woods Agreement and Dumbarton Oaks. The San Francisco parley is the fruit of his vision, the realization of his dreams, if it can be said of him that he dreamed dreams. He was, indeed, no mere dreamer; he was a doer. Between conception and action there was no dream area of indecision, confusion or frustration. He willed the things the whole world dreams of, and thereby he became the conscience of humanity and the spokesman of the common man. Yet he was not an austere Puritan or reformer. His strong will was tempered with humor, lightened with grace and charm. Thus, through patience and the gradualism of the statesman and practical idealist, he achieved the realization of a program of mounting scope in the affairs of men and nations.

The war he waged against the breadline and the economic challenge of the great depression became history in his own lifetime. The second chapter of his Presidency, his role in the extirpation of Hitlerism, is now coming to a close. The master builder held the line against Hitler's threatening victory—the repeal of neutrality, the creation of lend-lease, the triumphant battle of production, the crumbling of Festung Europa, the earth-shaking advances in the Far East.

But the Commander-in-Chief of the Army and the Navy never forgot that he was also the trustee of the peace. Throughout the years of war, he laid the foundations upon which will rise the structure of world order and more lasting peace. They are truly his offspring. Though he died in the pangs of its creation, he has left a monument to his glory. He lived to see the onrushing sweep of victory, but only the beginning of the peace. In humanity's Book of Life, peace must still be marked "unfinished business."

It is the sad fate of the Jewish people that its liberation remains in the area of the unfinished business of Roosevelt's life. He was a friend of the Jewish people, true and tried. There was no vestige of prejudice in him. He saw the immensity of Jewish woe, and he sought to stem that flood of suffering. With tremendous goodwill, he initiated the Evian Conference, helped establish the Intergovernmental Committee, called the Bermuda Conference, created the War Refugee Board—all palliatives, alas! that did not save from galloping destruction the doomed Jewish people of Europe.

Those failures could not but lead President Roosevelt to the acceptance of a complete Zionist program as the fundamental and primary remedy—without which all other efforts become hollow no matter how sincerely undertaken—for the solution of the Jewish problem.

The spirit of Franklin Delano Roosevelt calls us to the completion of the unfinished tasks for which he labored and in the service of which he died as a soldier in battle. President Truman, whose hands we uphold, has picked up the torch where it has fallen, and will carry it forward to that bright day so nobly conceived and bravely advanced by Franklin Delano Roosevelt.

F. D. R., Unforgettable Friend of Israel

BERNARD G. RICHARDS

AN ARISTOCRAT of the spirit by birth and tradition, a democrat by choice and conviction, a humanitarian by every instinct stemming from ancestry and enlightenment, Franklin Delano Roosevelt, our great peace-time and war-time President, whose sudden death has cast the whole civilized world into grief and mourning, through his life and work exemplified the finest traditions of Americanism. In the sense of true tolerance, love of fair play, complete devotion to the principle of the equality of all men and the recognition of merit and character regardless of any other considerations, this means that he was the staunch friend not only of the Jewish people but of all the races and nationalities of mankind, especially of those who suffered from tyranny, oppression, or injustices of any kind.

A lover of man and a natural born mixer, he mingled freely with all groups of society and if he was attracted to any particular persons or circles he was drawn to them by the admiration of traits of character, talent, ability and animating ideals which are the basis of all true friendship and cooperation. Antecedence, prestige, influence had little weight in the choice of his collaborators.

Franklin Roosevelt's association with outstanding citizens of Jewish identity goes back to the early days prior to World War I, when he served as Assistant Secretary of the Navy under Secretary

Josephus Daniels, one of the first of the non-Jewish American Zionists, under whose administration a United States war vessel was sent to render relief to the Jewish settlers in Palestine stranded by the outbreak of the war. Mr. Roosevelt undoubtedly then came into contact with the Hon. Louis D. Brandeis, Dr. Stephen S. Wise, who had such close association with President Woodrow Wilson, with the then Professor Felix Frankfurter, with the Hon. Julian W. Mack, and others of equal standing. It is clear that the Assistant Secretary of the Navy and future President, who was in Paris during the time of the Peace Conference, gained a comprehensive knowledge of the representations which were then made to the assembly of the nations, by the Jewish representatives in behalf of Palestine and the rights of the Jews in Eastern European countries.

President Roosevelt's utterances on the problems and objectives of the Jews sent to various bodies on different occasions and now scattered through various publications, would in themselves fill a book similar to the two books of his papers and addresses which were edited for publication by his close friend and adviser Judge Samuel I. Rosenman. For the purposes of this brief article, it is difficult to select the more notable of the late President's outstanding tributes to the genius of Israel and to Jewish services to humanity. Some of his expressions on Jewish aspirations in Palestine have lately been embodied in the volume "America and Palestine," edited by Reuben Fink. Most notable, however, among Mr. Roosevelt's utterances on the Jewish homeland is the half-forgotten letter in which he referred to the observations which he made in Paris in 1919. On October 31, 1930, F. D. R., then Governor of the State of New York, addressed a letter to the Zionist Organization of America, which was intended to be presented to the monster protest meeting at Madison Square Garden against the Simpson Report of the British Government. The letter was as follows:

"The events of the past two weeks have brought forcibly to my mind the days of the Peace Conference in Paris in the spring of 1919. As one who was in Paris that winter, and who talked with the national leaders there assembled, I can fully sympathize with the disappointment which is being expressed by the Jewish people at the new declaration which affects the administration of Palestine.

"It is my clear recollection that at the close of the war there was a general and wholehearted understanding, a moral agreement, from which no one dissented, that Palestine was to be set aside as a territory for the Jewish National Home. While it is true that in other countries in Europe and in Asia the theory of the protection of minorities was discussed and approved, nevertheless, in the discussion of the Palestine project the question of minorities did not enter in. It was assumed that it was the object of the powers to guarantee to the Jewish people all such rights and privileges as are inherent in the maintaining of a Jewish National home. It was, to the best of my recollection, not just a question of securing rights for the Jews as a minority group in Palestine.

"Eleven years ago this purpose of the powers assembled at the end of the war was universally acclaimed as one of the finest steps that had been taken in the history of mankind. It was acclaimed as an assurance to the Jewish people of a center where without hindrance or suppression or interference they might have an opportunity to recreate their great civilization."

As indicated before, Mr. Roosevelt's various statements on Palestine, his letters to the Zionist Organization, his meetings with Dr. Wise, Dr. Chaim Weizmann, Justice Brandeis and other leaders, his reception of various delegations and conversations with them constitute a chapter by themselves which one day will form part of the permanent record of historic achievements. If due to the stress and strain of unusual war conditions these consultations and representations did not eventuate in a triumphant conclusion, this does not mean that our cause did not remain close to the great heart of F. D. R. and that he did not intend later on to press the issue to a successful termination. Having been witnesses to his heroic struggle for the welfare of America and the freedom of all the oppressed in humanity, we cannot do otherwise than retain our faith and confidence in unswerving devotion to the causes to which he committed himself and for which he zealously labored all his life. Having had the privilege of personal contact with the radiant personality of F. D. R., the present writer heard from his own lips his warm assurance of deep interest in a reconstituted Jewish Palestine and these clear words left one with an abiding faith in the President's genuine devotion to our cause.

The advent of the Nazi menace in Germany and the ultimate threat which it offered to all free peoples and to civilization itself brought the colorful personality and powerful convictions of Mr. Roosevelt into bold relief, his words and actions becoming a bulwark of strength and resistance to the enemy for all the oppressed and persecuted peoples, and a symbol of freedom to all the world.

Beginning with June 10, 1934, when the attitude of the Roosevelt Administration toward the persecution of the Jews in Germany was voiced in a powerful protest by the late Senator Joseph T. Robinson from the floor of the Senate, continuing to July 30, 1938, when Congressman Emanuel Celler definitely assured a New York mass meeting of the deep feeling of resentment on the part of the President in the matter, including the address of the President at San Diego on October 2, 1935, and his letter of January 14, 1936, addressed to Dr. Alvin Johnson of the New School of Social Research, to various other occasions, F. D. R. voiced in no uncertain terms his feeling of outrage and horror at the persecutions and brutalities carried on by the new German regime.

Franklin Roosevelt's personal associations with outstanding personalities in the Jewish community began when he was Governor of the State of New York, through his close relations with his Lieutenant Governor, the Hon. Herbert H. Lehman; with a member of the New York State Assembly, Samuel I. Rosenman, who became counsel to the Governor; with the Hon. M. Maldwin Fertig, who later took the same position, and with many others who were among his co-workers. In the presidency there developed new relationships with Jewish citizens active in governmental affairs, and here there was again illustrated the recognition of merit as against any consideration of origin or social standing. Jews active in official life represent only the proportion, and even less than that, of Jewish citizenship to the rest of the population, but as the head of the Government symbolized a new era, a new attitude and a most enlightened outlook toward all questions of racial, religious and group differences, he naturally aroused the enmity of all those reactionary forces who stood for the very antithesis of this attitude, the bigots and the obscurantists and backlooking elements. To them the comparatively small number of Jews occupying positions in the government appeared like a tremendous host which was dominating the government and they of course made the most of the opportunity for extravagant misrepresentation, slander and attack. Hence we had the pasquils, pamphlets, leaflets and charts, issued and circulated by vermin, underground journalists and publishers, picturing a Jewish conspiracy to control the United States. With the triumph of enlightenment and true Americanism, however, precipitated and made certain by the events of the war, the "black hundreds" in America have disappeared from the scene and if some of them are still in hiding, their days are surely numbered. For the spirit of Franklin Delano Roosevelt and his immortal predecessor Woodrow Wilson will go marching on and their words, deeds, and examples will serve as the best proof and assurance against the return of that blindness and fanaticism which had almost brought destruction to the whole of our civilization.

He Loved Us All

RABBI HYMAN JUDAH SCHACHTEL

WE THE people of America and the people of the world have suffered an incredibly tragic loss in the passing of Franklin Delano Roosevelt. Not since the death of Abraham Lincoln has it seemed as if the very heart was torn out of our country as it now appears with the untimely death of President Roosevelt. We all leaned upon him—those who agreed and those who disagreed with him. And even those who disagreed with him often recognized that in his presence they were standing before true greatness. President Roosevelt was the very incarnation of America. In him there was the love of her 'rocks and rills,' her 'woods and templed hills.' He gloried in the beauty of America, her 'spacious skies and amber waves of grain,' her 'purple-mountained majesties above the fruited plain.' He loved the people of America, people from all countries of the world, people of every race, color and creed. He loved us all and we knew it. He loved the youth of America, our youth that is writing the chapter magnificent in heroism, faith and courage on the battlefields of this war; the chapter magnificent to which his own four sons are contributing their gallant share.

His gay confidence, his glorious smile, the noble wave of his hand, the friendly music of his voice made Americans feel that he was their own personal and beloved comrade. It was a joy to be living at a time when he was President. He was the first great leader to take the public into his confidence by means of the radio. There may be other Fireside Chats from other presidents in years to come, but all of us in the years ahead will be telling our children that there never was another man's voice that could come into your home through a mechanical instrument and grasp your hand and your heart in the clasp of friendship as did the voice of this greatest American of our age.

Our nation has never sustained a greater loss than in this untimely death of our Chief Executive. Franklin Delano Roosevelt, more than any of us, knew how to look unflinchingly into the eyes of trouble and danger and suffering. He knew this from personal experience. He was born into wealth and station. He was a handsome, tall, athletic young man. He rejoiced in the strength of his youth. Then at the age of 40 he was stricken with infantile paralysis. It is true that he was surrounded by affection and aided immeasurably by a brilliant and wonderful and thoughtful wife who helped to restore his fighting heart. Yet a lesser man would have succumbed entirely to the ravages of the disease which left his legs useless and withered. Never again could he run with the wind and walk like other men. Before him were years of leaning upon other's arms, of wearing steel braces, of relying upon other's physical support. Anyone looking into that sickroom 23 years ago, that is anyone who did not know the brave heart of Franklin Roosevelt, would have said that here was a life that was finished; here was a life that at best could not do much more than limp along stunned and crippled. Yes, anyone might say that who did not know Franklin Roosevelt; for there is greatness in the man, and power and faith and courage. There is glory in him, the glory of a radiant vision that saw life as the challenge to make this world a better place for his having been here. By one of those strange paradoxes of life, Franklin Delano Roosevelt was to do more for the spiritual welfare of humanity when he was afflicted physically than he ever did during the first 40 years in which he was strong and physically able. A new man and a new soul and a new heart were shaped in that crucible of pain 23 years ago. Out of it there emerged the man who, though he himself could not walk, was destined to carry upon his broad shoulders, like the legendary Atlas of old, the burdens and the problems and the hopes and the yearnings of the whole world. He became such a titanic spirit that none of us ever thought of him as a man physically afflicted. He had transcended all limitations of the body because his soul had wings; and with him as our guide we were rising to the heights of his own aspirations and dreams for a better world.

Can you ever forget those frightful, despondent days of 1933? Panic seized the hearts of all. Uncertainty was king. And then on the day of his inauguration there came the clear confident tones of the voice of him whom the nation had summoned in its darkest hour. In ringing tones of confidence he banished uncertainty and drove out panic and silenced confusion as he exclaimed, "We have nothing to fear but fear itself!" Here was a leader with a fighting heart—here was a man for the people. Here was a president of whom we could be proud. Here was a leader for whom we were waiting so anxiously and desperately. Yet in that very same year, across the seas, there had arisen a leader of Germany who was the enemy of both God and man. He was the personification of the Nihilism and bestiality which mankind must overcome before the curse of war can be banished forever from our world. Humanity arose against this evil and there were a number of leaders who won the devotion and loyalty of the people of the world, men like Winston Churchill and Joseph Stalin. But humanity took only one leader to its heart, to only one did it give its complete love and trust and faith, and that man was Franklin Delano Roosevelt. The very mention of his name in any country of the world is like the sound of the name DELIVERER, SAVIOR, FRIEND. The English love Churchill and the French, DeGaulle, and the Russians, Stalin, it is true; but there is a special shrine in the heart of humanity where the name of Franklin Delano Roosevelt is worshipped and adored. For he possessed the golden gift of making friends and being a friend. He himself personified 'the good neighbor' which he loved to say was the ideal that America cherished in her international relationships. Think of it! He was esteemed so highly as a friend that England's House of Commons adjourned for the day and Russia declared twenty-four hours of mourning upon news of his death—actions unprecedented in the history of the world. We are told that Prime Minister Churchill was with Lord Beaverbrook when the terrible news of President Roosevelt's death was brought to him. Immediately he exclaimed 'I must go to be at the funeral of my friend!' Only the strongest pleas from his associates prevented him from flying to America.

Ever since we have seen photographs of President Roosevelt since the Yalta Conference, we his countrymen have worried about his health. His face was thin. He seemed haggard and worn. We were shocked because we were so accustomed to seeing his radiantly healthy-looking handsome countenance. We had quite forgotten that for 12 years this man had borne our burdens, had often stood out alone against the evils of our generation. We thought and we hoped that he would live forever. The wish was father to the thought for all of us knew that we in the world had need of him. Thus even when we saw his haggard, thin face we still refused to believe that our great leader might die. His sudden death is like the frost that comes to an early spring. Although we know that the season goes on, yet our hearts ache tonight and we feel like children who yearn for the reassuring clasp of their father's hand, a father who has gone.

A great burden has fallen upon the shoulders of President Truman, a burden which every one of us must help to bear. The new President in his inspiring address to both houses of Congress has dedicated himself to carrying on both overseas and at home in the identical spirit of Mr. Roosevelt. The new President will not fail us and we shall not fail him.

Thank God that Franklin Delano Roosevelt lived long enough to see the certain signs of victory. This is the one light which illuminates our darkness. Thank God that he has already been able to shape the peace. The victory of Allied arms will be a monument to his memory. The establishment of a just and lasting peace will be the loftiest tribute that we shall pay to his glorious life. But above everything else, we and our children and children's children, the future generations of people all over the world, will cherish the memory of a man who though he walked with kings never lost the common touch; who defined for all mankind the nature of freedom and whose noble heart had room in it for a boundless love which embraced all of humanity. When the radiant soul of Franklin Delano Roosevelt, ten nights ago, appeared before the throne of God, I imagine that the Almighty Father did not address him by name; nor did the angels announce him by his earthly political attainments. Ah no, for God must have looked upon him with joy and the heavens resounded to the beauty of the divine voice as God said: "Welcome home, my son, my son. Welcome home. Blessed was your life upon earth. No child wept in loneliness whose cry did not reach your heart. No man was too lowly for your love to try and lift him up. You took my command that mankind shall live by justice and brotherhood and peace and made it the ideal of your life. As gold is refined in the fire so did I purify your spirit in the furnace of affliction. Never did you cry out against me but you came closer to me and ever called upon my Name. Many you led into the paths of righteousness. Welcome home my son, my son."

Franklin Delano Roosevelt in the words of his favorite song is now gone to his eternal "Home on the Range." Because of his life we are nearer to the fulfillment of that anguished yearning of all mankind for a world "where seldom is heard a discouraging word and the skies are not cloudy all day."

Roosevelt's Place in Jewish History

DAVID SCHWARTZ

THE rods of Moses and the rods of Pharaoh! You remember that story of Exodus. Terribly interesting imagery it is! The magicians of Pharaoh, the Hitler of his day, ruler over Egypt, the land of foremost ancient Kultur, which has decreed the extermination of the Jews, are manifesting their master race superiority over the Israelite leader, Moses. They toss out their rods and turn them into serpents and what not.

They finish their act, proudly, contemptuously looking at Moses, "Well, you can't do anything like this, even with the aid of your Jehovah and that New Deal you are offering the world!"

Then Moses, of whom it is written that he was marked apart for his humility, steps forth—and lo, the Eyptians are amazed when "the rods of Moses swallow the rods of Pharaoh."

This story comes to mind when we think back twelve years ago, when Adolph Hitler came forth "heiling" with his mighty rods, shouting of all he was going to do and, at the same time, the humble and friendly Franklin D. Roosevelt arose in the United States. Little did Adolph think then that the rods of Franklin would "swallow" those wonderful, masterful rods of his!

The rabbis in their eulogies of Franklin D. Roosevelt have compared him with Moses. Of course, they do not mean by that that Roosevelt spoke to God. And yet who knows? When one tries to live up to one's highest ideals, does not one then truly speak with God? When Moses brought down the tablets of the Ten Commandments, they were broken, and we are told that Roosevelt's Four Freedoms have been similarly broken.

One might go on making comparisons. Presumably, some of those rabbis, who in their eulogies of Roosevelt have compared him with Moses, were thinking at the time of the fact that Roosevelt, like Moses, was destined to see the Promised Land of victory only from a distance. Again, maybe they were thinking that, like Moses, Roosevelt suffered from a physical impediment, which he did not permit to interfere with the task to which Destiny had called him, but rather it mysteriously even aided him. Perhaps when they recalled F. D. R. standing and speaking to the world supported by his aide, they remembered it is written of Moses that he triumphed, too, only when the people held up his hands.

Moses, the great leader of the laboring people, of the common people, himself wasn't of the common people! He had been brought up at court as one of royalty, and Franklin Delano Roosevelt, who, it has been said, was the greatest labor leader America has ever produced, also was the son of wealth, member of a family which has been socially prominent from almost the first days of the country. . . .

Franklin D. Roosevelt came to the Presidency through the springboard of the governorship of New York, the state with the largest Jewish population. From the very beginning, Jews took to him, though in those beginning days, there was no thought that he would some day prove the great antidote to Hitlerism. Nazism was then no issue in America. Here and there, appeared reports in the papers of the doings of some fanatical anti-Semites in Germany, but no one in America foresaw what was to come to pass.

Roosevelt had first been associated with the candidacy of Al Smith. All over America, when Al ran for the Presidency, one heard as the theme song of the campaign, that tune:

"East Side, west side, all around the town."

It was something new in American history. The east side was where the Russian Jews and the Irish, where the immigrants and the poor people, lived.

And yet fundamentally it was not a new thing in American campaigns. Read the campaign songs of Andrew Jackson, of the log cabins of "Tippecanoe and Tyler too," and it will be seen that it is always the humble and the poor who are exalted.

Many Jews were active in the Smith campaign and when Smith receded from the picture, New York Jews gave strong support to Franklin Delano Roosevelt who had stepped into the position formerly occupied by Smith. It was a noteworthy fact that in Roosevelt's several races for the Presidency, north of the Bronx, his opponent would show the lead—but when he hit the Bronx and the other boroughs of New York City, the heavy vote of Greater New York with its large Jewish percentage would always bring Roosevelt into the lead.

Jews as a whole were strongly attracted to Roosevelt, and I see no reason why we should hide the fact. The German population in America has always boasted of its preponderant part in electing Lincoln in 1860. Of late, historians have been investigating and, alas, proving that their claims have been greatly exaggerated, but it is at least not wrong on the part of German-minded historians to try to prove the case, if it were so. So I say, it is not wrong for Jews to admit that they did like Roosevelt.

Roosevelt appointed a good many Jews to office, but the fact is, there was nothing wrong in this. The fact is, that Roosevelt did not appoint a disproportionate number of Jews to office considering the Jewish population of America.

The Jews did not ask any special favors of Roosevelt as Jews. The Nazis, of course, attacked him, charging him with being under Jewish domination and even insisted that Roosevelt was of Jewish descent. Of course, this was all nonsense. Mrs. Roosevelt once made a formal reply to the charge of his being of Jewish descent. She declared there was no Jewish blood on either side of her husband's family, but she went on to add, that the president had no prejudices, and in appointing anyone to office, he considered only one thing, his fitness for the office.

Roosevelt was distinctive from other American presidents in the remarkable knowledge he had of Jewish affairs. Jewish leaders who saw him spoke with amazement of his intimate knowledge of Jewish affairs. He knew even the details of the inner politics and rivalries of the several Jewish factions.

He wanted to make a significant and lasting contribution to straighten out the Jewish situation. Primarily, he looked for this achievement to be brought about by making the world order as a whole a more liberal, democratic order, but he showed a genuine sympathy with the Zionist movement, also, even though at times, Zionists felt he was not going fast enough in their direction.

Following the Yalta conferences, he tried to persuade the Arab leaders of the benefit Zionism would bring to them. He told Ibn-Saud that the Jews would be a greatly modernizing and transforming influence in the Near East. He admitted that he had not made headway in convincing Ibn-Saud, but already he was laying new plans to bring about the realization of a Jewish state.

The Miracle of F. D. R.

DAVID SCHWARTZ

WOODROW WILSON once spoke of the mystery of democracy unfolding itself in the coming of Abraham Lincoln to the presidency. Lincoln, at the time he was projected on the national scene was a man of relative obscurity. Seward, Chase, Banks, were all better known, and yet Lincoln was nominated and served during the great crisis of the Civil War, and somehow Lincoln gave the tragedy of the Civil War a beauty and a meaning that it would scarcely have had otherwise. It was as though Providence had reached out from the skies, looked down upon the America torn by fratricide and said, "Lo, I will give you a man who will speak for Me."

Abraham Lincoln was a miracle. His nomination was a miracle. His election was a miracle.

And we must have something of the same feeling as we contemplate Franklin D. Roosevelt. Here was a man who by all superficial tests, one might have expected, would long ago have passed out of the political picture.

At the age of forty, he was smitten with an affliction which would have downed an ordinary man and certainly put an end to his political hopes. And F. D. R. himself appeared reluctant to go on. We remember how Al Smith begged him to permit his name to be entered for the Governorship of New York to help Smith who was then running for the presidency. We remember how Smith got on the telephone and spoke with F. D. R. down in Warm

Springs, Ga., where Roosevelt was dreaming of walking again. "People don't know the pleasure of wiggling a foot," F. D. R. then said.

Reluctantly F. D. R. gave his consent to run for the New York governorship.

The Republicans had put up as their candidate for governor, a Jew, Albert Ottinger. A candidate other than F. D. R. might have been tempted to appeal to anti-Jewish prejudice, but F. D. R. was above all this. As a matter of fact, Roosevelt, as I recall it, got no little of his support from Jews. He was of course not the known figure he is today and his victory over Ottinger was by no great margin.

The subsequent steps in his career are fresh to all of us. The miracle of his career is that a man who has a great physical handicap which might have been expected to blast a political career, was the very one to break the powerful force of the two term tradition in American politics, and to win a third and a fourth term in the White House.

Miracles too, have, frequently, a rational explanation. How is this to be explained. In part, to be sure, it is to be explained by the fact that F. D. R. came to the fore at a time of crisis and Americans were averse, as the saying goes, to change horses in midstream.

But that is only a partial explanation. The other part of the explanation is to be found in the character and personality of F. D. R. I have now and then met people who are personally acquainted with F. D. R. and if you ask them for their personal reactions to the president, you will find that sooner or later they will speak of his "charm."

That is one of the facts of his personality. A Jew who was complaining to me about the fact that Roosevelt named a Jew as Secretary of the Treasury in his cabinet, I think, points to another quality. This Jew said that it was all right for the President to have named a Jew as a member of his cabinet, but he should not have named him to the Treasury portfolio, but, said this complaining

Jew, "Roosevelt is self-willed. If he decides on a thing you can't stop him."

I think this offers a second clue to the character of Roosevelt. His will is indomitable.

Now, both of these characteristics have some relationship to his physical handicap. The man who is beset by an affliction of this type, if he would survive, must acquire sunniness of disposition, and indomitable will, or he cannot go on.

To be sure F. D. R. was a genial, sunny and strong person before, but I think, the disease which his enemies have always made an issue against him, has rather helped to bring out the best in him. It has made him strong and yet humble, gracious and humorous as well as serious.

Moses, the Bible tells us, too, suffered from an impediment.

If I were a mystic, I could elaborate on this point. I would say that in the entire career of F. D. R. the hand of God is to be seen. I could point to the further "proof" of the miraculousness of his career in the fact that Roosevelt came to power in America at the same time that Hitler came to power in Germany. A Jewish proverb says that God always provides the remedy before the disease.

Anti-Semites have sometimes tried to charge that Roosevelt is of Jewish descent. Of course, there is nothing to this, but F. D. R. narrowly did escape having a Jewish name. It has always been a tradition in the Roosevelt family that the eldest child should be named Isaac, and when F. D. R. came along, he was scheduled for that billing, but his mother, a Delano, wanted him named after one of her family, so it was Franklin Delano instead of Isaac.

Yet, the name Isaac for F. D. R. strikes me as particularly felicitous. Isaac in Hebrew means to laugh.

F. D. R. could laugh and help the world to a little sunniness—when the whole face of the world is drab.

And there is something else unique about Isaac. Isaac has two sharply distinct periods in his life, according to the Bible. The second period, when he bore the name Israel, following his wrestling with the angels.

F. D. R. I think, began a second period of his life, when this son of wealth had to wrestle with affliction—and learned from it to wrestle with the affliction of a whole people—of a whole world.

And there is another similarity between F. D. R. and Isaac. Even the angels, the Bible said, could not beat Isaac.

Our Chief Has Fallen

RABBI MORRIS SILVERMAN

THIS is a day of national sorrow. Our country has lost its President. This is a day of international bereavement. The world has lost a leader, a great soul, a humanitarian. This is a day of mourning for Israel. Israel has lost a true friend.

At this moment we are reminded of the life of Moses. Moses stood upon Mt. Nebo looking out across the Jordan Valley into the Promised Land. He had spent forty of the best years of his life in an effort to bring the Israelites out of the bondage of Egypt into the land of freedom and opportunity. He had hoped to enter that land himself at the head of an advancing host. That was his goal. That was his purpose, his consuming desire. Yet, after all of his toil and effort, his disappointments and heartbreaks, he was not destined to set foot in the Land of Promise. He died in the desert just as he was about to realize the hope of his striving.

Thus was the life of Franklin Delano Roosevelt cut short just as he had reached Mt. Nebo, at the moment when the Promised Land appeared, when one phase of victory was in sight, the moment for which he had hoped and prayed and waited. And, like Moses, our Chief will not enter the Promised Land. He has fallen in battle.

For thirteen long and difficult years Franklin Delano Roosevelt was our leader. He led us from depression to recovery, from the humiliating defeat of Pearl Harbor to the victory which will come momentarily in Europe. He led us in war. Alas, he will not lead us from war to peace. A true lover of peace, a true lover of freedom, friend of all the oppressed, he would have given of his great statesmanship, of his political genius, of his vision, to the formulation of world peace. He would indeed have colored the peace table with his vivid personality. But Franklin Roosevelt will not be there.

Roosevelt has often been criticised. Most great men are criticized. That is as inescapable as fate itself. But although there may have been disagreement about many of his domestic policies, everyone agreed that in international diplomacy his leadership was peerless. In foreign affairs he was the equal of any of the Big Three.

It is tragic that our nation should have lost its leader at this critical time in world history. Well may we agree with Mrs. Roosevelt's first words: "I am more sorry for the world than for us." Our hearts go out in sympathy to the Roosevelt family, of course, for their personal loss is very great but our hearts grieve yet more for a world that is stricken of its leader. In the words of our Talmud, "Alas, our crown has fallen."

In Warm Springs, Georgia, today, there is an unfinished portrait. That portrait will never be completed because the man whose portrait it was to have been was suddenly called before the artist was through. There is other unfinished business. In Poland, in France, in Palestine, in other parts of the world there is left unfinished business because the master-mind has been summoned from his earthly tasks. However, while there is no one else who can take Roosevelt's place for the completion of his portrait, his unfinished business in Poland, in France, in Palestine must be completed by others who will be guided by the spirit of the genius who drew the plans, who perfected the machinery, who set the wheels in motion.

We Jews pray for the completion of Roosevelt's unfinished business. We pray that his promises for Zion will be fulfilled. His sustaining words pledging his assistance in the establishment of a

Jewish Commonwealth in Palestine buoyed up the drooping spirits of Jews all over the world. At a time when millions of Jews were being starved and slaughtered that pledge brought hope and strength and courage and comfort to our grief-stricken people. Roosevelt was the champion of all oppressed people. He was the champion of the Jewish people. We trusted him. We relied on him. We had faith that out of this war he would bring light and salvation to the scattered remnants of Israel. Franklin Roosevelt is no more. Well may we bow our heads in grief.

It is yet too soon to evaluate his place in history. Whether his name will be linked in history with the immortal Washington and Abraham Lincoln, time and historians will determine. It is enough for us now that he has bequeathed to us a heritage for all time, a deep concern for the forgotten man, a love for America, a love for democracy, a love for freedom. His example of victory over defeat will remain an American tradition.

In 1920 he was defeated for Senator of the State Legislature of New York. In 1924 he was defeated in his campaign for the vice presidency. But he never permitted his defeat to make him bitter. Defeat never broke him. Each stumbling block was an impetus to rise to new heights. The greatest test of his courage and his indomitable will came over twenty years ago when he was stricken with infantile paralysis. Such a catastrophe in the height of ones career would have crushed most people. Not Franklin Roosevelt. He considered it but another hurdle and he mastered that, too.

Five times he crossed the Atlantic to meet with Churchill and Stalin. On aeroplanes, over highways and rivers and oceans, risking his life and depleting his strength he traveled thousands of miles in the last years of his life. He was the Commander-in-Chief, it is true, but he fought his fight like a soldier in the ranks, risking life and limb in the performance of his duty. Woodrow Wilson was the greatest casualty of World War I. Franklin Roosevelt was the greatest casualty of World War II. Like Wilson he dreamed of a better world order. Like Wilson he never achieved it.

We shall remember Roosevelt for his utter fearlessness in times of great crisis. "We have nothing to fear but fear itself," he told us. He was great because of this fearlessness. Now, at this moment when all things have turned dark and discouraging because of his death, we must make his philosophy ours, "We have nothing to fear but fear itself." Like Roosevelt, we have faith in the American people. We have faith that right will be triumphant, that our armies even in the absence of their beloved Commander-in-Chief will carry on with yet greater vigor and consecration, that they will lead us to complete victory inspired by the spirit that will never die.

Like Palestine, America is a Land of Promise. When Moses died his mantle descended upon Joshua. The Children of Israel mourned their leader and rallied around Joshua. So, today, when the mantle has dropped from the head of our illustrious leader, there is another leader who will lift the mantle and make it his own. We must rally around our new President and give him fully of our faith, our trust, our cooperation. Because we loved Roosevelt and the things he stood for we must transfer our confidence, our loyalty, our devotion to the man whom he selected as his successor and who now takes his place.

It is one of the blessings of our democracy that we have orderly succession. In other countries at a time like this there might have been panic and confusion—perhaps revolution. We accept a new leader with the dignity that is befitting a land like ours. We are confident that he will call upon the best intellects to help him through his difficult task. It is to the glory of America that one who was a clerk, a timekeeper, a farmer, can be called to the highest office of the land.

Any day, any hour, the gates of victory in Europe will swing open. Our European port will be reached. Hearts will be lifted in praise and thanksgiving. We will rejoice that one phase of this bitter war is over. Yes, we will rejoice, but our Commander-in-Chief will not be here to rejoice with us.

We say with Walt Whitman when he addressed Abraham Lincoln:

"O Captain, my Captain, our fearful trip is done,
The ship has weathered every rack, the prize we sought is won,
The port is near, the bells I hear, the people all exulting,

My Captain does not answer, his lips are pale and still,
My Captain does not feel my arm, he has no pulse nor will.
The ship is anchored safe and sound, its voyage closed and done,
From fearful trip the victory ship comes in with object won;
Exult O shores, and ring O bells,
But I with mournful tread,
Walk the deck my Captain lies, fallen cold and dead.

My friends, soon there will be talk of a monument dedicated to Franklin Roosevelt. The best monument we can erect is to bring about the realization of his hopes and ideals. We must learn from the past. Let us not let him down as we did Woodrow Wilson. It becomes our sacred duty to make the post war world a world which Roosevelt envisioned—a world of brotherhood, a world of justice, a world of freedom, a world of Good Neighbors, a world of peace.

With this resolve in our hearts let us bow our heads in prayer:

O God, who art our strength and stay in time of trouble and sorrow, with hearts heavy laden we turn unto Thee for comfort and guidance in this fateful hour of our nation's history, as we mourn the passing of our President and the Commander-in-Chief of our Armed Forces. As we commend his spirit to Thy keeping we thank Thee for his life of consecrated service, for his fearless leadership, for his noble heart and his zealous devotion to the high principles of justice and freedom. Grant that his dauntless courage, his prophetic vision, his understanding sympathy for the oppressed everywhere arouse in us the determination to keep our country free from bigotry and strife, to knit us more closely one to the other in brotherhood and unity, to complete with unabated zeal the unfinished task to which he gave his life, to crush the forces of tyranny and to achieve a just and lasting peace for all men.

O Thou who guidest the destiny of men and nations, we implore Thy guidance upon our new president. Give him wisdom and courage and vision to bring to fruition the work so nobly begun.

Be with all those who walk in the valley of the shadow of death on land, on the sea and in the air. Bring them safely through this night of terror. Speed the day of victory when the dominion of arrogance will pass away and swords turned into ploughshares so that men shall not wage war any more. Then will the memory of our departed President be bound up in the bond of life and his memory be an everlasting blessing among us.

Memorial Sermon at Sampson Naval Base

CHAPLAIN JACOB K. SHANKMAN

"• • • A mourning nation is overwhelmed with a numb and unspeakable grief. We of the Navy, particularly—that navy which he served and loved—feel that we have sustained an irreparable loss. It would take the pen of a poet and the soul of a Psalmist to pour out the elegies of our weeping millions. In great sorrow, we cry: 'O weep for Adonais, for Adonais is dead.' David's dirge for his beloved friend Jonathan comes to mind—'Tell it not in Gath, publish it not in Ashkelon'; so too would we moan—'Tell it not in Berlin, publish it not in Tokyo, lest our agony and sorrow bring comfort to our foes!'

". . . This is not the place to assess the achievements of our great President. His place in history is secure. But there are some spiritual lessons which we can learn from his life upon which we can meditate with profit.

"F. D. R. was a glorious example of an affirmative approach to life. Through all his years, he gave a thrilling and convincing demonstration of a positive way of living. He was possessed of real spaciousness of soul; the dimensions of his personality were broad and limitless. He was warm and smiling and human. . . . He was an ardent sportsman, a fisherman, and a sailor. He loved stamps and he loved people. He said 'yes' to life. . . .

"In the fullness of that enthusiastic life, he was afflicted with a dread disease that might have laid him low. The grimness of paralysis consumed his strength. It might have soured and embittered him, stirred the fires of resentment within him, and frustrated and warped him. But with indomitable will and heroic spirit, he rose above the affliction and mastered his handicap. This was the sign of his healthy-mindedness, the symbol of his optimism, the token of his courage. He was the Happy Warrior incarnate.

'In the fell clutch of circumstance,
He did not wince nor cry aloud;
Under the bludgeonings of chance,
His head was bloody but unbowed.'

"Do you recall his greeting to Marjorie Lawrence? When that operatic star was similarly stricken and returned to the stage of the Metropolitan to begin her career anew, he saluted her with the words, 'Greetings from an old veteran to a raw recruit!' Even in adversity he could smile at life. Surrender and despair were not part of his make-up.

"How often have we chaplains listened to the complaints of men that they could not do their jobs in the Navy. They were troubled by sore backs, sore arms, sore feet, or mysterious headaches. Yet here was a man who could not walk, who had to wear pounds of steel to brace him, who had to rely on canes and wheelchairs, who had to lean on others so that he could stand, and yet not only was his spirit not frayed, but he assumed the responsibility of the greatest job in the world. This was the secret of his personality: he knew how to live triumphantly and affirmatively.

"In countless villages and hamlets of this land, in mansion and in hovel, thousands of parents could comfort their children, who were likewise afflicted, by pointing to his example. 'He did the impossible—he became President—you can do it, too.' What power in that life! What glory! What inspiration!

". . . And he lived that way to the end. He died in harness. On the very last day of his life, ashen and gray, with the crushing weight of a tragic war and the burdensome problems of fashioning a just peace on his mind, on that very last day—he was at his job. What a lesson to those in whose vocabulary the words 'goldbrick' and 'fluffing off' are so prominent!

"How touching were the words sent by the desolate wife and grief-stricken mother to her children embattled all over the world: 'Your father slept away this afternoon. He did his job to the very end.' This is a lesson to those of us who must sometimes send the tragic news to loved ones far away that a dear one has slipped away from the family circle. He did his job to the very end!

". . . F. D. R. was a man of flaming and radiant idealism. He fought evil and resisted tyranny. . . . They said that it was paradoxical that this scion of aristocratic traditions, this heir to magnificent ancestral estates, this man who was reared in fashionable Groton and lived on Harvard's exclusive Gold Coast—one who truly inherited the purple of class distinctions—should be conscious of the lot of the under-privileged and dispossessed and should be animated by the will to improve their welfare. . . . They said that he betrayed his class; they called him names; they threw brickbats at him; they accused him of hypocrisy and insincerity. . . . But like Moses who left the palace of the Pharaohs to liberate a nation of slaves, like Isaiah who was born to princely luxury but who cried out with impassioned fury for justice and righteousness, like Tolstoy who abandoned the wealth and privileges of nobility to dedicate himself to the weak, downtrodden and impoverished, so did F. D. R. devote himself to the welfare of his fellow men. The Century of the Common Man may not have been his phrase, but he labored with indefatigable zeal and with bold, pioneering vision to create a New Deal in which the wealth of the nation, its fabulous resources and untold riches, could be harnessed for the greatest good of the people. . . .

"He came into office at a time when the nation, in Ezekiel's words, was a valley of dry bones. Farms were idle and factories were shut; jobs were scarce and banks were failing; the country was hopeless and men were depressed. And he infused new courage and hope into America. He covered the dry bones with sinews and flesh, and he breathed the breath of a new spirit into them. He dispelled the gloom. 'There is nothing to fear but fear,' he cried, and his own faith, confidence, and determination rallied men to recovery and progress, to new growth and expansion, and to broader bases of economic justice. . . .

"Yet it was not only in domestic affairs that he showed his towering greatness; it was in the field of foreign relations that he revealed his practical wisdom. His heart was right, but so was his head! He saw clearly, if not more clearly than any other American of his generation, that there is a clean-cut and irreconcilable distinction between what has been termed 'We or They,' between reaction and progress, between barbarism and civilization, between death and life. He saw, as Lincoln saw, that the world could not be half slave and half free. . . . He knew that there could be no compact with appeasement, no refuge in isolationism. . . . He realized that America must not only be armed, but must become embattled. . . . His vigorous policies and his decisive actions turned seeming defeat into certain and inevitable victory. . . . He was not only the champion of freedom, but its savior. . . .

"Not that he glorified force! Two days after the treacherous attack on Pearl Harbor he said: 'The true goal we seek is far above the ugly field of battle. We Americans are not destroyers, we are builders. When we resort to force, as now we must, we are determined that this force shall be directed toward ultimate good as well as to immediate evil.' . . . He never lost sight of that ultimate good; it was ever his objective. The Four Freedoms were not honeyed phrases on his tongue. The Atlantic Charter was to him a manifesto of a new world, in which stronger nations would protect the weak, and in which the ties of justice would bind men together in enduring peace. This is why Polish peasants and Chinese coolies, Ukrainian farmers and workers in the French underground trusted in him and revered him. . . . He concluded one of his greatest speeches with the words, 'I still believe in ideals' . . . that belief persisted to his last breath . . . those words will reecho through eternity. . . .

"It is one of the tragedies of life that men do not always live to see the fruition of their dreams. With success almost in their grasp, they fail to reach it. Like Moses on Mt. Nebo, they can see the Promised Land, but they are denied entrance into it. So it seems to be with F. D. R. The victory which he planned is certain—but it is still to be won! The peace for which he laboured must yet be fashioned out of our common pain and our common sacrifice. . . . He has now joined the martyred Lincoln and the idealistic Wilson, in dying before the work was completed. . . .

"The pathos and sadness of Lincoln's words, spoken when he left his friends and neighbors at Springfield, come forcibly to mind: 'I now leave, not knowing whether ever I may return, with a task before me greater than that which rested upon Washington. Without the assistance of that Divine Being who ever attended him I cannot succeed. With that assistance, I cannot fail!' Roosevelt is gone, but the strength of his character, the greatness of his soul, the brilliance of his ideals—these remain to guide us and to challenge us. . . . It is a tribute to our democratic structure that with determined spirits and united will we shall follow the trails which he has blazed. . . .

"We bow our heads in grief this day. By the death of our Commander-in-Chief, the Navy has lost a devoted shipmate, the Nation has lost one of its immortal giants, and the world has lost one of its noblest sons. . . . Stevenson's Requiem might well be read for him.

'Under the wide and starry sky
Dig the grave and let me lie.
Glad did I live and gladly die.
And I laid me down with a will.

'This be the verse that you grave for me:
Here he lies where he longed to be,
Home is the sailor, home from the sea,
And the hunter home from the hill.'

"With bowed heads and humble hearts let us march to the victory whose foundations he laid and to the free world whose structure he envisioned."

Champion of Justice

RABBI HARRY J. STERN

"How doth the city sit solitary,
That was full of people!
How is she become as a widow!"

THE whole civilized world is this day overwhelmed by mourning and the world's life is indeed poorer in consequence of the sudden passing of Franklin Delano Roosevelt. Free men everywhere mourn his death as a personal loss—the departure of a dear member of the family. Everywhere lovers of freedom have come to look upon Mr. Roosevelt as their fatherly spokesman, interpreter and guide.

All here are acquainted with his biography. At a young age out of Harvard Law School he soon occupies a seat in the New York State Senate. In World War I, he occupies the important post of United States Undersecretary of the Navy. Then at the age of thirty-nine tragedy overtakes him; he is struck down by infantile paralysis. For some years he battles with this dreadful disease. Another less courageous would have given up the combat—not Franklin Roosevelt! He mastered his physical handicap and surprisingly to all who thought otherwise, he with great courage re-entered the arena of public life. Twice he was elected to be the chief-executive of the great State of New York and unlike any other in the history of the United States he was elected for four terms as President of the United States.

Though of patrician intellectual background, Franklin Roosevelt ever identified himself with the problems and struggles of the common people. He truly loved the common folk! He knew no arrogancy. The masses always recognize genuine humbleness and these have most generously responded to Franklin Roosevelt's love for them. His incomparable friendly smile won for him multitudes of devotees. He was indeed a lover and friend of man—of all races and creeds.

Franklin Roosevelt championed justice for the dispossessed and disinherited of America and of the world. As President, he created methods by which to help raise the standards of living thus enabling people to enjoy the benefits of freedom. As statesman he has ever rejected the idea that the world's problems are incurable. He who has held personal combat with physical disability, has kept to the conviction that every social disease can eventually be conquered. In his Second Inaugural Address, he insisted that he and his government dedicated themselves "to the fulfilment of the vision to speed the time when there would be for all the people that security and peace essential to the pursuit of happiness."

Yes, Franklin Roosevelt true to the teaching of the great prophets of Israel fought in the cause of social justice and righteousness. He, true to the prophetic dared to make often enemies of those in high places who negated the rights of the little fellow. He fought for the democratic way of life which spells appreciation for the sanctity of the life of every human being.

No one felt more deeply than this man the outrage of the Nazi assault upon humanity. No one gave nobler utterance to America's horror of the systematic slaughter of the Jewish population on the continent of Europe by the ghouls of Berlin and no one was more anxious for the speedy salvage of the doomed victims of Nazi barbarism.

President Roosevelt by word and deed has shown his great friendship for the Jewish people. But a few weeks ago he reaffirmed the pledge he made in his historic message of October 15th last, addressed to the Forty-Seventh Annual Convention of the Zionists of America, in which the chief executive promised "to effectuate the establishment of Palestine as a free democratic Jewish commonwealth." He said, "I made my position on Zionism clear in October. That position I have not changed and shall continue to seek to bring about its early realization."

All peoples great and small have come to see in Roosevelt the great architect of a new society whose personal friendship with the two other great architects, Stalin and Churchill, was the primary factor that made possible a turning point desired by all humanity from carnage to universal peace as shown by the principles laid down at the Yalta Conference and by the hopes we now have for the San Francisco Conference. Be sure it was the magnetic friendly personality of Franklin Roosevelt that to a large extent helped bring about the Grand Alliance which is now dealing out such deadly blows to the Axis partners and crushing the enemies of freedom.

But in the mysterious dispensation of God, Franklin Roosevelt alas, was not destined to taste the sweets of peace he had so zealously labored to establish. Like unto Moses, who had brought the children of Israel from the land of bondage within sight of the promised land so he brought the free peoples of the world within the reach of victory and peace—the great boon he sought to obtain.

Only in time of death we seem to be truly human. This explains why now Mr. Roosevelt's erstwhile opponents and bitter enemies heap this day encomiums upon his great life and achievements. Why have these failed to speak words of appreciation when this truly great man could have been sustained and encouraged in the challenging labours for an improved society?

This solemn hour calls for dedication. How shall we honour the memory of this humanitarian? We can best honour the memory of Franklin Roosevelt by pledging to follow his creed: that we resolve to labour unselfishly in the building of world security and world order based on justice and righteousness. We must begin this by our own personal living and striving in our daily dealings with fellow man.

Thank God that a man of such moral stature as Franklin Roosevelt was in the White House to give leadership when the world was attacked by a ruthless barbarism which threatened to overrun civilization and negate human progress. Franklin Roosevelt was not a ruler, not a dictator, not even a king. What was he then? A servant! We measure life truly by the number of people a man serves. Like unto Moses, the servant of God, Franklin Roosevelt served the God of all humanity and millions of people. He like unto Moses did not really die. In the language of the Rabbis this beloved servant too was but kissed by God and the Heavenly Father took him unto Himself.

We close our tribute with the lines of Robert Louis Stevenson found pinned to a book which President Roosevelt presented to a friend:

> Under the wide and starry sky,
> Dig the grave and let me lie.
> Glad did I live and gladly die,
> And I laid me down with a will.
>
> This be the verse you grave for me:
> "Here he lies where he longed to be:
> Home is the sailor, home from the sea,
> And the hunter home from the hill."

Vision Fulfilled

RABBI LEON STITSKIN

ON THE day when Abraham departed this world, all renowned men of the nations of the world stood in line and said: "Woe to the world that has lost its leader. Woe to our ship whose helmsman is gone!"

We have become a bereaved nation. Our country has sustained a grievous loss. We have lost our President of the United States, our peerless leader, our great humanitarian. But more than that we are overcome by a deep sense of personal loss. Some of us never realized that President Roosevelt was so close to us. The evaluation of his political, economic and diplomatic achievements we may leave to the historian. To us what meant most was the grandeur of his life; his smile, the heart throb of the masses that palpitated through every gesture, syllable, sentence of his outpourings. He was a friend of the people. He had faith in the innate goodness of man. He had faith in the infinite possibilities of mankind. He had warmth, fascination, crusading zeal.

There are three kinds of leader: One who emphasizes the civilization of the head and regards as the highest good the acquisition of knowledge. He, therefore, advances the cause of science and inventive genius. But often such civilizations become decadent and destroy themselves. They are like a tree with a beautiful foliage but too few roots.

Then again there are leaders who emphasize the civilization of the hand. They strive after mechanical perfection and technological skill. But because their emphasis is too materialistic and competitive, they often destroy themselves.

Finally there is a third kind of leader who believes in the civilization of the heart, whose chief concern is the civilizing of the hearts of man—cultivating his sense of compassion and enhancing his spiritual values.

Such a man, such a statesman was our great late President. He displayed this quality to the utmost. He possessed a rare gift of the human heart. He had the common touch. That's why we suddenly discover that the rock upon which we have leaned has suddenly toppled over and we are as it were dangling in mid-air.

Who can ever forget the year 1929. Hunger was rampant. Shivering men were standing in long bread lines. And then came a voice that resounded with increasing intensity and challenge: "The only thing we have to fear is fear itself."

What hope he inspired. What confidence he engendered, what visions he fulfilled! It was indeed difficult to realize that the man whose magnetic personality has captured the hearts of Americans was bound in iron braces and since 1921 moved about in a wheel chair. Stricken with the dread affliction of infantile paralysis his whole life was a struggle to ameliorate the woes and handicaps of all people. He was the very incarnation and symbol of democracy.

For humanity he gave his life. May his memory remain a beacon of light for all of good heart to follow. Let us resolve that the light which he ignited shall be fanned into a bright torch for all mankind.

Roosevelt—The True Man

RABBI MORRIS TELLER

LIKE a thunderbolt out of the clear blue came the stunning news on Thursday, April 12, that our President is dead. His death caused not only women and children to cry but men as well. Even after a few days have passed the sorrow has not passed. He was a world-figure and the world mourns his loss. As his illustrious widow so tersely phrased it, his demise was a greater loss to America and to humanity than to his own family. He consecrated his life to America and to humanity and he practically sacrificed his life for America and humanity. Beginning his presidency in the depth of the depression, he soon saw the menace for this country and for all humanity in the rise to power of the satanic maniac in Germany. A man of insight and foresight was needed, a man of keen mind, stout heart, vivid imagination, diplomatic skill, dynamic persuasiveness, unbounded enthusiasm, courageous self-reliance and faith in the ultimate triumph of righteousness. Providence blessed America and mankind with such a man. He was the right man. At the right time he was ready and was chosen to give his utmost and to do his best with his divinely endowed gifts and qualities for his country and his fellowmen.

Our beloved lamented Roosevelt was a unique person. Perfectly at ease with the most exalted of men, he sought to put at ease the common man, to provide him with the needs and comforts of decent living. He never forgot "the forgotten man" and he planned and struggled with those who differed with him so that the forgotten man shall not be long forgotten. His respect for human personality prompted him to exert all efforts to make it possible for people in modest station to maintain themselves with self-respect. His new deal program may have had some shortcomings, but his purpose in introducing it was to provide a square deal for all classes of Americans. He was willing to incur the ill-will of "economic royalty" because he believed fervently in economic democracy. He talked and wrote in modern terms and phraseology; but his thoughts and ideals were based on the ancient biblical teachings. In his addresses and fireside chats he constantly sought to impress his listeners not only with his fine voice and with his superb eloquence, but also and more so with his sincerity of purpose to bring about the realization of the hopes of the ancient prophets for an era of righteousness, justice, loving-kindness, and peace. Far from being a war-monger he loved peace. But he would not purchase peace at any price. It had to be peace with honor, peace with justice. To insure such a peace it was his aim to reorganize this one world at the cessation of war in such a manner as to bring about the messianic era in international affairs.

Physically handicapped since he had been stricken with disease while still young he was not embittered nor cynical. His spirit was too courageous, his outlook upon life too optimistic to allow himself to become self-pitying and morose. Because he was handicapped his heart beat in sympathy with the suffering of others. He realized all the more how handicapped individuals and handicapped groups must be helped. What he did to help and inspire others to help the victims of infantile paralysis is a glorious chapter in American philanthropic history.

To us, the Jewish people who are so handicapped and so restricted and who therefore need the aid of those who are in a position and able to help us, Roosevelt was a tower of strength. Among the charges levelled at him by his enemies was that he was too friendly to the Jews. Sometimes we Jews felt that he might have done even more than he did for our people in our frightful emergency. But we loved him so much and had so much faith in him that we justified what we thought was his occasional neglect of our plight by ascribing it to his heavy and numerous burdens or to his inability to do as much for us as we needed or as he wanted to do. We instinctively felt that he commiserated with us in our great tragedy, that he wanted to do his utmost for us and that he, himself afflicted, understood our afflictions and was eager to come to our assistance as a humanitarian as well as a friend of our people.

Now that he is no longer in the land of the living vexing thoughts come to our minds. What of the future? How will America fare without him whom we trusted and loved so much as to give him an unprecedented tenure of office? How will humanity manage without him? Was it not his holy purpose to help the entire human race by making all people good neighbors? Nor can we Jews be blamed for our grave concern about our people since our protector and our friend has gone to eternity. Such thoughts have been perplexing us since the ship of state has lost its faithful and capable captain to whom all the inmates of the ship were dear.

But if we are to compare our beloved leader to Moses, as he has been compared by many who have eulogized him since his death, because, like Moses he could only get a glimpse into the promised land of victory and abiding peace and was not permitted to enter and enjoy it, let us remember that following Moses, Joshua his disciple, became the leader and Joshua succeeded in conquering the promised land and in consummating the unfulfilled tasks and hopes of Moses.

Carlyle in his "Heroes and Hero-Worship" discusses the question of leadership. Does the great man make the generation great by his leadership or does the great generation develop the great man and leader? The past twelve years needed the type of leadership that Roosevelt could give us and did give us. He served diligently, most capably and for the most part very successfully. He was among our greatest presidents, and one of the world's greatest leaders who will be revered for ages to come.

Now what of our new President, Harry S. Truman? The events that will now take place on the American scene and in world affairs may require the talents, temperament and traits of President Truman and he will, with Divine aid and with the loyalty of America, help conquer and win the peace as Roosevelt by his wisdom and strategy and skill helped win the war.

As for us Jews, who because of our uncertain lot are, as a rule, inclined to ask whenever a change takes place, "will it be good or bad for Jews," we too need not fear the change. Yes, we deplore the demise of our friend, the humanitarian par excellence, but we look with hope to our new President that he will be a true man, true to his promises to carry on the general policies and principles of his illustrious predecessor, true to the platform of his party which he promised to follow and in which one of the outstanding planks is the establishment of the Jewish commonwealth of Palestine.

When he spoke in Chicago at a protest meeting against Nazi

atrocities a few years ago when he was U.S. Senator from Missouri, he hurled invectives against Nazism abroad and against any form of Nazism or Jew-hatred in our country. He was sitting next to some venerable orthodox Rabbis and the reverence and courtesies he showed them although they had addressed the large assembly in Hebrew and Yiddish was really heart-warming and reassuring. Recently he gave a St. Patrick's Day address in which he vehemently denounced the snakes and lizzards who would poison the "body-politic of America." He was too close to Roosevelt not to have been imbued with his spirit of humanitarianism which does not tolerate intolerance and does not sanction bigotry that would mask with an "America First" false face.

As Americans, as Jews, as members of the human race, we now pledge our loyalty to our new leader while we are grief-stricken at the loss of our lamented leader. We pray to our merciful Father to guard the soul of the deceased President and we beseech Him to guard the life and safeguard the health of our new captain. May he be granted the privilege of steering the ship of state safely out of the stormy seas of war into the calm currents of a peace that will be just and abiding.

PRAYER

O ETERNAL GOD, Almighty in Mercy!

Thou hast decreed that all who are born shall eventually die, the greatest as well as the most humble. The mortal remains must be returned to the earth, but the spirit remains immortal, the soul returns unto Thee, its divine source. Here on earth the departed ones continue in the respectful and revered remembrance of those to whom they were precious. Their good deeds and blessed life are an inspiration to those who survive them.

We pray unto Thee, O Merciful Father, to whom is entrusted the spirit of all flesh, spread Thy sheltering tabernacle over Franklin Delano Roosevelt who has gone from his glorious labor on earth to his eternal heavenly rest. May the illustrious record of his life and achievements inspire all who would honor his memory to consecrate their own lives with holy thoughts, lofty inspirations and noble deeds.

Bless Thou the soul of Franklin Delano Roosevelt with that ineffable good which Thou hast in store in Thy heavenly abode for those who have lived righteously on earth and who have been a blessing to their fellowmen. Amen

---

Designer of a New Age

RABBI JAMES A. WAX

TONIGHT, as we sit here with hearts that are heavy and spirits that are tried, there travels a train through the mountains of the Atlantic Coast, carrying the shell which sheltered the greatest spirit of the 20th century; a spirit that is comparable to the greatest teachers of humanity, to the greatest moral mentors of mankind —a name that will be inscribed in the academy of the great, that will be recorded in the books which posterity will read and that will inspire generations yet unborn.

It is so easy for a people shocked by grief for a great man to forget the source of his greatness—for a people to forget the fountain of his inspiration. The man who yesterday drew his last breath and bowed to the inevitable without pain and without suffering is mourned by all liberty-loving men, and even those who could not always agree with the ideals which he espoused, with the noble purposes which he pursued, are grief-stricken and today articulate their admiration and their affection.

What made this happy warrior who only yesterday was called "that man in the White House," today the most priceless memory of our century? Franklin Delano Roosevelt was good because he was godly; he was fine because he was faithful; he was humanitarian because he was human. He who possessed so much power; he in whose hands lay the destiny not only of his countrymen but even of the world felt that his power was not supreme, that all things were in the hands of God, and that He was the fountain of life and the ruler of men. Few in high places have ever relied upon God with such constancy and with such fervor. God to him was not an abstraction but a force which sustained him from affliction to life, from defeat to victory, from annihilation to fulfillment. Because he was acquainted with suffering, because he was acquainted with the strength that comes from God, he triumphed over sickness and made it his servant.

Allegiance to altruism, coupled with pursuit of high purpose, made him a lovable person, a name which men respected, a personality which men prized. The greatness of Franklin Roosevelt lies in his own humanness. He was the child of wealth but one to whom material bounty meant little. Faithful to mankind, he forsook the caste into which providence placed him. To him all men were alike. To him all men shared the same basic needs and ultimately aspired to the same common goals. Men laughed and he laughed with them. He was a man among men. Yes, he had some of the weaknesses and frailties from which all of us suffer, but he had more than that, a spirit of humanity, for he himself was a human being. His godliness, his faithfulness, his humanity have made him immortal. The spirit which animated the lives of Jeremiah, Isaiah and Jesus permeated the life of Franklin Delano Roosevelt. His idealism and devotion to high cause placed him in the succession of Washington and Lincoln. What Washington was to his generation, what Lincoln was to his century, Franklin Delano Roosevelt is to the world today. Architect of utopia, builder of a better world, designer of a new age, Franklin Roosevelt was a symbol of hope. His name is linked with freedom, with liberty, with justice, with peace.

We thank God that we benefitted by his daring and dauntless

leadership, by his burning conviction and his heroic courage—that we shared his companionship, though we knew him not by proximity. In our gratitude for his life and his labors, for his ideals and his inspiration, let us resolve that upon the foundation which he laid, we will build the household of humanity for which he hoped, and in the fullness of faith, we proclaim, as have our fathers in every generation at a moment like this, "The Lord giveth, the Lord taketh away. Praised be the name of the Lord."

The Victorious Leader

RABBI STEPHEN S. WISE

OUR country has not been as bereft as it is today since that day of April, 1865, when another emancipator passed out of the Presidency into history. We will not be bereft again in our generation—indeed, it may not be for generations!—as we are this day, for there is no Franklin Delano Roosevelt left to die. Living, he had joined the ranks of the immortals; his death merely reveals anew his immortal stature, moral and spiritual.

How unvisioning are they who have said of him, "How tragic that he died before victory!" The truth is that President Roosevelt not only did not die on the eve of victory, but his Presidency marked a series of American victories, of which the inevitable victories at Berlin and Tokyo are to be only the last.

On the day of his first inauguration, March 4, 1933, he moved the American people to adopt a new principle for democracy—namely, that Americans, individuals and families alike, were not to be permitted by starving to bear the entire burden of the economic disaster which unwise social planning had brought to many millions of American homes. He acted with courage, with wisdom, with initiative in averting what, under a leader of lesser capacity and quality, might have proved an overwhelming disaster to many millions of Americans. He laid down the incontrovertible principle that "the test of our progress is not whether we add more to the abundance of those who have much; it is whether we provide enough for those who have little." And this principle he uttered with the deep and heartening faith that "this great nation will endure as it has endured, will revive, and will prosper." To which utterance he added the winged word which our nation will never permit itself to forget: "The only thing we have to fear is fear itself." At no time throughout his more than three Presidential terms did Roosevelt yield to fear. Economic disaster, partisan foes, Nazi threats, military peril alike beat in vain upon the citadel of his own unconquerable faith.

In order to measure the stature of Roosevelt, one need but consider what might have been if Roosevelt had not been at the helm to guide, to lead, to inspire. In the crisis beginning March 1933, he saved the nation and averted what might have become civil strife between the "haves" and the "have-nots" by laying down the law that a nation owes a duty to its dispossessed sons and daughters, that it belongs to them, that it must suffer with them and save them in their hour of avertible trouble and preventable need.

He did not die on the eve of victory. He died long after, in the name and in the spirit and mood of his country, he had won the war against economic depression, which is only another name for social bankruptcy, for that disaster which comes from the failure to use with wisdom the strength of a country in order to bring some measure of substance and hope to all its people.

The second victory which he achieved came not when he led us into war—for he did not lead us into war. At one and the same time he kept us out of war, while prophetically utilizing the vast resources of his country in order to avert the crushing of human freedom which the British Commonwealth had for a time been left alone to safeguard and to defend. Throughout this period of his leadership, on the one hand he dared to appeal to the conscience of mankind to "quarantine" the aggressor nations, while at the same time, steadily, patiently, and vigorously, he prepared the mind and mood of the nation for the struggle which he rightly forefelt could not be avoided. They who today are among the loudest acclaiming him victor over death and strife, were among those who basely used their leadership in the political life and newspapers of our country in order to keep us out of a struggle from which we could not keep out without yielding almost immediately the freedom of the European democracies and ultimately our own freedom. History will not forget the wisdom, the foresight—indeed, the prescience—of this man who from the day of the rise of Fascism saw more clearly than any other American leader that American democracy must in one way or another resist the aggressions of Fascism, or it would in the end yield its own freedom, only to be broken and trampled upon by the ruthless power of aggressor Fascist nations.

Roosevelt died not on the eve of victory, for he beheld the day of victory. He had done all that a great leader could do to ensure that victory. And before his eyes were closed, he beheld the American and British armies in the West and the Soviet armies in the East approaching one another. And his passing from earth virtually coincided with the day of the merging of these mighty armies into an irresistible force, a force not only destined to crush the crumbling German armies, but proclaiming to the world that humanity is done forever with tyranny and Fascism, that the day of freedom has dawned for all men. The soul of Roosevelt was not liberated from its earthly form until after he had told his countrymen in his last inaugural address: "It is America's purpose that we shall not fail . . . the purpose of the American people in their righteous might to win through to absolute victory . . . We will not only defend ourselves to the uttermost, but will make it certain that this form of treachery shall never again endanger us."

President Roosevelt did not die before the dawn of victory. He had not failed to prepare for the peace of the common man. Wisely and nobly he had proclaimed the Four Freedoms, which meant not only peace for the immediate future but it may be, as he willed it, a peace abiding throughout future centuries. This man, this simple democrat, knew how to work with men as different as Prime Minister Churchill and Marshal Stalin. His friendliness, his simplicity, his human qualities, gave him the power of cooperating with the leaders and with the peoples of other lands, who trusted him as they trusted Wilson before the First World War was won, as all the world came to trust Lincoln.

He died not before victory. For the San Francisco Conference, which is to establish an International Security Organization, is his monument. The cornerstone is to be laid in his own country; but the over-arching structure is to embrace the whole world. Let not partisanship lay disfiguring and vandal hands upon the San Francisco Conference which is the testament of Roosevelt to mankind. The San Francisco Conference is to be a reiteration of Roosevelt's insistence that the world shall not remain unorganized; that it be organized into warlessness; that nothing shall be permitted to stand in the way of a warless world and of world security; that warless world which will mean the end of the aggressor nations; that warless world which is not only to prevent German aggression, but aggression by any nation, by any people; that warless world in which we have come to see that the democracies alone can keep and safeguard and defend the peace.

Happily Roosevelt was our leader during the years throughout which we faced the problem, "Shall America permit England and freedom to go down to disaster? And what will be our own fate if that comes to pass?" Against groups of bitter and rancorous enemies, in addition to multitudinous partisan foes, he took his stand long before we were bombed into war at Pearl Harbor, and prepared the nation for the mighty crisis, which is about to end in triumph because, with the help of well-chosen military and naval commanders, he led us from victory to victory. He died not before the war is ended, for the European war is ended. The armies of the United Nations, East and West, are at the gates of Berlin, and the Nazi gangsters are gathered at the gates of hell!

Roosevelt's glory of leadership sounds the triumph of this immortal hour.

I do not wish now to dwell upon Roosevelt as a friend of the Jewish people, though I can hardly forget what he wrote to the American Jewish Congress on February 9, 1944, when he declared in words that will live:

> The attempt of Adolf Hitler and the Nazi party to rule Germany, to rule Europe and then to rule the Western World was based on two brutal devices: organized terror and organized anti-Semitism. Terror put Hitler in power and kept him there. Anti-Semitism was the terror's counterpart in propaganda. In the name of the self-styled master race, Hitler robbed, first his own people, then the peoples of Europe, and tomorrow, by his own boast, would have robbed the world. In the past months we have defeated Hitler's plans for world conquest. We have recovered some of his stolen gains, and in the months to come we shall recover more, and we shall meet and defeat Hitler on his own ground.

Sorrowfully, withal gratefully, I recall his word to me as President of the American Jewish Congress, when, addressing a solemn message to the meeting in Madison Square Garden on July 17, 1942, he declared:

> Americans who love justice and hate oppression will hail the solemn commemoration in Madison Square Garden as an expression of the determination of the Jewish people to make every sacrifice for victory over the Axis powers. Citizens, regardless of religious allegiance, will share in the sorrow of our Jewish fellow citizens over the savagery of the Nazis against their helpless victims. The Nazis will not succeed in exterminating their victims any more than they will succeed in enslaving mankind. The American people not only sympathize with all victims of Nazi crimes but will hold the

perpetrators of these crimes to strict accountability in a day of reckoning which will surely come. I express the confident hope that the Atlantic Charter and the just world order to be made possible by the triumph of the United Nations will bring the Jews and oppressed people in all lands the four freedoms which Christian and Jewish teachings have largely inspired.

Other occasions will arise, and I will tell the story of the concern he felt for the misery of the Jewish people in Europe, of his compassion with their suffering, of his resolute will if possible to bring them healing and redress.

President Roosevelt was a warm and genuine supporter of the Zionist cause. Again and again he did not hesitate so to proclaim himself. Who is base enough to maintain that he did this in the hope of partisan advantage? When last we were together, on March 15, he told me at great length the story of his purpose to make the Near East leaders understand the miracle which the Jewish rebuilders had wrought in Palestine, and that nothing but good would come of the continuance and the emulation in neighboring lands of their toil and sacrifice for a great ideal. If he felt a sense of failure in respect to his recent mission in the Near East, as far as our aims are concerned, it was only because he may have attached too much importance to some super-subtle counselors in the State Department of our own country and of the Colonial Office in England, who exaggerated the importance of the most conspicuous and picturesque of the ruling figures in the Near East. And while there was a momentary sense of failure, at the same time he had already planned for another and, as he believed, more effective method of approach to the problem, the solution of which was bound to be the establishment of a free and democratic Jewish Commonwealth in Palestine.

It is not my wish to emphasize Roosevelt particularly as a friend of the Jewish people. He was a friend of man and men. No man was more genuinely free from religious prejudice and racial bigotry. He faced men as men, a man as a man. He hardly knew or seemed to remember in his daily contacts, whether a man belonged to one or another race or faith. This I know, that though he was—it may indeed be because he was—firm and unshakeable in his own faith as a Christian, he knew and revered Jewish values and held Jews as he held all men, in the reverence which men as men deserve.

It was the genius of Franklin Delano Roosevelt to bring back to the thought of the American people "the forgotten man." There was no "forgotten man" in his life. Though himself a child of fortune, he never forgot the children of adversity. I remember as early as March, 1933, how his soul rebelled at the Nazi doctrine of "superior" or "inferior" races! More than any American since Lincoln, he brought the common man back to the remembrance and the conscience of all Americans.

As one who counts it among the precious privileges of a lifetime to have been a friend of the President, I say about this beloved and immortal figure, as my fathers in their ancient and beauteous tongue were wont to say of the man who had passed: "*Adonoy natan, v'Adonoy lakach: y'hi Shem Adonoy m'vorach.*" God gave Franklin Delano Roosevelt to America; God has chosen to take his mortal presence out of the life of his country and of mankind.

As freedom this day sings the requiem of Roosevelt, may God touch all the nation with healing and benediction in his memory. He did his work, he lived his life, he served his country, he helped to liberate all mankind. *Zecher Zaddik l'vrachah.* The memory of this righteous man be blessed, and remain a blessing to us, his countrymen, who loved and followed him living, who will execute his purposes and translate his last will and testament into a world organized for peace with justice, forever to be bound up with the immortal name of Franklin Delano Roosevelt.

We Will Carry On

MRS. STEPHEN S. WISE

ALL the world has lost a friend in the passing of President Roosevelt, and we of the Women's Division send our deepest, truest sympathy to Mrs. Roosevelt, who ceases nominally to be the First Lady of the land, but who, because of her dedication to the causes of the people and her gallant bearing in this hour, will long remain the First Lady in the hearts of her countrymen, including the Women's Division of the American Jewish Congress to whom she spoke with such warmth and wisdom at our last Annual Luncheon.

We can hardly think of America, and indeed of the world, without our great President and all the magnificent activity he brought to bear against the destructive opposition that so often meets great leadership. I quote the words of Dr. Wise in his memorial tribute, "President Roosevelt was a friend of Jews only in the sense that he was a friend to all men, all peoples, all races, all faiths." He was the incarnation of the spirit of tolerance, and more than tolerance, the understanding and sympathetic relationship which is that of the "good neighbor" to other peoples, though they dwell afar. We of the Women's Division are proud to think of the messages, which from time to time he sent to the Congress, including his famous utterance on anti-Semitism. "Whoever condones or participates in anti-Semitism plays Hitler's game. There is no place in the lives or thoughts of true Americans for anti-Semitism."

We have suffered an irreparable loss which we shall not cease to mourn, but we shall carry on in his spirit—the democratic ideals which made and will keep our country great. In the brave words of Mrs. Roosevelt to her children, "He did his job to the end as he would want you to."

We women will carry on our job to the end.

MEMORIAL PRAYERS AND POEMS

Franklin Delano Roosevelt, 1882–1945

MOSES BENMOSCHE

DO NOT speak of "great mind, great heart," as though
They alone were attributes to bow to—
As separate virtues to mark the man.
These loose terms show our paucity of words—
How inadequate our powers of speech.
Anemic the written word, meaningless
The jumbled sounds that fall on mortal ears.
No language has the soul of man, except
Those soundless tones, eternal in the heavens,
With which to gauge the soul of any man,
Much less our Leader's soul, our President,
Our trusted, trusting friend and servant, too.
For, finite man has only finite stuff
That reaches only finite depths in man.
But, that vaster world beyond the finite
Holds that tenuous thread of spiritual man,
Which, like a beam of light, now bright, now dull,
Lights the path of his faltering physical self.
Our mortal eyes may not behold the light
That burned within the soul of this Roosevelt.
But by all his works shall we discern it;
Perhaps not now but in what the future holds;
Perhaps not in our own generation,
But in all the generations to come.
Time has marked our President for its own.
His spiritual power reaches far
Beyond the limits of our visible skies,—
In tune with that great cosmic symphony
Of peace, of freedom, of hope, and of love,
Into the souls of people here at home
And wherever there are homes, forever.

Franklin Delano Roosevelt

MARIE CHERRY EDELSON

DEAR God, Why did You take him—
Thy ways, we cannot know;
We only know we needed him—
Why did he have to go.

He was our inspiration—
He was our guiding light;
His winning smile lent courage—
It made the sky more bright.

So fine and unassuming,
To all he was a friend;
His instantaneous passing,
We cannot comprehend.

In this our darkest hour,
All hearts are fraught with care;
A nation now is mourning—
With heads bowed down in prayer.

His "Fireside Chats" so intimate,
Stirred every human soul;
His plea for worldly brotherhood,
Was heard from pole to pole.

A great humanitarian—
Noble were his deeds;
A champion of all peoples,
Whate'er their faith or creeds.

If last words he were given,
He'd say: Friends, do not mourn;
Hold firmly the Four Freedoms—
Americans, carry on.

His name will live in history—
Unto the end of time;
So great—and yet so humble—
Indeed he was sublime.

We never can forget him—
Though from us he did part;
His memory we hold sacred—
He lives in every heart.

Dear Lord, Thou art the Master—
Our fate is in Thy hand;
Forgive me that I question;
'Tis hard to understand.

Why did'st Thou take him from our midst—
To lie beneath the sod;
His noble task unfinished—
Pray tell me why—oh, God.

Each pulse is beating faster—
His death is keenly felt;
We place within Thy keeping,
Our beloved Roosevelt.

Prayer

RABBI JULIAN B. FEIBELMAN

THY ways, O Lord, are past our finding out. Thy words and Thy thoughts exceed our finite powers. In abject humility we bow in submission before Thine inexorable will which removed from us our leader, our champion, our friend, Franklin Delano Roosevelt, President of the United States of America.

As Thou hast given, so hast Thou taken. Now we rise to praise Thee for so beneficent a gift. Our fathers have taught us to say, Blessed be the Righteous Judge. We knew not how much Thou gavest, until Thou hast taken away. As the gift of his life's blessing was shared by our Nation, indeed by all peoples, so is grief and sorrow meted out unto all the children of men. As Thou hast called him, Thy son, unto Thyself, so Thou callest all men to acknowledge Thy law. As within the houses of the great, so is it in the hut of the simple. Man is of few years, and destined from the cradle to begin his pilgrimage unto the grave.

Our hearts fill with pride, even as our spirits droop in sorrow, that Thou vouchsafed to him the glorious gift of leadership until he could see the fruition of consecrated effort, and the vindication of his great courage and spiritual convictions. Thou gavest him to see the Promised Land. It is now our task to walk into it alone, bereft of his leadership, and to strive to build the new world which he foresaw and planned, and to erect the new Freedoms for all mankind, for which he diligently labored.

All men are to call Thee Father, Thou hast made them all. So are all Thy children to love their fellowmen as themselves, for Thou art the Lord. Sadly, we confess, and in the midst of great strife, that we have transgressed Thy Law, and resorted to power. Yet, through this pall of hatred and beyond the pale of warfare, we were given a Charter, a breath of new freedoms for men who have never sensed liberties, and to those who have long since forsworn their dreams, to rear their children in the full light of Thy Sun. Franklin Delano Roosevelt was this friend of man. He was possessed of both vision and courage, and although born in high place, he gave his great power and rare voice and keen sight into the lives of the lowly. We are the more sorrowfully proud of the generation, nay the great historic epoch, we shared with him. In Thy light, he saw light, and sought to affirm that the basis of our civilization, and the inspiration of all human touch, was Thy Law, Thy teachings, Thy way.

As Thou wast his light, O Lord, be Thou now his Salvation. And give us a portion of Thy Spirit that we go forward into the new lands, seeking our brethren, loving our fellowmen, and revering Thy name through service to them. Enable us to possess the pride of his memory as a consecration, dedicated to the gigantic and manifold tasks, unfinished and incomplete, which he bequeaths to us. As Thou didst establish his work for good, so help us in our braver, truer and nobler efforts. Preserve our Nation, uphold its new leader, lead us to complete victory, that Thy Spirit may prevail over strength and power and might, so that Thy children, everywhere, may know Thee, and walk humbly with Thee, doing justly, loving mercy, and sharing the privilege of praising Thy name, forever and ever. Amen

---

Prayer

CHAPLAIN JESSE JOEL FINKLE

ETERNAL Master of the Universe and Father of all mankind, with hearts full of grief, we pause to pay tribute to our beloved Commander-in-Chief who has gone unto his eternal reward.

We especially mourn his passing at a time when the world crisis is rapidly approaching its climax, and the victory for which he so zealously labored is assured. His inspiring leadership, idealism and grasp of the problems of international relations will be sorely missed not only by Americans, but by all liberty-loving peoples for whom he sacrificed so much.

Merciful Father, grant comfort and consolation to his bereaved ones in this hour of sorrow and strengthen them as they strive to carry on in the spirit of their loved one.

Help us in the armed forces together with our fellow-citizens back home, to pay tribute to his memory not only with words of prayer and praise, but even more with such deeds as will speedily bring to reality his high hopes for the establishment of world peace and brotherhood.

Strengthen the hands and heart of his successor as he now shoulders the tremendous burdens of national leadership in this crucial hour. We pledge our loyalty to him and fervently resolve to work with him and his counsellors in keeping our blessed country a beacon light of justice, truth and brotherhood unto all the nations of the world. So may the memory of Franklin Delano Roosevelt ever be for a blessing and speed the day when at last "nation shall not lift up sword against nation, neither shall man learn war anymore!"

He Did His Best

RUTH SUSAN FISCH (AGE 10) *

HE DIED, his soul left the earth.
But his spirit did not go.
It lingers on in memory
Of a great president we know.

* Member of Congregation.

God took him when we needed him.
Needed him so bad.
And we mourned deeply for his loss,
And it was oh, so sad.

He died for his country
And for his country men.
He died so that the whole world
Could be free again.

The work he started
He never lived to see.
But now it is finished
And now all men are free.

God took him away.
To the so much needed rest.
He gave his life for his country.
He did his very best.

He died, his soul left the earth.
But his spirit did not go.
It lingers on in memory
Of a great president we know.

Memorial Prayer

RABBI LEO M. FRANKLIN

O UNIVERSAL God, in Whose hands are the destinies of men and nations, we come into Thy presence in this hour of our nation's bereavement—indeed, perhaps the most tragic hour in the history of a great people—our hearts burdened with the weight of our sorrow and yet with a prayer of thanksgiving on our lips. Though we cannot, as yet, grasp the enormity of the loss that has come upon our nation and upon the world, and though we know that a prince and a great man has fallen at the very moment when most we needed his guidance and his example of courage, of fidelity and of selfless devotion to a great cause, we are grateful that we have been privileged, through these years of bitter conflict, to have him as our heroic leader and our constant inspiration. A man of his type cannot die. Only they are dead who are forgotten. And he shall never be forgotten.

Wherever men love liberty; wherever men fight for freedom; wherever men exalt right above might; wherever men long for justice and brotherhood; wherever men hope for a world at peace; and where all who are clean of hand and pure of heart hope to dwell in security, each under his own vine and fig tree, the memory of Franklin Delano Roosevelt shall inspire them, strengthen them and guide them.

For his example of indomitable valor in overcoming physical infirmity and in facing handicaps before which most men would have quailed and many succumbed, we are grateful for his defense of the weak, the poor and the disadvantaged. For his desire and his work to give every man, irrespective of creed or color or national origin, his chance to live a full, free and happy life, we are deeply grateful. Though like Moses of old, he was not privileged to enter his Promised Land of universal peace, but only to see it from afar, it was he who led us to its very border, and it is he whose spirit shall go before us in our attempt to build a better and a saner world.

For the manhood, the valor, the physical and moral heroism of this man, we thank Thee. May his mantle descend upon his successor in office, to whom, O God, give something of his spirit, something of his courage, something of his faith, something of his practical idealism, and let us all, even amid our grief, turn in confidence and unshaken faith to Thee, O God, who hast given and hast taken away and Whose name shall be forever blessed. Amen.

Memorial Prayer

CHAPLAIN ROLAND B. GITTELSOHN

OUR God and God of our fathers, we turn to Thee in moments of gladness and sorrow alike. Today our hearts are heavy with grief as we mourn the loss of our Commander-in-Chief and President, Franklin Delano Roosevelt. In the words of our fathers we say, "The Lord hath Given; the Lord hath taken away. Blessed be the name of the Lord."

We cannot mourn the death of a great man, O God, without thanking Thee first for his birth. Our teachers said of old that a people depends upon its leaders even as a bird in flight rests upon its wings. We are exceedingly grateful that in the many crises which have faced our generation Thou didst give us this man, so great and fine a leader. We thank Thee for his breadth of spirit and depth of feeling. We thank Thee for his intense love of our nation's common folk and for the dedication of his strong will on their behalf. We thank Thee for his high vision of one humanity and for his tireless efforts to weld all peoples and nations into one world of peace. We shall feel the pain of his parting ever more sharply as time goes on.

We pray, O our God, that even as Thy blessing rested on Franklin Roosevelt to inspire him, it may comfort and strengthen all of us who now mourn and follow him. Grant a goodly portion of wisdom and strength especially to Harry Truman, whose task is overwhelmingly heavy. Help the American people to uphold his hands, to see the world in terms of human beings and human life even as Franklin Roosevelt did, to think and labor tirelessly for that just and decent peace which alone can justify the ghastly sacrifice of this war. Make each one of us understand, we pray Thee, that we can honor best the name and memory of our greatest President since Lincoln not by words alone but by devoting our strength, our efforts, and if need be, our lives to the fulfillment of his visions and dreams.

We thank Thee, O Eternal our God, that for more than a dozen years when we needed it most, we were blessed with Franklin Roosevelt's leadership. Out of the depths of our sorrow, and grief, we pray now that we may prove worthy of that great gift, to the end that government of the people, by the people, and for the people, may indeed never perish from this earth. Amen.

May the Words

RABBI SAMUEL H. GOLDENSON

O THOU who are the Father of the fatherless and the Friend of the friendless, in the hour of the great bereavement that has befallen our beloved country and mankind, we turn to Thee for strength and comfort. We know not the meaning of the darkness that has so suddenly enshrouded us and the mystery that has engulfed us.

We pray Thee to let Thy presence shine upon us and enable us to see why we should now be denied the leadership of Franklin Delano Roosevelt, the leadership that we have so earnestly sought and the guidance that we have so sorely needed. Help us, we beseech Thee, to understand why he who has labored with mind and heart and soul for the day of victory should have been denied the joy of the victory so close at hand, the victory over those who turned light into darkness, called bitter sweet, trampled upon all that is good and true and holy, and peopled the whole world with widows and orphans, with maimed and broken men.

We know not, O Heavenly Father, why this new disaster has befallen us. And yet even in this dark bereavement we are conscious of the many mercies wherewith Thou has blessed us.

We thank Thee for the lesson taught us by one who had it within him to turn his own affliction into a source of understanding of the heart of all those in want, in fear, in pain and distress. May we, too, turn our loss into high resolve to stand at the side of all those in need of support, protection and reassurance.

We thank Thee for blessing us with this good and wise man at a time when our stricken world needed to be lifted from the slough of despondency and the hopelessness of depression. For his fortitude and fearlessness, we thank Thee, Lord.

We thank Thee for his wisdom to discern so clearly the meaning and the danger of the world struggle for dominion, and we praise Thy name for his intrepid courage and superb resourcefulness to resist the powers of darkness and the forces of evil.

We thank Thee for the eloquence of speech, the cogency of thought, and the earnestness of spirit that enabled Franklin Delano Roosevelt to persuade multitudes to see the light as he saw it. We thank Thee for men's faith in him and for all the good they enjoyed through his life and labors.

We pray Thee, O Heavenly Father, to bring comfort and healing to his bereaved family, to his noble companion in life and to their children. Give them strength to bear the burden of their great sorrow.

We pray Thee for his successor, our new President, Harry S. Truman, and for all those associated with him in places of leadership. Grant them, we beseech Thee, counsel and understanding. Strengthen them with the might of high purposes to the end that they may carry forward to fine fulfillment the high and humane purposes, hopes and dreams of Franklin Delano Roosevelt.

May the day soon come when right will prevail among men and victory resound throughout the earth. And may the new society of righteousness and peace be established as a memorial to him whom we now mourn and to all other good men who through the ages have striven and sacrificed to build the better world, the world in which "all men shall live in their own habitations in peace, and none shall make them afraid." Amen.

Memorial Prayer

RABBI MORRIS A. GUTSTEIN

ALMIGHTY God! We pray unto Thee in this hour of our affliction for the comfort and grace which come from Thee, even when we walk in the shadow of death. Our hearts are indeed overwhelmed with heavy sorrow, as we think of the precious life which has been taken from our midst. Franklin Delano Roosevelt, who was not only a humanitarian, statesman and friend, but whose deeds were emblematic of the soul in man, has now been taken from the realm of this earth to enter into the eternal world—the heavenly world—to rejoin the spirits of those whom he dearly loved in life.

Grant, O Eternal Father, in Thine infinite loving kindness that he may reap in fullest measure the fruits of righteousness which he wrought here upon earth; that he may dwell under the cover of Thy heavenly throne with the souls of the pious men and women of the world who have fulfilled their parts in life, worthily, and have gone to their rest with honor and reverence.

Vouchsafe that President Roosevelt's influence for good may always hover over the destinies of our great and glorious republic and democracy, and over the entire world, that it may help to consolidate all the forces of light and decency throughout the world, and help to materialize the yearnings and aspirations of all peoples for a world of freedom, liberty and equality; that it may cause contentment and peace to reign throughout the world after this bloody conflict between man and man ceases and help to conserve the bond of lasting peace between the nations of the world.

At this hour we would raise our eyes to Thee, and pray that Thou wouldst send Thy heavenly consolation unto the mourners of the President's family, and that Thy mercy may descend upon them in the hour of their sore trial.

Be Thou, O God, we pray Thee, with our new President, who has assumed his office in this crucial hour of the world, and in this hour of our nation's grief. Be Thou with him, and guide him in his difficulties and needs. Enlighten and sustain him with Thy power, and enable him to lead us safely from this quagmire of blood, into the paths of peace, justice and righteousness.

Fill the hearts of all with the spirit of true devotion to the cause of a common brotherhood of man, and the recognition of the reign of the Fatherhood of God amongst man. In the words of our lamented President, of sacred memory, grant that all those who fought and fight "whether by life or by death, they may win for the whole world the fruits of their sacrifice and a just peace." Amen.

Prayer

RABBI DAVID LEFKOWITZ

IN THIS early morning hour we articulate the reverent, solemn matin prayers that rise from the heart of grief-stricken America while our great President awakes to his first eternal morning which never changes to afternoon, evening or night.

O Thou God full of compassion who dwellest on High, yet art also near to the pain and sorrow of all Thy children, we raise to Thee our tear-dimmed eyes and stricken hearts and voices, in deepest grief but also in humble resignation to Thy will.

We, O Father, have lost our country's leader, our nation's commander-in-chief, and the world has been called upon to surrender one who was destined to march to the very climax of his great, epochal historic task of fashioning a cataclysmic chaos into a lasting peace. Almost in the hour of the final consummation, when all that he hoped for, prayed for and strove for was about to come to pass, he was called unto Thee. In Thy wisdom Thou didst say to him, "Your work is done, my servant. Come home and rest from your vast labors."

We bow to Thy will, assured that Thou knowest best when a man's work is done. Our prayers are not for Franklin Delano Roosevelt, for he always walked with Thee in steadfast faith and it is well with him. We pray for his stricken and bereft wife and children that they may stand strong before the blow which has fallen on them, with the same faith and trust and courage that were his shining armor. May they be upheld by a great pride in the tremendous historical work he performed in the world, and in the high place he has attained in the history of all times.

May they be assured that—

> There is no death, the stars go down
>   But rise upon some other shore,
> And bright in heaven's jewelled crown
>   They shine forever more.

And we pray for this great nation of ours, America, now that it has lost its dauntless and wise leader. May we prove worthy of him of that tremendous outpouring of all his physical and mental resources for the attainment of a decent world, of human security and justice even to the humblest and least of all Thy children, and of the fervor with which he opposed tyranny and inhuman cruelty to bring about the world of free men. Consecrate us, in this trembling hour of our grief, that we may continue his dreams and his task to complete the victory and to achieve the peace through a confederation of the nations of the world. May it be that now our great nation pledge itself that we will not falter as we take up the work which has fallen from his inert hands, but march with the rest of the United Nations toward the goal of international organization for permanent peace.

Into Thy hand we humbly, solemnly and yet with unbounded

gratitude for the gift of his life, give back to Thee our great president, praying that his soul he bound up in the bundle of eternal life. Amen.

In Memoriam

RABBI IRVING LEHRMAN

IT IS with bowed heads and broken hearts that we pay tribute to the immortal spirit of our great and beloved president, Franklin Delano Roosevelt. Every American regardless of race, color, and creed, cries out at this bitter moment, "Woe unto our ship, that has lost its captain!"

Our hearts are too full, our eyes too wet, and we are altogether too much shocked and numbed by this sudden great bereavement to be able to evaluate the man or the hour.

Only one thing we know.

This is not a moment for despair, for grief and remorse—but rather for dedication and prayer.

And so we turn to our heavenly Father, for strength and guidance.

Thou, oh God, hast seen fit to lay upon us this heavy burden. In this most crucial moment in the history of mankind, Thou hast taken from us one whose heart beat for all humanity.

He was the master architect of a new world order—the intrepid pioneer, in search of a happier human society—the great lover of democracy, who brought courage to the weak and faith to the downtrodden—the dedicated, loyal American, who gave his life for his country.

Grant, oh Lord, that his death shall not have been in vain. Inspire us with his vision, his faith and courage, so that our beloved America may carry on the crusade, for the cause of universal peace, justice, and brotherhood.

We invoke Thy blessings, oh our Father, on Harry S. Truman, who has been called to fill this great void. Grant him the wisdom and the power to bring to fruition the great work which is yet undone. And may that peace, for which Franklin Delano Roosevelt died, speedily come, and bring healing to this grief stricken world.

We pray Thee, oh God, gather into Thy heavenly vessels the copious tears that have been shed for him this day, by grieving mankind, and may they be sufficient to wash clean the misery, and suffering, and heartache of all peoples on earth.

Oh Lord, receive Thou his soul.

May it be bound up in the bond of eternal life. Amen.

Prayer

RABBI ISRAEL H. LEVINTHAL

HEAVENLY Father, Lord of the Universe,

Our Sabbath peace and joy are marred by the overwhelming tragedy which befell our beloved country. Like a thunderbolt from a clear blue sky came the terrifying news that Franklin Delano Roosevelt has been summoned to his eternal rest. Verily, we are all orphaned today. We have lost friend, counselor, guide. We leaned upon him so heavily. He was not only the heart of America, but also the heart of all humanity. We, of the House of Israel, have lost a brother in spirit, who felt our sorrow, who shared our woe, who understood our need.

We pray, O God, for Thy consolation. We pray Thee, comfort his bereaved family. Comfort the citizens of our beloved America in their loss of a great and true leader, who was their inspiration for the life of genuine Americanism.

We thank Thee, O God, for the service he has rendered, for the devotion and selfless loyalty which he gave to every endeavor to promote the welfare of our country and the happiness of all mankind.

We thank Thee for his leadership as Commander-in-Chief of

our armed forces, in leading the democratic peoples toward victory in their war against the barbaric forces which threatened to sweep the world. We thank Thee for his vision of world peace, for which he strove and for which he gave his life.

We pray Thee, in this hour, to bless the new President of the United States, Harry S. Truman. May he be accorded the wholehearted support and cooperation of all our citizens. Grant him, O Lord, the strength and the wisdom to lead our country in the spirit of his matchless predecessor.

We pray Thee that all the citizens of our glorious America may ever remain loyal and faithful to the memory of our departed chieftain by clinging to his ideals, by cherishing his visions, by carrying on his service in behalf of our country, and in behalf of all mankind.

We pray Thee, God, bless America in this its great sorrow and need.

In submission to Thine inscrutable will, all of us assembled in this House of God, now join in reciting the hallowed words of the Kaddish, in the cherished memory of our unforgettable and beloved Franklin Delano Roosevelt. Amen.

Prayer

RABBI WALTER PEISER

OUT of the depths, do we call Thee O Lord; Lord, hearken unto our voice. Sadly, solemnly, reverently do we ask Thee, in Whom alone we can find comfort in our grief, from Whom alone we can obtain consolation in our heartrending bereavement, we ask Thee to be with us now, and with all our fellow Americans everywhere, and with all the peoples of the world—who looked to Franklin Delano Roosevelt as the man, annointed by Thee, to lead this world through the wilderness, years of stupidity, confusion, oppressions, and war to the promised land of human brotherhood and everlasting peace. Joined is he now with the Choir Invisible of all the prophetic voices of the ages, with

Lincoln and Jefferson, with Amos and Hosea, and with that divinely inspired genius, who, like himself, longed for the time when 'swords would be beaten into ploughshares and spears into pruning hooks, when nations would no longer lift up sword against nation nor learn to war any more, but when, instead, each man would sit safely under his own vine and fig tree with none ever to make him afraid again.'

Our President, our Commander-in-Chief, our friend and loved one, is at peace with Thee. He needs not our prayers. He has well earned his Heavenly reward. His own deeds, his thoughts, his unselfish yearnings that took into them every man, woman, and child in all the world, the most humble of them with the greatest of them, these will speak for him in Thy presence, better than can our meagre words.

It is on ourselves, rather, that we implore Thy blessing, upon our whole world bereft of his advice and counsel, upon our Nation with the awful task of war, though now trending toward Victory, not yet won, certainly not yet over, and with the problems of the peace upon which he was capable of shedding so much light, not yet solved.

It is for living human beings, all over, and their sufferings, and needs, their dilemmas and bewilderments, that we beseech Thy mercy, now that their greatest earthly friend is no longer of this world but of Thine. It is upon the new President, especially, that we invoke the guidance, and inspiration, and the strength of spirit that come alone from Thee, and that his predecessor, our beloved departed, had from Thee in so rich and ample measure. It is for all the leaders of the people, in charge of our destiny and our happiness, that we are pleading now, that they may continue to feel and be inspired with the personality of the departed leader of leaders, to carry on his hopes, his dreams, his prayers for the United Nations, the Atlantic Charter, and above all for the four freedoms—of religion, of speech, from want, and from fear.

God be with our Happy Warrior, who fulfilled in his life the vision of the poet:—

"Who doomed to go in company with Pain
And fear, and bloodshed, miserable train—
Turned his necessity to glorious gain.
Who labored good on good to fix; and owed
To virtue every triumph that he knew.
Who when he rose to station of command
Rose there by open means; and there did stand.
Who comprehended his trust, and to the same
Kept faithful with singleness of aim.
And who when called upon to face
Some awful moment to which Heaven had joined
Great issues, good and bad for humankind,
Was happy as a lover; and attired
With sudden brightness, like a man inspired.
Who not content that former worth stand fast
Looked forward, persevering to the last.
Found comfort in himself and in his cause
And, while the mortal mist was gathering, drew
His breath in confidence in Heaven's applause.
This was the happy warrior; this was he
Who every man in arms should wish to be."

May the Words

RABBI NATHAN A. PERILMAN

O GOD, who are master of life and death, we know how finite is our wisdom, how limited our vision. One by one the children of men pass along the road of life making their impress upon their fellowmen, only to disappear from our sight. We know that in life we are in death, and that none can escape their latter end. Thou ordainest Thy children unto life. Thou dost guide and direct them by paths which Thou designest. Some are destined to greatness, some to obscurity, but for all, the latter end is one. In thine own time, and in thine own way, thou callest them home to thee.

Knowing all this, we yet cannot find solace in the great sorrow that has fallen upon the righteous among the children of men in the death of him in whom their hopes did abide, Franklin Delano Roosevelt. How ill the world can afford to lose its great spirits in this hour when greatness is so sorely needed. Now, when all of the values which we cherish are hanging in the balance. We pray that Thou will show us Thy love that we may find the wisdom and courage and strength to meet the challenges which lie ahead. Be with him upon whom the mantle of responsibility has fallen, our new President, Harry S. Truman. Guide and sustain him in the grim tasks of the war and in the grave problems of reconstruction that will follow the war's end. Help us to uphold him, that his labors may be blessed and that he, too, may be worthy of the benedictions of the righteous.

Hasten the day when peace and justice and righteousness will dwell in all the earth when the high purposes for which Franklin Delano Roosevelt lived and died, will be established for all men. Let peace on earth be Thy reward for the sorrow we now feel. Then will the righteous know gladness again, and the pious rejoice for Thy will shall have been fulfilled. Bring comfort to those who are heavily laden and peace to the oppressed in heart. Amen.

Benediction

CHAPLAIN ELIHU RICKEL

HEAVENLY Father,

We offer up our hearts in gratitude for the life and works of our departed Commander-in-Chief, Franklin Roosevelt. With Thy sustaining hand, he led us through dark days. Through the storms of confusion and conflicts, he guided us and the free people of the world to the threshold of a new day and a hope for a better life.

We beseech Thee, O Lord, to bless and favor his successor who now assumes his burdens and responsibilities. Grant him the strength and wisdom to guide us past the pitfalls and obstacles which separate us from a speedy victory and a peace that will endure.

Bless Thou the work of his hands; and through him give us the patience, courage and integrity to help in the establishment of Thy Kingdom on earth. Amen.

F.D.R.

RABBI HYMAN E. SCHEINFELD

PRAY, where can you find
In the history of generations
Such a lover of mankind
Realizing its fondest aspirations?

A tragedy like that of Job
He knew during his life's span;
Yet his heart embraced the globe,
With love as no other man.

Though an aristocrat by birth;
New deals he has undertaken,
For those crushed to the earth,
The forgotten and forsaken.

Optimism was his shield,
Faith his shining spear;
With these he won't yield
To tyranny and fear.

With his charm and smile,
He kindled mankind's imagination,
With words in prophetic style
He saved all civilization.

Extinguished is the light tower,
Radiating courage and inspiration;
In America's darkest hour,
A crucial moment for every nation.

Silent his eloquent grace,
The great heart is stilled;
And the world's every place
With sorrow is filled.

He is lamented by old and young
Who cry and shed a tear,
For him whose life's brave song
Banished cowardice and fear.

Soldiers of whom he was fond
Mourn his passing with deep grief;
While heroes in the Great Beyond
Now hail his Commander-in-Chief.

Source of comfort and love!
Humbly we bow to Thy will;
For the sake of him now above,
Continue to guide our destiny still.

Prayer

RABBI NATHANIEL S. SHARE

O LORD our God, Refuge of the afflicted and Comforter of the bereaved, we lift our hearts to Thee in prayerful entreaty for Thy help in this dark hour for our nation and for all the world. Shocked and humbled by the tragic passing of our great President, we beseech Thee for vision and strength to persevere and bring to triumphant fulfillment the tasks that have fallen from his dying hand.

We are grateful that Thou didst bless us with a leader whose social vision and faith in democracy were an inspiration during these years of testing. His love of mankind, regardless of station, creed or race, his championing of the cause of the disinherited and the underprivileged in the spirit of the Prophets of old have left their impress upon the history and institutions of our time and have become a foundation on which future generations will build.

Extend Thy sheltering protection over his spirit now returned unto Thee. Give him his heavenly reward for a lifetime of labor in behalf of humanity. Sustain and comfort his sorrowing near ones and give them strength to rise above their loss. Grant solace unto all who mourn the world over and teach us to recognize that our grief can be transmuted into healing blessing if it impel us to labor, in devotion to humanity and love of freedom equal to his, for the building of that better world which was his dream and his goal.

In resignation to Thy will, we say, "The Lord hath given and the Lord hath taken away. Praised be the name of the Lord forever and aye." Amen.

We Mourn, We Hope, We Pray

RABBI SAUL SILBER

WE MOURN the passing of a great man—Franklin Delano Roosevelt—because, endowed with prophetic vision, he foresaw the world of chaos and cautioned guidance and preparation. We mourn him because he was endowed with a genius for statesmanship. It was he who took the ship of state through the peaceful waters of evolution in contrast to the other nations who suffered bloodshed through revolution. Through his guidance our democratic form of government was preserved. We mourn him further because out of his greatness he learned to love all mankind and worked unfailingly in their behalf.

We hope that the ideas and ideals which he so wisely brought to our people and the world will stay alive long after his tombstone is erased by time. According to the Rabbis of ancient times, the righteous grow greater after death. They then lose all opposition and loom as sterling characters and their greatness is enhanced. We hope that the seeds of love and peace which Franklin Delano Roosevelt has planted in the minds and hearts of the people of the world over will bear fruit in days to come.

We pray that all those peace-loving nations of the world who cherish honor and dignity will take unto their hearts the message of Franklin Delano Roosevelt, who believed that the small and the weak, who constitute the great multitudes of the world, are the mighty. . . . We pray further that our new President, Harry S. Truman, will take the high banner of courage into his steady hands and carry the fight for unconditional surrender against greed, poverty and prejudice to its very end. We pray the Almighty God shall endow President Harry S. Truman with a heart of understanding, and that all people of the nation unite in a common effort to help him in the task that destiny has thrust upon him. Amen.

Prayer of Tribute, Dedication and Hope

RABBI MILTON STEINBERG

O LORD and King who art full of compassion, in whose hand is the soul of every living thing and the breath of all flesh, to Thine all-wise care do we commit the soul of Franklin Delano Roosevelt, lover of mankind and servant of Thee who no less actually than any of the soldiers he led has given his life for our country, for human freedom, and for the achievement of a just and lasting peace among nations.

O Lord, full of compassion do Thou shelter him ever more

under the covert of Thy wings. May his memory and influence abide among us that through us Thou mayest establish the work of his hands, aye the work of his hands mayest Thou establish it. In Thy presence God of man's heart we here highly resolve that he shall not have lived and died in vain. We pledge ourselves to the goals to which his spirit was consecrated; to a new birth of freedom at home and throughout the world to justice, mercy, and dignity for all men; to the coming of the day when the last sword is beaten to a plowshare and men shall have ceased to hurt or harm on all Thy holy mountain; when the earth shall be full of the knowledge of Thee as the waters cover the sea.

Our God and God of our fathers, we invoke Thy blessing on the new President of the United States Harry S. Truman who yesterday succeeded to a high and exalted office and to the gravest, most solemn responsibility that has ever devolved on any human being. Do Thou guard him in life and health. Give him vision equal to his opportunities, strength sufficient to his duties, and courage commensurate with the perils that beset America and mankind. May America and the world find in him a fitting successor to the prophet and prince who has left us. As once Moses died but Joshua arose to lead the children of Israel into the Promised Land; as once Elijah departed this world but the mantle of his light and truth found a fitting successor on whom to rest, so in our day may Harry Truman stand strong and firm in the place of Franklin Roosevelt. To Thy glory the welfare of America and the service of all mankind. Amen.

Prayer for F. D. R.

RABBI JACOB J. WEINSTEIN

"HOW are the mighty fallen!
Tell it not in Gath, publish not in the streets of Askelon
lest the daughters of the Philistines rejoice—
Ye mountains of Gilboa, let there be no dew,

Neither let there be rain upon ye, nor fields of offering.
Ye daughters of Israel, weep over him who clothed you in scarlet,
who put on ornaments of gold upon your apparel—
How are the mighty fallen and the weapons of war perished!"

We are orphaned. We are bereft—our guiding star is fallen. The beacon of fire by night, the pillar of cloud by day has been veiled in the seamless robe of death. As a tree is best measured when it is down, so do we now realize the stature of the man we delighted to honor as our leader. Through the bitter grief of this black hour we cannot help but see his shining image—how he won from the Pharaoh of reaction the privilege to lead us through the red sea of poverty into the wilderness of transition toward the promised land of security; how he scotched the reptiles of reaction and smote the rock of tradition until sweet water poured for the thirsty; how he turned from the native dragons to face the challenge of the alien despots and gave the cry of alarm which was as the voice of one crying in the wilderness until the masses saw with his eyes; how he mobilized the nation against the arrogant satan of the double cross and gave armored shield and flying spear to all the victims of aggression; how by his profound subtlety and the magic of his conciliator's art he held together the spectrum of parties within us and the Allies from warmest scarlet to frozen white; how he gave heart to them that were dispirited and hope to them that were cast down——

And now with the noise of victory in the air and the hour of final triumph at hand, he is summoned to the Mount and gathered to his fathers with the kiss of God as was Moses at the very brink of the Jordan—as was Lincoln whose mantle he wore with comely grace—— Amen.

EDITORIALS AND RESOLUTIONS

Roosevelt's Jewish Associations

BALTIMORE JEWISH TIMES

FRANKLIN DELANO ROOSEVELT'S political emergence marked an historic milestone in American life, and it is by reason of this that his Presidency had probably more Jewish associations than that of any other President in American history.

Roosevelt has frequently been compared to Jackson. Jackson, like Roosevelt, had a so-called Kitchen Cabinet corresponding to Roosevelt's brain trust. Jacksonian democracy meant an advance over the Jeffersonian democracy just as Roosevelt's New Deal meant an advance over the Jacksonian democracy. But Rooseveltian democracy was a reversal of Jacksonian democracy in one very significant way. Jacksonian democracy was the coming to power of the frontier—the rural and new settlements of the population. Rooseveltian democracy on the other hand was the coming to power of the urban elements. In Roosevelt's days, the cities, with their great concentration of population, came to exercise the balance of power.

It was because of the fact that the city had reached this powerful position, that we must trace these Jewish associations. F. D. R. first emerged politically we remember, when he rose to place in nomination for the Presidency, "Al Smith," the pride of New York's east side.

It will be recalled that Al Smith had strong support among the Jews of New York. A Jewish woman, Mrs. Henry Moskowitz, was then regarded as Smith's leading political adviser.

But Smith was not destined to win out, and, instead, the figure of the man who had nominated "the Happy Warrior," Franklin Delano Roosevelt, loomed to the fore.

When Roosevelt first ran for the Governorship of New York, young Herbert H. Lehman, wealthy banker who liked to devote most of his time to settlement work, was induced to run as Lieutenant Governor on the Roosevelt ticket. The association of Lehman and Roosevelt was to continue to the end. After Governor Lehman had served ten years in the gubernatorial mansion at Albany, President Roosevelt appointed him as head of UNRRA.

Among the other Jews who have been prominent in their association with President Roosevelt are Henry Morgenthau, Jr., a neighbor of the President at Hyde Park, Judge Samuel Rosenman, commonly regarded as one of the intimates of his "Brain Trust," Felix Frankfurter whom Roosevelt named to the Supreme Court, Bernard Baruch, who began his friendship with F. D. R. in the Wilson days of the first World War and David Lilienthal, the director of T.V.A.

The Nazis have long tried to paint Roosevelt as being under Jewish domination and, in fact, even repeatedly charged that he was of Jewish descent. Of course, this is all nonsense—and the fact of the matter is, that Roosevelt has not named an excessive number of Jews to office. In fact, the number of his Jewish appointees is probably much less than one would expect from the proportions of the Jewish population.

In the Ladies' Home Journal, Mrs. Eleanor Roosevelt once answered a query which had come in about the alleged Jewish descent of the President. She wrote at that time:

"As far as I know, there's no Jewish blood on either side in my husband's ancestry. I do not think he favors any nationality particularly, and neither does he have any prejudice. He looks upon people, as people, regardless of their race, religion or color and when he is trying to find the right person to do a job, I think he tries to think exclusively about the qualities of mind and character which are essential for that job and I doubt whether any other consideration enters into his decision."

Mrs. Roosevelt was undoubtedly right in this. The President has become identified as a friend of the Jews principally perhaps because he has been an outstanding leader in the fight against Nazism.

It is no secret that the Nazis hated President Roosevelt even more than they hated Churchill—and President Roosevelt rather enjoyed the fact that he was not on their love list. Once when an American correspondent returned from Germany and told the President that he was the prize hate of the Nazis—that he was hated more than Churchill and Stalin—the President laughed and said he hadn't had such good news in a long time.

Jews liked to point to the fact that Roosevelt came to power in the same year as Hitler. Just two months after Hitler came to power shouting about the New Order, which he would introduce into the world, Roosevelt came into office proclaiming the New Deal. Had another man come into office instead of Roosevelt in this critical year, the picture of the world today might be vastly different. If America had not, through Roosevelt's policy, immediately begun the "cash and carry" provisions which enabled England to begin buying armament in America, if America had not gone through with the Lend Lease which enabled England and Russia to gird themselves more strongly for the fight, if America had not thrown the full weight of its military force on Germany, today instead of anticipating early victory, we might anticipate a world really dominated by the Nazis—we might have seen that "new order of a thousand years" about which Hitler shrieked so much.

God called forth Franklin D. Roosevelt to clean out the scourge of Nazism and prepare for the foundation of a higher civilization. Franklin D. Roosevelt now belongs to the immortals. In Jewish history, too, his fame remains secure.

AMERICA MOURNS

It is not often when we think of a modern statesman that we make Biblical analogies. Statesmanship has come to be too much associated with politics, and politics is too secular a thing to be compared to the sacred. And yet in the minds of hundreds of thousands of Jews there must have occurred, this past week, the simile of the President dying, just as victory over the Germans was nigh, and of Moses dying as he saw the Promised Land from a distance.

The Biblical story has a parallel in the modern story in other ways. The story of the Exodous is also the story of an attempt at an extermination of a people. Egypt and Germany might well be the synonyms for one another.

Yes, it is easy to read the sacred, the hand of Providence, in the life of Franklin D. Roosevelt in a multitude of ways. Roosevelt came into power in the very same year as Hitler came into power. It was as if Providence had taken care to see that there should be an anti-toxin to this plague of Adolph Hitler. To speak of it thus is not to indulge in extravagant language, for if ever there was a plague in history, that plague was Nazism. Between the bubonic plague of the Middle Ages, spread by rats, and the plague of the Nazis there is little to choose from.

Franklin D. Roosevelt gave himself to conquer this modern plague and died in the cause—a true battle casualty. We mourn the death of this great and good man, but let us be happy also that he did live to see the day when victory over the enemy was assured. When we mourn, let us be thankful also that there did arise a man in our midst who said that this accursed thing of Nazism shall not spread over the world, and helped raise and organize an America not only to prevent its spread, but to choke it in its very roots in Germany.

Ours is the task now of completing the work he began. It was not only the ending of this war for which Roosevelt fought, but for some degree of world organization which shall make future catastrophes of the same kind—future Hitlers—impossible. Wisely Roosevelt went about this. No leader of the world—not Churchill and not Stalin—had the same faculty for making nations cooperate as Roosevelt. He was the one man seemingly best fitted to lead us into that plane on international cooperation—and now we have him not. That is the terrible part of the loss.

And yet we may be thankful that, before he died, he had successfully laid much of the groundwork for this international co-operation and collaboration. We have but to build upon it.

Let our mourning for Roosevelt be transmuted rather to this task. If he could speak to us now, he would say—"Do not weep for me, but finish this thing which I began to do."

They Do Not Die

B'NAI B'RITH MESSENGER

HE IS NOT DEAD! He, who but yesterday strode high among the giants of the earth, is not dead. He is not dead, who but yesterday spoke humbly with the humblest of men. Franklin Delano Roosevelt is not dead!

They do not die who heal the lame and halt and make the crippled children to walk again. They do not die who feed the hungry and shelter the homeless. He is not dead!

They do not die who lead the children of men out of the desert of despair to the Land of Peace. They do not die who love peace and hate war. They do not die who know justice and do justice. He is not dead!

They do not die who of themselves give all that others, even the lowliest, may gather hope and strength and life! They do not die who lay down their lives for their fellow men! He is not dead!

He cannot die whose whispered name brought the only spark of hope in the charnal houses of Europe! He cannot die whose word lifted high the hearts of Africa and Asia! He cannot die whose wisdom gathered segments of a disintegrating America and made it whole again! He is not dead!

They do not die whose hearts are touched by the finger of God! They do not die whose souls are seared with prophetic fire. They do not die who leave behind a spark of themselves in their fellow man. They cannot die for whom strong men stand on streets and unashamedly weep. He is not dead!

Roosevelt lives! He lives as Washington, as Jefferson, as Lincoln live! He lives as Moses lives! He lives as the Prophets live! Nor war, nor pestilence, nor ageless time shall erase his name from the heart and minds of men!

—"Well done, good and faithful servant;
Enter thou into the Kingdom of God."

In Memoriam—Franklin Delano Roosevelt

THE JEWISH ADVOCATE

BELOVED of nations, the President of the United States, Franklin D. Roosevelt, who was elected for the fourth time, was born on the thirtieth of January, 1882, to his father, James—the second in the Roosevelt family—and to his mother, Sarah Delano. She was his father's second wife and bore him an only son, Franklin.

Franklin Roosevelt gained his deep knowledge of languages through extensive travels, accompanied by his parents, to various European countries. He visited Europe ten times or more in his childhood. He is a complete master of the French tongue, reads German with ease, and also Spanish and Italian.

An interesting anecdote is told concerning young Franklin: when he was five years old, his father took him to visit the incumbent President, Grover Cleveland, who was a great friend of the elder Roosevelt. Taking young Franklin on his lap, President Cleveland said: "I want to wish for you, my dear little friend, from the depths of my heart . . . that when you grow up you will not have to taste the bitter fate of living in the White House as President of the United States." President Cleveland's wish in that direction was not fulfilled, nor was his warning heeded. . . . Franklin D. Roosevelt has had the courage to take upon himself the responsibilities of the presidency for three consecutive terms . . . in order that he might help rescue his people from the evil powers that rule the world and help end the reign of tyranny from the earth, and thus march toward a brighter future.

After his father's death, Franklin entered Harvard College. His mother closed her mansion in Hyde Park and rented two rooms in a hotel in Boston in order to be near her son. . . . At college, Franklin was an average student . . . he excelled, however, in the field of literature . . . edited the famous "Harvard Crimson" . . . was a member of many student societies . . . yet, in spite of his pedigree, one society at Harvard, "Persilion," refused to accept his membership.

Later, he matriculated at Columbia University in order to study law . . . but before he was accepted at Columbia, he fell in love with Eleanor, also of the Roosevelt family . . . a very old and distinguished family. (The founder, Claus Van Rosenvelt, arrived with other early settlers at New York—then known by the Dutch name of New Amsterdam—in the year 1644. It was his son, Nicholas, who changed his Dutch name by a brief contraction, by omitting the "Van" and the "n" in "Rosenvelt." The thirty-second President of the United States belongs truly to one of the pioneering, constructive families of the country . . . related and bound up with other prominent families of their country and with other presidential families—the Washingtons, the Adams', Harrisons, Tafts, Grants and others. The twenty-sixth President of the United States, Theodore Roosevelt, was an uncle to Franklin.)

Eleanor captivated the elder Mrs. Roosevelt's heart. An orphan, she received her training at the home of her grandmother, Mrs. Hull, who brought her up . . . after her schooling in America, she studied at a fashionable private school in England . . . at 18 she finished her courses of study; at 19, became engaged to young Franklin; and was married on March 17, 1905, at the home of a friend on Fifth Avenue, New York. Theodore Roosevelt, who was then President, left the problems of state to attend the wedding of his relatives.

Inclined from early youth to problems of the community, Franklin became more and more attracted to the social and political phenomena of his day. His interest in political life was strengthened by the fact that his uncle, Theodore, was President; and during the period of his presidency, Franklin had more than one occasion to discuss with him political conditions in America . . . Franklin's concern with national and world political problems and with various communal questions did not detract from his longing for nature and for the sciences that he loved from his childhood . . . all of his spare hours he devoted to swimming, boatting, to nature and to the sea. From his early youth he dreamed of being a sailor . . . persevered in the study of maritime service; and, therefore, this influenced his general studies at the university.

About a year after their marriage, the Roosevelts had their first child, a daughter, Anna Eleanor. When Franklin finished his studies at Columbia, he was the father of three children.

He received his diploma in the field which he decided he would pursue the rest of his life. He decided to engage in law . . . his apprenticeship was spent in the offices of a prominent lawyer for five dollars a week; and it was not until 1907 that he began to practice the profession for himself, founding a partnership with two other young lawyers. However, his heart was not tied up in legal interests, but in communal work, the welfare of society. The very month he opened his office, he announced his candidacy for the New York State Senate, to which he was elected by a great majority. From then on, his work in the field of law practically ceased and he became a statesman . . . revealed an individual willpower and a clear decision characteristic of the fighter who knows what he wants and who believes in the steadfastness of his ideals . . . a man without compromise for his righteous and straightforward thoughts . . . had the courage to oppose the heads of his party, those leaders of that political bloc which had elected him. . . . His friends in the Democratic party recognized in this young warrior an upright courageous statesman who walked in straight paths and who would not cater to anyone who was prejudiced.

Franklin Roosevelt was seen at first as a man dry and prosaic; as a man utilitarian to the 'nth degree. Later it was realized that in the heart of this man there beat a wealthy stream of noble poetry, true poetry: his jealousy for honesty; love for truth; ideals for righteousness; profound hate for political chicanery, party collusion, bribery, self-interest and protectionism.

When he reached his 40th birthday, his personality was known beyond his own state. His many efforts in behalf of his people had made him an accepted political personality throughout the country. Then, in the year 1920, when he had already attained many successful political accomplishments and when he had started the climb to the highest office in his state which was the first step toward the presidency of the country, he was struck with infantile paralysis . . . family doctors declared him incurable . . . internationally known specialists decided he would unquestionably be paralyzed for the remainder of his natural life. . . . A few made the doubtful observation that only with superhuman will power might he miraculously succeed in moving part of the paralyzed limbs . . . a powerful will was required—a will to live in order to overcome the malady . . . many of his best years did Roosevelt wrestle with this affliction . . . he worked on his body not only according to the instructions from his physicians, but also according to his own ideas. . . . His efforts bore fruit. Roosevelt regained his health; only his legs did he find difficult to manipulate. . . . And it was from this illness that he came through with greater courage and renewed vigor to work for the benefit of the poor among his people whose fate had been unemployment and starvation.

In 1932 Franklin D. Roosevelt was elected, for the first time, to the Presidency of the United States . . . at the time of the election, his paralysis was utilized by his opponents as a target at which to shoot. They called attention to his illness and endeavored to thus weaken his position in the eyes of the voters. But in one of his campaign speeches, Roosevelt pointed to his activity in the past and his preparedness to carry the burden for the good of his country. This promise he kept after he was elected by the New Deal measures which were initiated by Mr. Roosevelt himself.

From the days of Abraham Lincoln there has not been a President so beloved by the people as Mr. Roosevelt. More than any of his predecessors is he the people's President, despite family background. He loves the common people . . . Roosevelt turns to his people by way of radio on subjects which he feels concerns them very much. It is said that in order to know the effect that his speech will have on the common man, Mr. Roosevelt invites to his private room a working man—an average citizen—and has that man listen to the speech before it is broadcast. If the speech is understood by the listener, then will the President read it to the people. His speeches have become famous throughout the land and have made him beloved by the masses of citizens . . . they have warmth, a feeling of love of mankind, love for all the creatures that were created in the image of God.

Roosevelt ascended to the Presidency after Mr. Hoover's term expired—ten years after World War I which ruined the economy of the entire world . . . there were close to fourteen million unemployed . . . from this impoverished condition, President Roosevelt saved the country through his "New Deal" measures . . . provided economic means which removed the fear of unemployment in the land; promised bread for the hungry; activated the land economy . . . an enlightening example is the famous Tennessee Valley Act . . . one of the most interesting in the program of rehabilitation.

But not only is President Roosevelt distinguished as a lover of his own countrymen—he is also famous as a lover of humanity in general . . . many nations have sought shelter and protection through him. Countries faced with difficulties turned to him for aid and advice; and help was extended to them in accordance with their needs—whether small or large.

All the world democracies saw in Roosevelt the only anchor of refuge in troublous times—especially when the enemy of mankind, Adolph Hitler, rose to power. Roosevelt came forward . . . and, therefore, is he truly worthy of the name "Beloved of Nations." And in the mouths of universal Israel is he also called by that title. . . . The Bible is the Book of Books in his opinion . . . on more than one occasion has the President expressed his high esteem for the Jewish people. He has even surrounded himself with advisors from our people . . . Bernard Baruch, Felix Frankfurter and Henry Morgenthau . . . each in his own field.

In February, 1936, the President sent his greetings to the Palestine Rehabilitation Conference:

> "I am very happy to extend greetings to this National Conference of Palestine which has gathered in Washington and which has stirred American Jewry to constructive work for the progress of the Jewish National Home in Palestine. Every American knows and evaluates the love of the Jewish people for his land, which is tied up with the noble history of the Jewish nation. . . . The faith in the resurrection of Palestine was crowned with success through the foundation of the Jewish National Home which is based on the principle of righteousness for all residents of the land. I am sure that the American people, which has already demonstrated its sympathy for this great aim . . . through the acts of its presidents and unanimous decisions of Congress and Senate . . . will be ready to cooperate generously in the United Palestine Appeal whose aim is to create a haven of refuge for Jews who seek refuge. My hopes are that the American people will help in the never ending development of the Holy Land, where, I am sure, the Jewish people will continue to spread light and learning for the entire world."

It is doubtful if there is another statesman in the world who understands the Jewish question with all its entanglements and who views its solutions so favorably as this President . . . it is for this reason that the Jewish people rejoiced in his re-election: the Jewish community of America . . . of the dispersed lands . . . and the Jewish settlement in Eretz Israel. . . . Every Jew looks at his election from the viewpoint of benefitting world statesmanship . . . and hopes that on the day when peace and its details will be outlined, we, too, will be considered. . . . We have confidence in him . . . In a letter to the Catholic Conference for Human Rights and Against Religious and Racial Discriminations, the President points out the great danger of anti-Semitism:

"One must fight with all vigor against the hate of the Jew which imperils the fundamental rights of all Americans. I hope that this conference will continue its battle with all the means in its possession."

To all he showed his gigantic spirit and breadth of heart. Thus his name is great in all corners of the world; and concerning him, too, it is written in the prophecy of Malachi that "from the rising sun in the East, until its setting, thy name is famous among the nations." This is what the Bible means by the expression "lover of nations"; and as the prophet Malachi says: "Have not we all one Father? Has not one God created us? . . ."

Therefore, I saw fit—as a son of the faithful in Israel—to relate unto all who may hear my words the numerous kindnesses which this eminent and noble President has shown, and I want to engrave in everlasting tribute in his portrait these very things in the language that is left to our keeping—the Hebrew language. And for all the good deeds of this great and exalted President may the Lord of kindness repay him, this (President) Lover of Nations, in accordance with his loving kindness and depth of his charity, and may his name be well thought of for many generations to come.

Franklin Delano Roosevelt

HARTFORD JEWISH LEDGER

IN THE book of Job we read: "Shall we receive only the good from God and not the evil as well . . . The Lord has given; the Lord hath taken; The Lord's name be blessed."

These words came to mind after the first numbing shock of the news of the death of Franklin Delano Roosevelt. If ever there was a man in modern history in whose memory these words could be said, that man was Franklin Delano Roosevelt. When he was alive, he was the embodiment of the truth that God never forsakes His children and that in every hour of crisis He summons the leaders who become the instruments of His will and the tools in His hands, as it were.

There were conceivably other periods in which a man of the stamp and stature of Franklin Delano Roosevelt might not have been the creative, challenging leader that he became. He was the right man at the right place in the right hour. He came to leadership at a time when this country was frightened, was literally dragging itself through the slough of despair. Everything seemed to be collapsing about us and people spoke the dread word, Revolution. And then by the providence of God, Franklin Delano Roosevelt appeared, a man of stout heart, of daring vision, of compelling will, of genial personality, a man who has known sorrow and tribulation, suffering and pain, a man who, though crippled physically was endowed with a spirit no pain, no malady, no affliction could cripple or break. "We have nothing to fear but Fear itself," he told us and somehow his own example, his own gallantry, his own will to reject defeat communicated itself to 130,000,000 in America and the people rallied and proceeded to a period of enterprise and endeavor unequalled in human history.

There came then the rumblings of war. And again the stout

heart, the clear vision, the consecration of spirit were manifested and again he summoned his people and the world to resist evil everywhere, to prepare for combat, if need be, and the spirit of the truly great and the far-seeing prepared the country for the battle that was clearly coming whilst at the same time he led his people to a realization that they who were then in the front lines were to be given our unstinted support as a matter of our own defense as well as an act of justice and in the protection of our cherished institutions.

He bore burdens few men in history have been called upon to bear. He accepted challenges that were hurled at few men in all the ages, and throughout all, he remained the envisioned prophetic spirit in the body of "the happy warrior" who believed in his cause, who believed in his country, who believed in its institutions, who believed in his people, who believed in himself and over and above all had faith, a strong, abiding faith in the triumph of righteousness and of justice.

Thus endowed, he, of necessity, was the friend of those who are known as the little men, the underdog. He became the defender of the weak and the hungry, the disadvantaged, the discriminated against. He was the continual defender of the rights of minorities everywhere and the uncompromising champion of the dignity of every human personality, of the dignity of man as a human being.

We Jews knew Franklin Roosevelt. We loved him. We honored him. We revered him. He was a proven friend, a tried and tested friend. He has found a place in the annals of Jewish history even as his name will go ringing down the ages as one of the prophets of a new day.

In the midst of our grief, we find the urge of our hearts to offer praises. In the midst of the shock that we experienced, we can hear his voice, gay, yet solemn, brave and earnest, summoning us to battle, the battle in which he has fallen, challenging us to carry on.

He did not live to see the victory of which he was one of the supreme architects and fashioners, but the victory is certain. He toiled well and faithfully.

He laid the plans for the peace beyond the battle. These we and our chosen leaders of today will have to translate from blueprint to reality. We hear his voice: "We have nothing to fear but Fear itself," and fearless and undaunted, as heirs of his spirit, as the generation the best of whose soul he symbolized, we shall go on to save, to heal, to restore, to build the bright world, the happy, peaceful world which he envisioned. As we go forth, let us do so with thanksgiving, thanking God for the life and the spirit, the example and the heroic qualities of Franklin Delano Roosevelt.

May His Memory Be a Blessing

THE RECONSTRUCTIONIST

NEVER before in the history of mankind has the death of a public person so deeply moved vast numbers of the human race as has that of Franklin Delano Roosevelt. No other death has ever left so many people feeling personally bereaved. Multitudes had become familiar with his expressive countenance as flashed on the screen and with the modulations of his voice as it came over the radio in those addresses so aptly characterized as "fireside talks." People came to feel toward him as toward a friend and neighbor who talked intimately to them about matters close to his heart and to theirs. There was thus added to their appreciation of his statesmanship a warm affection, an emotional loyalty. Not only women and children but also strong men wept when they learned of his death.

An ancient legend has it that God gathers in a special vessel the tears shed on earth and that, when the vessel is filled, the Messiah will come. There can be no doubt that the tears shed for our late President will speed the coming of the Messianic era. They are testimony—much needed testimony in view of the evidence of ruthless and wanton cruelty provided by dispatches from Germany—that men all over the world can be united by a common love of what is truly great and good.

It is not our intention to appraise the greatness of Roosevelt. Standing at the foot of a mountain, one is too near to sketch its contours or estimate its mass. Only after the passing of years has given us a perspective in which to view Roosevelt's career and achievements will it be possible to evaluate them. We can but comment in passing on some aspects of his character and his endeavors.

The heroism of his soul was displayed when he survived the dread disease which almost killed him in the prime of his life. His struggle against the paralysis that attacked his body and that, in a person of less heroic mould, would have invaded his spirit and subjected it to despondency and self-pity, is symbolic of the struggle in which he led the nation and mankind.

When he was inaugurated as President for his first term, the country was in the grip of economic crisis. Productive processes were at a standstill. Depression, amounting almost to despair, seemed to render our whole social and economic organism impotent and inert. Roosevelt grasped intuitively that the economic crisis was essentially a disease attacking the nerve centers of American life. To combat it required a great act of will, a vigorous affirmation of faith in the nation and its potentialities. Assuring the people that they had "nothing to fear but fear itself," he projected one measure after another for ameliorating conditions and immediately checked the defeatist mood of the nation. Whether all of those projects were wise or not is not here the question. He himself regarded them as more or less tentative and did not hesitate to modify some of them in the course of time. But he conquered the paralysis of the nation. He rallied its will to recovery, to life. He sensitized it to the need for action to abolish poverty and insecurity. He made of government a dynamic factor in developing the health, security and freedom of the people.

In international affairs he played a similar role. Fascism was another and aggravated symptom of that same moral paralysis that had afflicted the nation. It attacked the coordinating nervous system of mankind and prevented the different members of the human race from cooperating for the survival and well-being of the whole. Fascist intimidation had succeeded in almost completely isolating the nations from one another, thereby threatening the whole organism of human civilization.

Roosevelt was among the first to perceive this danger. Courageously disregarding the charge that he was a warmonger, he rallied America's will to live as a member of the human race and to combat fascist aggression. Largely as a result of his leadership, humanity is so far on its way to recovery that, even as we go to press, the Conference of the United Nations to effect a world security organization is opening in San Francisco. Certainly Roosevelt is principally to be credited with having cured America of its paralyzing isolationism and restored it to functioning in concert with other nations of the world.

To be sure, there is still a great way to go before world peace is firmly established. We will miss Roosevelt's presence and wise guidance. But his leadership will not cease with his death. The mass emotion which that tragic event called forth will rather add momentum to the movement for establishing a democratic peace on earth.

We Jews have always felt particularly close to Roosevelt. He understood us and the nature of the attacks upon us. He never hesitated to call upon the services of competent Jewish advisors. Let fascist-minded politicians lampoon his policies by labeling them the "Jew Deal," he would not let that interfere with his utilization of Jewish talent and character in the service of America and of humanity. What a light is cast on the nature of Judaism by the fact that Roosevelt, who bespoke the moral conscience of mankind, was a friend of the Jewish people, while Hitler and his accomplices in the conspiracy against humanity are, to a man, its enemies!

As Americans and as Jews, we are grateful to God for having fashioned the soul of Franklin Delano Roosevelt and having exalted him to leadership in these critical times. May all who have expressed grief at his death remain faithful to his leadership until the task begun by him has been completed. Nothing less will serve as an appropriate monument to his memory than a united world enjoying freedom, security and peace.

The President

YESHIVA COLLEGE COMMENTATOR

"O weep for us who live to mourn
And not for him whom we have lost!
For HE has to his rest been borne,
WE—in a sea of grief are toss'd."

NEARLY a week has transpired since the passing of our president, and our thoughts are yet wholly with him.

Perhaps we are not possessed of the clarity to visualize the shape of things to come, but our limited vision permits an appreciation of the president's majestic greatness which Death, in its sullen morbidity, has all too clearly revealed.

We cannot eulogize the president, for the mouthings of man are grossly inadequate. We can only regard him as a symbol, a spirit of surging and unbounding inspiration. To this generation he is the proponent of a new age—an age in which Man is raised from the lower depths and is given the opportunity to act and live in accord with his will and penchant. All the eulogies of and dulcet tributes to the "intrepid commander-in-chief" and "sagacious president" in essence were indicative of one fact: the waging of war and the inauguration of domestic measures are means to his one end of the universal freedom of man.

Were we assured that the idealism of the president would pervade the minds of men in time to come, then our grief would be somewhat mitigated. If posterity will remember these words of our departed guide, then his spirit shall have transcended the borders of mortality and all terrene limitations: "We are a nation of many nationalities, many races, many religions—bound together by a single unity, the unity of freedom and equality. Whosoever seeks to set one nationality against another, seeks to degrade all nationalities. Whoever seeks to set one race against another seeks to enslave all races. Whoever seeks to set one religion against another seeks to destroy all religion. I am fighting for a free America—for a country in which all men and women have equal rights to liberty and justice. I am fighting as I have always fought, for the rights of the little man as well as the big man—for the weak as well as for the strong, for those who are helpless as well as for those who can help themselves."

We, as Jews, felt a singular, egregious hurt for in the president we had a champion of human rights. We do not venture to say that the solution of Jewish problems would have certainly been effectuated by the president had he been granted a longer stay. All we know is that the president had an understanding of and was sympathetic to our cause. He was the most firm crutch among the powers-that-be upon which we could lean. We can but hope that his successor will be imbued with equal understanding.

That consummate interest and understanding of our president was not the passive concern ordinarily exhibited by those men of great place. His was a sincere desire to liberate the shackled and oppressed—and the very existence of countless refugees is a living testament to his beneficence. Little wonder that so many the world over virtually worshipped him as a divinely-inspired personage, almost a Moses.

To those for whom he secured a sheltered haven, as well as to us for whom he laid the foundation of a tranquil future, he signified the flouter of the Pharaohs, the guide through the walled sea, the leader through the wilderness. And now the time had come for The Promised Land.

"And the Lord spoke unto Moses, saying, get thee up into this mountain of 'Abarim, unto Mount Nebo . . . and behold the land of Canaan . . .

"And Moses went up from the plains of Moab unto the mount of Nebo . . . and the Lord showed him all the land . . . And the Lord said unto him, This is the land which I swore to Abraham, unto Isaac, and unto Jacob, saying, Unto thy seed will I give it; I have let thee see it with thine eyes, but thither thou shalt not go over.

"And Moses the servant of the Lord died there in the land of Moab, according to the order of the Lord."

Resolution

Adopted at the 41st Annual Convention of the Zionist Organization of America Held at Detroit in July, 1938. President Roosevelt's Name Was Inscribed in the Golden Book of the Jewish National Fund.

WHEREAS Franklin D. Roosevelt, President of the United States of America, by his great act of historic and humanitarian significance of March 24th, 1938, has revitalized mankind's conscience by convoking the International Conference of European and American Democracies to consider ways and means for bringing relief and succor to the refugees from the land of oppression;

WHEREAS This renewal of America's great moral leadership in the protection of minorities against the oppression of tyranny has found a warm response on the part of 31 European and American nations whose representatives will gather at the International Conference on Refugees on July 6th, at Evian, France;

WHEREAS the Jewish National Fund, in response to suggestions from many quarters, has decided to dedicate a volume of the Sefer Ha'Zahav (Golden Book) in Jerusalem to the name of Franklin Delano Roosevelt as a means of expressing this widespread feeling in a manner employed in this and in other countries to manifest recognition of the services rendered by the outstanding thinkers, statesmen and humanitarian leaders of our generation;

WHEREAS The President has indicated his pleasure at receiving from the Jewish National Fund a replica of the said volume, the original of which will forever repose in the City of Peace together with the other five volumes, which constitute Israel's Roll of Honor;

THEREFORE, be it resolved by the delegates of Zionist Districts and Organizations to the 41st Annual Convention of the Zionist Organization of America meeting this day in the City of Detroit, Michigan;

1. To express their wholehearted approval and to pledge their support of this singularly appropriate tribute to the President of the United States;

2. To invite all affiliated and cooperating organizations, groups and individuals to register their esteem of and appreciation for President Roosevelt through entering his name in the special Sefer Ha'Zahav volume on the basis of their contributions of $100 for each inscription in order to enable the Jewish National Fund to extend the land area of Jewish freedom and hope in Eretz Israel;

3. To urge all Jewish organizations in the United States to cooperate to the fullest extent with the Jewish National Fund to the end that the Franklin Delano Roosevelt Volume when presented at the White House, be as representative by the number of inscriptions as this historic action requires.

ROOSEVELTIANA

Message on the 15th Anniversary of Balfour Declaration

NOVEMBER 4, 1932, TO JUDGE MORRIS ROTHENBERG

DEAR MR. ROTHENBERG:

I greatly regret that I shall be unable to be present at the meeting to commemorate the fifteenth anniversary of the Balfour Declaration to be held under the auspices of the Zionist Organization of America.

As you know, I have on prior occasions expressed my fullest sympathy with the purposes of the Balfour Declaration. Out of the World War came a matter of great spiritual significance—the establishment of a Homeland for the Jewish people, recognized as such by the public law of the world. In the realization of this aim, the United States played a leading role. I know how close it was to the wish of President Wilson. The formal terms of its expression during the war, the so-called Balfour Declaration, had his personal approval and he did much to have it written into the peace treaty. The subsequent unanimous endorsement of the Balfour Declaration by both Houses of the United States Congress gave further proof of the deep interest of the American people in the purposes of the Declaration and in the fulfillment of the moral obligations which it involved.

Jewish achievement in Palestine since the Balfour Declaration vindicates the high hope which lay behind the sponsorship of the Homeland. The Jewish development in Palestine since the Balfour Declaration is not only a tribute to the creative powers of the Jewish people but by bringing great advancement into the sacred land has promoted the well-being of all the inhabitants thereof.

I shall personally watch with deep sympathy the progress of Palestine. I extend to your organization my sincerest wishes for continued success and achievement.

Very sincerely yours,
FRANKLIN D. ROOSEVELT.

Letter Addressed to Dr. Stephen S. Wise

I AM glad to greet the National Conference for Palestine which is meeting in Washington to mobilize American Jewry behind the constructive effort to further the rebuilding of the Jewish homeland in Palestine.

Every American knows of the love of Jews for the land associated with the great beginnings of their history and every Jew must rejoice that this undying loyalty has been crowned by the establishment of a Jewish National Home resting upon the sure foundations of justice and well-being for all the residents thereof.

The American people which has, by the action of Presidents and a joint resolution of Congress, attested its sympathy with the great purpose of a national Jewish home in Palestine will, I am persuaded, be ready to cooperate generously with the United Palestine Appeal which aims to provide a home for homeless Jews. I confidently hope that the cooperation of the American people will contribute to the further progress of the Holy Land, which, I am sure, will continue to give light and leading to all the world.

Very sincerely yours,
FRANKLIN D. ROOSEVELT.

Letter Addressed to the Hon. Grover A. Whalen

JULY 16, 1936

MY DEAR MR. WHALEN:

We need, from time to time, to renew our faith in those eternal verities which are and which must forever remain the bases of human betterment. First among these is the common aspiration of mankind to seek communion with the Great Ruler of Human Destiny and next is the love of the homeland, which is a natural aspiration of our devotion to family life.

The interest which I have had and have frequently manifested in the rebuilding of the ancient Jewish homeland is, I am persuaded, an interest which is shared by all who recognize that every people has the inalienable right to life, liberty and the pursuit of happiness. It is a source of renewed hope and courage, that by international accord and by the moral support of the peoples of the world, men and women of Jewish faith have a right to resettle the land where their faith was born and from which much of our modern civilization has emanated.

Very sincerely yours,
FRANKLIN D. ROOSEVELT.

Letter to Pope Pius XII

DECEMBER 23, 1939

IN THEIR hearts men decline to accept for long the law of destruction forced upon them by wielders of brute force. Always they seek, sometimes in silence, to find again the faith without which the welfare of nations and the peace of the world cannot be rebuilt.

I believe that while statesmen are considering a new order of things, the new order may well be at hand. I believe that it is even now being built, silently but inevitably in the hearts of masses whose voices are not heard, but whose common faith will write the final history of our time. They know that unless there is belief in some guiding principle and some trust in a divine plan, nations are without light and peoples perish.

Because the people of this nation have come to a realization that time and distance no longer exist in the older sense, they understand that that which harms one segment of humanity harms all the rest.

Message to the American Palestine Committee

MAY 23, 1942

(Addressed to Senator Robert F. Wagner of New York, its co-chairman)

DEAR BOB:

Will you please convey my greetings to all of those assembled at the Second Annual Dinner of the American Palestine Committee, being held in Washington.

As you know, I have on several occasions expressed my interest in the efforts of those seeking to establish a Jewish National Home in Palestine. I think that we all take renewed encouragement in the fact that the immediate military danger to Palestine, which existed some time ago, has been very definitely removed.

The great physical, economic and educational development which has taken place in Palestine in the last two decades has been a perfect example of what can be accomplished by a free people, working in a democracy. We are all looking forward to the day when that type of development may be continued in peace and harmony in the general march of mankind toward the accomplishment of the Four Freedoms everywhere in the world.

I know that all of you assembled at this anniversary dinner will always have clearly in mind the duty and responsibility resting upon all of us to work and fight toward attaining this great objective in the days to come.

Very sincerely yours,
FRANKLIN D. ROOSEVELT.

Message to the Zionist Organization of America

OCTOBER 1, 1942

MY DEAR JUDGE LEVINTHAL:

I have received your and Mrs. Pool's letter of September ninth, regarding the forthcoming joint convention of the Zionist Organization of America and Hadassah.

At this time when our country is at war it is fitting to note the substantial contribution which Palestine is making to the war effort of the United Nations. That contribution is due in great part to the work of your organizations in the past and the present.

I am sure that your deliberations will have primarily in view the great struggle in which we are engaged, and I know that you will share fully in the hard work and sacrifice required for the total defeat of our enemies.

Sincerely yours,
FRANKLIN D. ROOSEVELT.

Statement by President Roosevelt

MADE FOLLOWING THE SUSPENSION BY ARGENTINA OF THE PUBLICATION OF JEWISH NEWSPAPERS, OCTOBER 15, 1943.

I HAVE been informed that the Argentine Government has suspended the publication of the Jewish newspapers, some of which have been in existence for many years. While this matter is, of course, one which concerns primarily the Argentine Government and people, I cannot forbear to give expression of my feeling of apprehension at the taking in this hemisphere of action obviously anti-Semitic in nature and of a character so closely identified with the most repugnant features of Nazi doctrine. I believe that this feeling is shared by the people of the United States and by the people of the other American republics. In this connection I recall that one of the resolutions adopted at the Eighth International Conference of American States at Lima in 1938 set forth that "any persecution on account of racial or religious motives which makes it impossible for a group of human beings to live decently is contrary to the political and juridical systems of America."

A Message to Robert Szold

"I THINK that we all take renewed encouragement in the fact that the immediate military danger to Palestine, which existed some time ago, has been very definitely removed.

"The great physical, economic and educational development which has taken place in Palestine in the last two decades has been a perfect example of what can be accomplished by a free people working in a democracy. We are all looking forward to the day when that type of development may be continued in peace and harmony in the general march of mankind toward the accomplishment of the Four Freedoms everywhere in the world."

Whoever Participates in Anti-Semitism Plays Hitler's Game

February 9, 1944

DEAR DR. WISE:

The attempt by Adolf Hitler and the Nazi party to rule Germany, to rule Europe and then to rule the Western World, was based on two brutal devices: organized terror and organized anti-Semitism. Terror put Hitler in power and kept him there. Anti-

Semitism was the terror's counterpart in propaganda. In the name of the self-styled Master race, Hitler robbed, first, his own people, then the peoples of Europe, and tomorrow by his boast, would have robbed the peoples of the world. . . .

Some of the sources of anti-Semitism in this country were created to serve Hitler's purpose. Let every American look to his own mind and actions so that while we defeat Hitler's armies we also defeat his poisonous propaganda. Whoever condones or participates in anti-Semitism plays Hitler's game. There is no place in the lives or thoughts of true Americans for anti-Semitism.

FRANKLIN DELANO ROOSEVELT

Statement Released by White House

MARCH 24, 1944

THE United Nations are fighting to make a world in which tyranny and aggression cannot exist; a world based upon freedom, equality, and justice; a world in which all persons regardless of race, color or creed may live in peace, honor and dignity.

In one of the blackest crimes of all history—begun by the Nazis in the day of peace and multiplied by them a hundred times in time of war—the wholesale systematic murder of the Jews of Europe goes on unabated every hour. As a result of the events of the last few days, hundreds of thousands of Jews who while living under persecution have at least found a haven from death in Hungary and the Balkans, are now threatened with annihilation as Hitler's forces descend more heavily upon these lands. That these innocent people, who have already survived a decade of Hitler's fury, should perish on the very eve of triumph over the barbarism which their persecution symbolizes, would be a major tragedy.

It is therefore fitting that we should again proclaim our determination that none who participate in these acts of savagery should go unpunished. The United Nations have made it clear that they will pursue the guilty and deliver them up in order that justice be done. That warning applies not only to the leaders but also to their functionaries and subordinates in Germany and in the satellite countries. All who knowingly take part in the deportation of Jews to their death in Poland or Norwegians and French to their death in Germany, are equally guilty with the executioner. All who share the guilt shall share the punishment.

We call upon the free peoples of Europe and Asia temporarily to open their frontiers to all victims of oppression. We shall find havens of refuge for them. . . .

In the name of justice and humanity let all freedom-loving people rally to this righteous undertaking.

Prayer by the President of the United States

JUNE 6, 1944

MY FELLOW AMERICANS:

In this poignant hour, I ask you to join me in prayer:

Almighty God: Our sons, pride of our Nation, this day have set upon a mighty endeavor, a struggle to preserve our Republic, our religion and our civilization, and to set free a suffering humanity.

They are men lately drawn from the ways of peace. They fight not for the lust of conquest. They fight to end conquest. They fight to liberate. They fight to let justice arise, and tolerance and goodwill among all Thy people.

And, O Lord, give us faith. Give us faith in Thee; faith in our sons; faith in each other; faith in our united crusade.

Message to the 47th Annual Convention of the Zionist Organization of America

OCTOBER 14, 1944, ADDRESSED TO
SENATOR ROBERT F. WAGNER

DEAR BOB:

Knowing that you are to attend the 47th Annual Convention of the Zionist Organization of America, I ask you to convey to the delegates assembled my most cordial greetings. Please express my satisfaction that in accord with traditional American policy, and in keeping with the spirit of the Four Freedoms, the Democratic Party at its July convention this year included the following plank in its platform:

"We favor the opening of Palestine to unrestricted Jewish immigration and colonization, and such a policy as to result in the establishment there of a free and democratic Jewish Commonwealth."

Efforts will be made to find appropriate ways and means of effectuating this policy as soon as practicable. I know how long and ardently the Jewish people have worked and prayed for the establishment of Palestine as a free and democratic commonwealth. I am convinced that the American people give their support to this aim; and if re-elected I shall help to bring about its realization.

With cordial regards and best wishes,

FRANKLIN DELANO ROOSEVELT.

Statement of March 16, 1945

DR. STEPHEN S. WISE talked with the President for three-quarters of an hour, and an official statement issued later quoted the President:

I made my position on Zionism clear in October. That position I have not changed and shall continue to seek to bring about its earliest realization.

Immigration into Palestine

LATE Wednesday evening, November 23, 1938, on the eve of the Palestine debate in the House of Commons, President Roosevelt from the Temporary White House in Warm Springs, Ga., made an unexpected announcement expressing gratification with the information reported here that the number of Jews allowed to enter Palestine would be increased. President Roosevelt's statement was as follows:

"It is reported that the number of refugees to be permitted entry into Palestine will be materially increased and in particular that many children and young people will be given refuge there.

I have no means of knowing the accuracy of this report, but I hope that it is true."

According to later reports in the press, the announcement of the President was intended for "consumption beyond the borders of the United States."

No Approval of White Paper

DR. STEPHEN S. WISE and Dr. Abba Hillel Silver, co-chairmen of the American Zionist Emergency Council, were received by President Roosevelt in Washington on March 19, 1944. After the interview which lasted one hour, the two Jewish leaders issued the following statement:

The President has authorized us to say that the American Government has never given its approval to the White Paper of 1939. The President is happy that the doors of Palestine are today open to Jewish refugees, and stated that when future decisions are reached, full justice will be done to those who seek a Jewish National Home for which our Government and the American people have always had the deepest sympathy—and today more than ever in view of the tragic plight of hundreds of thousands of homeless Jewish refugees.

Roosevelt's Letter on Religion

THE following letter to Dr. Samuel H. Goldenson, Rabbi of Congregation Emanu-El in New York City dated February 28, 1945, is probably the late President's last expression on religion:

"The gravity of the times which mark the one hundredth anniversary of the establishment of Congregation Emanu-El quickens in the hearts and souls of thinking men and women an appreciation of their dependence on the strength that can be found only in the everlasting reality of religion.

"It seems, therefore, fitting that I should again declare that no greater thing could come to our land today than a revival of the spirit of religion—a revival that would stir the hearts of men and women of all faiths to a reassertion of their belief in God. I doubt if there is any problem that would not melt away before the fire of such a spiritual awakening.

"The great majority of Americans find religious unity in a common Biblical heritage—the heritage of the Old Testament. Whether our allegiance is to the tenets of Christian Revelation or to the ancient teaching of Israel, we all hold to the inspiration of the Old Testament and accept the Ten Commandments as the fundamental law of God.

"It is well for us, therefore, in the face of global war and world upheaval, to emphasize the many essential things in which we, as a nation, can find unity as we seek solution of the momentous problems before us."